Robert Pippin and Film

Series Editors:

Lúcia Nagib
Professor in Film at the University of Reading
Tiago de Luca
Associate Professor in Film & Television Studies at the University of Warwick

Advisory Board:
Martine Beugnet, Université Diderot Paris
Thomas Elsaesser, University of Amsterdam
Catherine Grant, Birkbeck University
D.N. Rodowick, The University of Chicago
Ágnes Pethő, Sapientia University
David Martin-Jones, University of Glasgow
Philip Rosen, Brown University
Laura U. Marks, Simon Fraser University

Film Thinks is an original book series that asks: how has film influenced the way we think? The books in this series are concise, engaging editions written by experts in film history and theory, each focusing on a past or present philosopher, thinker or writer whose intellectual landscape has been shaped by cinema. *Film Thinks* aims to further understanding and appreciation, through sophisticated but accessible language, of the thought derived from great films. Whilst explaining and interpreting these thinkers' ideas and the films at their origin, the series will celebrate cinema's capacity to inspire and entertain – and ultimately to change the world. Aimed at film fans as well as specialists, *Film Thinks* is devoted to knowledge about cinema and philosophy as much as to the pleasure of watching films.

Published and forthcoming in the *Film Thinks* series:

Adorno and Film: Thinking in Images
By James Hellings

Georges Didi-Huberman and Film: The Politics of the Image
By Alison Smith

Judith Butler and Film
By Temmuz Süreyya Gürbüz

Noël Carroll and Film: A Philosophy of Art and Popular Culture
By Mario Slugan

Roland Barthes and Film: Photography, Myth and Leaving the Cinema
By Patrick Ffrench

Slavoj Žižek and Film: A Cinematic Ontology
By Christine Evans

Stanley Cavell and Film: Scepticism and Self-Reliance at the Cinema
By Catherine Wheatley

Queries, ideas and submissions to:
Series Editor: Professor Lúcia Nagib – l.nagib@reading.ac.uk
Series Editor: Dr Tiago de Luca – T.de-Luca@warwick.ac.uk
Senior Commissioning Editor at Bloomsbury: Anna Coatman –
Anna.Coatman@bloomsbury.com

Robert Pippin and Film

Politics, Ethics, and Psychology after Modernism

Dominic Lash

BLOOMSBURY ACADEMIC
LONDON • NEW YORK • OXFORD • NEW DELHI • SYDNEY

BLOOMSBURY ACADEMIC
Bloomsbury Publishing Plc
50 Bedford Square, London, WC1B 3DP, UK
1385 Broadway, New York, NY 10018, USA
29 Earlsfort Terrace, Dublin 2, Ireland

BLOOMSBURY, BLOOMSBURY ACADEMIC and the Diana logo
are trademarks of Bloomsbury Publishing Plc

First published in Great Britain 2022
This paperback edition published 2023

Copyright © Dominic Lash, 2022, 2023

Dominic Lash has asserted his right under the Copyright, Designs and Patents Act, 1988, to be identified as Author of this work.

For legal purposes the Acknowledgments on p. xi constitute an extension of this copyright page.

Cover design by Charlotte Daniels

All rights reserved. No part of this publication may be reproduced or transmitted in any form or by any means, electronic or mechanical, including photocopying, recording, or any information storage or retrieval system, without prior permission in writing from the publishers.

Bloomsbury Publishing Plc does not have any control over, or responsibility for, any third-party websites referred to or in this book. All internet addresses given in this book were correct at the time of going to press. The author and publisher regret any inconvenience caused if addresses have changed or sites have ceased to exist, but can accept no responsibility for any such changes.

A catalogue record for this book is available from the British Library.

A catalog record for this book is available from the Library of Congress.

ISBN: HB: 978-1-3501-8289-9
PB: 978-1-3502-9016-7
ePDF: 978-1-3501-8290-5
eBook: 978-1-3501-8291-2

Series: Film Thinks

Typeset by Newgen KnowledgeWorks Pvt. Ltd., Chennai, India

To find out more about our authors and books visit www.bloomsbury.com and sign up for our newsletters.

In memory of Nicholas Lash (1934–2020), without whom this author would have been nonexistent.

Itzt besteht darum die Arbeit nicht sosehr darin, das Individuum aus der unmittelbaren sinnlichen Weise zu reinigen und es zur gedachten und denkenden Substanz zu machen, als vielmehr in dem Entgegengesetzten, durch das Aufheben der festen bestimmten Gedanken das Allgemeine zu verwirchlichen und zu begeisten.

Nowadays the task before us consists not so much in purifying the individual of the sensuously immediate and in making him into a thinking substance which has itself been subjected to thought; it consists instead in doing the very opposite. It consists in actualizing and spiritually animating the universal through the sublation of fixed and determinate thoughts.

Hegel, The Phenomenology of Spirit (Preface, §33)

Contents

List of Figures	x
Acknowledgments	xi
Introduction: "I'm Just Trying to Understand the Goddamn Film"	1
1 Modernism, Self-Consciousness, and Film	27
2 The Political Psychology of the Wild West	59
3 Worlds Apart: Polanski and Malick	89
4 Film Noir and Agency: Do We Know What We're Doing?	109
5 Unknowing One Another: Film as Practical Moral Psychology	147
6 Pippin and Film Studies	179
Afterword: On the Nonexistence of Pippinian Film-Philosophy	211
Notes	217
Bibliography	245
Filmography	259
Index	261

Figures

1. Blink and you (literally) miss it: the first flash in *Rear Window* (before, during, after). *Rear Window* directed by Alfred Hitchcock © Paramount 1954. All rights reserved — 23
2. *The Head of White Horse*, 1810–1812, by Théodore Géricault (1791–1824), oil on canvas, 65 x 54 cm. France, 19th century. Paris, Musée Du Louvre (Photo by DeAgostini/Getty Images) — 40
3. Living myth in *Stagecoach*. *Stagecoach* directed by John Ford © United Artists 1939. All rights reserved — 70
4. Hallie's reaction at the end of *The Man Who Shot Liberty Valance*. *The Man Who Shot Liberty Valance* directed by John Ford © Paramount 1962. All rights reserved — 73
5. "Romantic fantasies" in *The Thin Red Line*? *The Thin Red Line* directed by Terrence Malick © 20th Century Fox 1998. All rights reserved — 107
6. Considering the need for "immediate, creative improvisations" in *Out of the Past*. *Out of the Past* directed by Jacques Tourneur © RKO 1947. All rights reserved — 122
7. *Talk to Her*: merger or failure? *Talk to Her* (*Hable con ella*) directed by Pedro Almodóvar © El Deseo 2002. All rights reserved — 154
8. A series of profiles in *Vertigo*. *Vertigo* directed by Alfred Hitchcock © Paramount 1958. All rights reserved — 171
9. *All That Heaven Allows*: an ironic conclusion? *All That Heaven Allows* (1955) directed by Douglas Sirk © Universal 1955. All rights reserved — 196

Acknowledgments

My heartfelt thanks to …

… Kate for encouragement and homemade hummus throughout, and some extremely helpful comments on specific passages, including a phrase or two I have shamelessly stolen.

… Lúcia Nagib for the warmth and enthusiasm with which she received my initial proposal, Tiago de Luca for his further support, and the three anonymous reviewers of that proposal for their very constructive comments.

… Pete Falconer, Hoi Lun Law (to whom extra thanks for turning me on to Pippin in the first place), Martin Shuster, Mario Slugan, and Dan Yacavone, each of whom read some or all of the book in manuscript and offered comments that were encouraging just when I needed it while also pulling me up on things when *that* was necessary. Many thanks also to the two anonymous reviewers for their valuable responses to the penultimate version of the manuscript. The remaining shortcomings—all my own work—are far fewer in number thanks to all your efforts.

… Everybody at Bloomsbury, and Veidehi Hans in particular, for making the publication process such a pleasure.

Introduction: "I'm Just Trying to Understand the Goddamn Film"

Robert Buford Pippin was born on September 14, 1948. During his highly distinguished academic career he has specialized in the often-daunting terrain of German Idealist philosophy and its aftermath. In the last ten years or so, however, he has drawn on an enduring interest in cinema and published five books about film: *Hollywood Westerns and American Myth: The Importance of Howard Hawks and John Ford for Political Philosophy* (2010); *Fatalism in American Film Noir: Some Cinematic Philosophy* (2012); *The Philosophical Hitchcock: Vertigo and the Anxieties of Unknowingness* (2017); *Filmed Thought: Cinema as Reflective Form* (2020); and *Douglas Sirk: Filmmaker and Philosopher* (2021).[1] Pippin's writings on film combine astute and attentive readings of individual films with an original approach to the relationship between philosophy and film, one that is informed by his extremely rich philosophical competence but wears this learning lightly and is expressed with an admirable dedication to clarity. This body of work has had, to date, only limited impact on the wider fields of Film Studies and film-philosophy. *Robert Pippin and Film* argues that this is unfortunate and attempts to articulate something of the nature and the value of what Pippin's writings on film have to offer. I personally believe it would be to the good if Pippin's work on cinema was widely seen as central to the philosophical study of film. Given that such a situation is currently difficult to imagine, however, this book aims at least to show that, whatever position it ultimately comes to occupy within these fields, Pippin's work on film deserves not to be marginalized.

Theory and Philosophy

Much of Pippin's work is concerned with the history of philosophy. The lion's share of his career has been dedicated to interpreting the writings of canonical philosophers, chief among them Georg Wilhelm Friedrich Hegel (1770–1831). This work, however, subverts any preconceptions we might have about the distinction between scholarly pedantry and original philosophical thought. Pippin demonstrates that textually and historically scrupulous analysis can be, as Raymond Geuss wrote about Pippin's first major work, "genuinely philosophical" (1989: back cover). This work was a book called *Hegel's Idealism: The Satisfactions of Self-Consciousness*, which defends an interpretation in which Hegel's thought is "far less obscurantist and far more interesting philosophically than has traditionally been understood" (ibid.: 11). According to the influential and controversial philosopher Richard Rorty:

> In point of originality and daring, Pippin is comparable to [Stanley] Cavell, whose readings of Austin and Wittgenstein are both unlike anybody else's and parts of a larger project of retelling the story of modern philosophy. Pippin's readings of Kant and Hegel are equally original, and form part of a project conceived on a similar scale.
> (Rorty 2002: 354)

For his critics, on the other hand, Pippin's "project" makes Hegel far too Kantian; Peter Osborne, for example, has referred to Pippin's "one-dimensionally Kantian Hegelianism" (2013: 21). Another distinction that Pippin subverts, then, is that between "analytic" and "continental" philosophy. As Rorty puts it, he "has no hesitation in cutting across the grain of most contemporary Anglophone moral philosophy, but his approach is equally remote from that of most so-called 'Continental' philosophers" (2002: 354). Pippin's dedication to clarity and argument suggests the former—he is certainly committed to what the philosopher Robert Brandom, his tongue firmly in his cheek, calls "the fundamental analytic credo—*faith* in reasoned argument, *hope* for reasoned agreement, and *clarity* of reasoned expression (and the greatest of these is clarity)" (2002: 2)—and yet the central figure in his thinking, namely Hegel, is often seen as emblematic of the division between the two traditions; indeed, "the creation myth of the analytic tradition is that its identity is taken to have been forged in opposition to the murky depths of Hegel's thought" (Lumsden 2011: 89).

Despite this formidable intellectual armory, however, Pippin once said about his book-length study of Alfred Hitchcock's *Vertigo* that he was "just trying to understand the goddamn film" (2017b). What does a remark like this signify? Coming from a man who has devoted much of his life to Hegel's rebarbative intricacies, it can hardly indicate a hostility toward abstract thought. Does it perhaps suggest that thinking about film is merely a diversion for Pippin, a bit of light relief after a hard day's work at the coalface of the *Phenomenology of Spirit* or the *Science of Logic*? On the contrary; it is very much *not* Pippin's version of the philosopher Colin McGinn's claim that "there is nothing better after a hard day of philosophical thinking and writing than a 'mindless' movie" (McGinn 2005: 136). However, as we shall see, Pippin does believe that taking a philosophical approach to film can be something very different from constructing theories about film. In this respect, Pippin's work resonates with Andrew Klevan's recent arguments about the usefulness for film-philosophy of what is often referred to as "ordinary language philosophy." Pippin would, I think, concur with Klevan that philosophy can "be continuous with film criticism," as opposed to "the more common assumption that philosophy is continuous with film theory" (Klevan 2020: 34, n. 48). The way Pippin's reading of philosophers such as Hegel informs his work on film, however, demonstrates some of the ways in which theoretical forms of philosophy can usefully inform a non-theoretical approach to film. (Contrast Klevan's remark that "if we are hoping to study film philosophically but not theoretically then I advise that we look to a practice within philosophy that is not theoretical" [2020: 1].)[2] What this means will, I hope, become clearer over the course of this book.

And what of the relevance of film to philosophy (rather than of philosophy to film)? Pippin notes that, by now, he is confident he can simply presume agreement with the proposition that

> the battle over the issue of whether "Hollywood movies" merit close, sustained attention as serious works of art (and not merely as revealing artifacts of use for sociology, history, or anthropology) has been settled on the side of Hollywood, and that one can hold such a view without being committed to any particular version of auteur theory, and without a commitment to any particular film theory.
>
> (Pippin 2010a: 159, n. 13)

I will explore the rationales for, and consequences of, this position throughout *Robert Pippin and Film*, but one immediately obvious aspect of Pippin's writings on film that is strongly informed by this stance is that while it is not replete with the terms of art that pepper some other forms of film-philosophy (most notably—and, for some, notoriously—Gilles Deleuze's "movement-image," "time-image," and so on; see Deleuze 2005a and b), neither does it include lengthy exegeses of philosophical concepts which are then "applied" to particular films. This is because Pippin conceives the way he critically engages in detail with individual films as itself philosophical. This book aims, likewise, to keep specific films in mind for as much of the time as possible, but it will also fill out some of the context of Pippin's readings by making more detailed reference to his purely philosophical work than he tends to when writing about film. His explicit remark in the first chapter of *Filmed Thought* that its "major premises ... are Hegelian" is rather unusual; the rest of the book contains only five more references to Hegel that are not relegated to the footnotes (Pippin 2020a: 9). In going into the philosophical background in a bit more detail, then, my practice will clash just a little with Pippin's own way of going about things. His clarity of exposition means, however, that there is less need than with some other film-philosophers for somebody simply to provide an approachable exposition of his ideas. To bring out more explicitly what Pippin usually allows implicitly, or at least relatively unemphatically, to underpin his writing on film will help clarify both the status of that writing and its relation to other aspects of his work. A few concepts will be central to this endeavor. These include, most importantly, "modernism," "autonomy," "normativity," and "apperception," all of which will be unpacked and explored in what follows. But it must be stressed that while such material will be, I hope, usefully amplificatory, it is by no means strictly *necessary*. To think that Pippin thinks that one cannot approach film philosophically (or read and understand his own philosophical writings on film) without the benefit of decades spent in gloomy libraries poring over Hegel would be a gross and unfortunate distortion.

In what follows I cover Pippin's first three books on film—the books on Westerns, on film noir, and on *Vertigo*—in the sequence in which they were published, but it has seemed most useful to divide up the coverage of *Filmed Thought* (which consists, for the most part, of essays that Pippin had previously published elsewhere), discussing its chapters whenever the material they contain seems most to resonate with the material in the other books. I should also note another methodological decision, which is that I will not restrict myself strictly to conveying Pippin's own interpretations, but also engage in interpretive work of my own, in dialogue with Pippin's writing. Not to do so would neglect the spur to further inquiry that is one of the main attractions of reading Pippin's work on film.

The structure of the book is as follows. The first chapter, "Modernism, Self-Consciousness, and Film," sets out some of the most important philosophical contexts for Pippin's work, covering his understanding of modernism, the centrality to his thought of Kant's initially rather recondite-seeming notion of "apperception," and concluding with an account of Pippin's few explicitly theoretical treatments of film and the philosophy of film. The next chapter, "The Political Psychology of the Wild West," focuses on *Hollywood Westerns*. This is followed by a shorter chapter that bridges those that precede and follow it and explores the senses in which a film can be said to have a "world." "Film Noir and Agency: Do We Know What We're Doing?" then sets out Pippin's account of agency—the most indispensable component of his account of what a philosophical treatment of narrative film might amount to—and explores how it plays out in his studies of film noir and the work of the Dardenne brothers. Chapter 5, "Unknowing One Another: Film as Practical Moral Psychology," explores the Nietzschean dimensions of this concept and how they inform Pippin's readings of Hitchcock's *Shadow of a Doubt* and *Vertigo* and Almodóvar's *Talk to Her*. The last chapter, "Pippin and Film Studies," looks at Pippin's work through a more comparative lens, considering the role of the canon in Pippin's treatment of film, his engagement with cinematic style (something he has been accused of neglecting), and the relation of his work to analytic and continental traditions of film-philosophy. The book concludes with a brief afterword.

To prepare the ground, the remainder of this introduction is divided into two sections. In the first, some of Pippin's central philosophical and methodological assumptions are concisely set out, while the second starts to get our critical hands dirty by engaging with Pippin's reading of Hitchcock's *Rear Window* and introducing Pippin's account of what it means for film viewers—and indeed films themselves—to be self-conscious.

Approaches

In this section I want to stress two points about Pippin's approach to film. In his first book on film, he thanks the philosopher Mark Wilson, "who some thirty years ago disabused me of my Europhile prejudices about 'art' film and introduced me to the wonders and depths of classic Hollywood cinema" (Pippin 2010a: x). No comparable shift of emphasis has taken place regarding his attitude to European philosophy.[3] From his earliest publications, Pippin's philosophical interests have centered around the likes of Kant, Nietzsche, and—above all—Hegel. Pippin tells us at one point that, whereas "Cavell's philosophical touchstone is Emerson, and to some extent Heidegger and Wittgenstein," his touchstone "has been Hegel on the link between self-knowledge, agency, and the knowledge of others" (2020a: 120, n. 8). So the first point is that Pippin is a Hegelian. Although things have changed in recent years, an interest in Hegel was for a long time as deeply unfashionable in analytic as in many continental philosophical circles.[4] To go so far as actually to refer to oneself as a Hegelian was as unacceptable to Bertrand Russell as to, say, Emmanuel Levinas. Given the implausibility of many of the things Hegel is—still—commonly held to have believed, this rejection is hardly surprising. So it is crucial to Pippin's project that to be a Hegelian does not mean what it has often been held to mean.

But what, then, *does* it mean to describe oneself as a Hegelian today? A number of the details of Pippin's answer to this question will emerge over the course of this book, but it is important to be very clear from the outset that it does not mean a belief that the world is made of thoughts, that history is really the activity of a mystical World Spirit becoming ever more conscious of itself, or that history came to an end in nineteenth-century bourgeois German Lutheranism. In the first paragraph of *Hegel's Idealism*, Pippin indicates that Hegel's influence (despite the paradox that he is "both extraordinarily influential and almost completely inaccessible") centers on his introduction of the idea of "historical subjectivity" (1989: 3).[5] For, say, Descartes as much as for Kant, what it is to be a rational being—whether approached from the "outside," or from within (experientially, phenomenologically)—is not something that can be said to change across time. For Hegel, however, subjectivity is ultimately unintelligible unless we take account of how it has changed and developed through time. As the editors of a collection of essays on Hegel in honor of Pippin put it, his Hegelianism:

> takes the form of a general account of a kind of historical progress, now without any straightforward, triumphant culmination in some ideal, reconciled "end of history," but rather as leading to the "problem" of modernity, a challenge both to human beings collectively and to individuals to interpret and reinterpret their own histories, cultures, and normative claims.
>
> (Zuckert and Kreines 2017: 3)

The idea that subjectivity itself might change—might have a history—or, as Terry Pinkard puts it, "the conception of our basic norms being indexed to very specific situations" (2017a: 100) is still rather difficult to get one's head round, and conflicts with many deep-seated intuitions and assumptions. Furthermore, to defend any notion of historical progress is certainly controversial and might seem to align Pippin with figures such as Steven Pinker, whose views are in fact very distinct from his. These complications notwithstanding, the idea of historical subjectivity is certainly much more promising than the highly abstract and implausible beliefs often ascribed to the comic-book Hegel.

Of course, "self-knowledge, agency, and the knowledge of others" (the factors above that we saw Pippin highlight as central to Hegel's influence on his approach to film) are not entirely synonymous with "historical subjectivity." Nevertheless, the point is that the former are, in the final analysis, forms or instances of the latter. Alternatively, one could say that it is only by thinking in terms of "historical subjectivity" that Pippin, following Hegel, thinks we can adequately tackle questions about "self-knowledge, agency, and the knowledge of others." In later chapters we will see in much more detail what possibilities are afforded by setting out from such a position. But for now, we might say that Pippin is a Hegelian in the first instance because historical subjectivity is his central interest—and thus it is, ultimately, what his explorations of film are directed at elucidating.

Of course, this would be unpromising were it not for the fact that films prove to be excellent sites for such explorations. In response to the objection that for writing to be "historical" it must draw on contextual, perhaps archival, research (see Abrams 2017 for a related complaint), Pippin would reply that simply by attempting to understand a film one can, among other things, learn something about subjectivity at a time, on the assumption that subjectivity is something *social* which *changes*. Pippin acknowledges that "it remains quite controversial to assume that there can be such a form of collective subjectivity" but declares that his work on film is intended to contribute to a demonstration of the idea "that we do not understand the meaning of so-called 'thick' normative terms—in the American case, terms like 'freedom,' 'individual,' 'right,' 'nation,' 'race,' 'woman'—without such a narrative working-out" as one finds in, among other places, great works of cinema (2016a: 220). This does not mean that a film need be deliberately designed to "say something" about them. Making a contribution to our understanding of such terms is, for Pippin, an inevitable consequence of any film that explores them in an interesting way. This is why Pippin has remarked that it is impossible for Shakespeare "to show us something important about Lady Macbeth's ambition without showing us something about *ambition*" (ibid.: 229; emphasis in original) and that "the play *Othello* cannot be about, be a way of understanding, Othello's jealousy without also being about, showing us something about, jealousy in general" (2021b: 241).

This position, obviously, places a great deal of weight on *interpretation*, which is the second point I want to stress at the outset. In Film Studies terms, Pippin's instincts concerning interpretation are much closer to those expressed by V. F. Perkins (to whom *The Philosophical Hitchcock* is dedicated) in the essay "Must We Say What They Mean?" than with those of David Bordwell, whose book *Making Meaning* was the occasion for Perkins's piece. In Pippin's view, although interpretation certainly involves the nonobvious (we often need to work at understanding a film), it is not necessarily helpful to say that "comprehension is concerned with apparent, manifest, or direct meanings, while interpretation is concerned with revealing hidden, nonobvious meanings" (Bordwell 1989: 2), because, among other things, "implication is a form of expression, not of concealment" (Perkins 2020: 249).[6] Interpretation can rearrange and reorientate our understanding of the very distinctions that are at issue. This means that, for example, there is no way of knowing which aspects of a film are a matter of "mere" description and which will require more extensive interpretation in advance of the attempt to comprehend, to describe, and to interpret. We cannot know what kind of interpretation is required without attempting an interpretation. In this, interpreting a film offers something like a microcosm of a whole tradition of post-Kantian philosophy concerned with rejecting what Pippin describes as Kant's "assumption that a determination of what could or could not be a meaningful assertion could, in advance as it were, let us know what could or could not be a legitimate philosophical, moral, religious, or scientific question" (1982: 231). It is therefore unsurprising that Pippin's account of interpretation holds as much for the interpretation of (at least some) films as of (at least some) philosophical texts. He has no interest in overreading films but also agrees, I suspect, with Cavell's remark in *Pursuits of Happiness* that "most texts, like most lives, are underread, not overread" (1981: 35). Pippin has remarked, for example, about *Thus Spoke Zarathustra* that since its first publication Nietzsche's book has either "remained basically inaccessible" or been "taken to be obviously accessible, which amounts to the same thing" (1988: 45–6).

Pippin's philosophical writings attempt to interpret the writings of Kant, Hegel, and so on, but never attempt to replace the need to actually read them. In this respect, they are not so unlike his writings on film. He would be horrified to think that anybody might think it desirable to read his book on *Vertigo* rather than watch *Vertigo*, like a kind of York Notes for students short on time or motivation. In this, if in nothing else, he lies in the mainstream of Film Studies (what kind of Film Studies wants to dissuade people from watching films?), but this position does distance him from some of the sites wherein film and philosophy intersect, namely those where films serve primarily to give philosophy some initial material to chew on. This is not to say that this kind of writing wants to put people off watching films, of course, but merely that, *qua* philosophy, whether the reader has actually had the experience of seeing the film does not make a great deal of difference.[7] Some philosophical reflection on *The Matrix*, say, doesn't need much more from the film than: "What we believe to be reality is a computer-generated illusion; we are really human batteries powering the machines that have created this illusion in order to keep us from realizing what is actually going on" (see, e.g., Dreyfus 2003). This is not the kind of philosophical treatment of film that Pippin finds most rewarding.

Cinema as Reflective Form: *Rear Window*

What kinds of films, then, and what kinds of treatments of them, *do* interest Pippin? He credits Kant with the view that "the only way to understand a philosopher's text is by *thinking* along with him [or her], actively probing what seem weaknesses or unclarities, asking continually whether a philosopher was entitled to the claims he [or she] makes, imagining how a position could respond to objections other than those posed in the text" (Pippin 2008: 33; emphasis in original). Something similar holds, Pippin believes, for understanding films philosophically. We need to "think along with" the film we are watching. Pippin's manner of so doing has a number of affinities with the "filmosophy" proposed by Daniel Frampton, which posits "a filmic kind of thought" involving a "filmind" ("the theoretical originator of the images and sounds we experience") whose activity can be detected by understanding a film's "action of form ... as the dramatic thinking of the filmind" (2006: 6). Frampton finds a sentence by Gilles Deleuze about Alfred Hitchcock's *Rear Window* useful to help explain what he means by this:

> One particular sentence in Deleuze's *Cinema* is helpful in understanding film-thinking: "It is the camera, and not a dialogue, which *explains* why the hero of *Rear Window* has a broken leg (photos of the racing car, in his room, broken camera)." The film surveys the tenement courtyard before returning to Jeffries [*sic*], asleep in his chair, his leg in a cast, at which point it then moves through his apartment to show the photo of a crashing racing car and a smashed camera. Film-thinking is thus the action of film form in dramatizing the intention of the filmind.
>
> (ibid.: 7; emphasis in original)

Deleuze's remark involves what is almost a kind of pun. Facts are often said to "explain" something, which could be considered a harmless anthropomorphism (the hole in the roof explains why the carpet is wet). Being inanimate, facts cannot "really" explain anything, but we are able to construct explanations by attending to them. Deleuze's point is that when, in a film, facts "explain things" there is also a more active kind of explaining going on. *The film* can be said to explain things in a fashion analogous to the way a person would do so. The *reason* the camera shows us what it does of L. B. Jeffries (James Stewart) in the way it does is to help the viewer come to know and understand certain things; we are really speaking about matters to do with narration, which in film can be achieved without verbal language.

Pippin might be skeptical of the need for neologisms like "filmind," preferring the term "reflective form," and perhaps makes clearer than Frampton that to speak of the film itself thinking is to speak metaphorically, but he is completely in agreement about the need to think about film form and meaning in terms of intention. In his own essay on *Rear Window*, Pippin writes:

> When we do notice [the director's narrational control], the visible narrational element is what gives the film its reflective form. Such a narrative form cannot but suggest a purposiveness, a point, and so manifests that the aesthetic object bears a conception of itself, a source of unity and ultimately interpretive meaning. It seems odd to say that filmed fictional narratives are in this sense "self-conscious," embody an awareness of themselves, but this is just an elliptical way of saying that the director is self-conscious of the point of the determinate narrative form.
>
> (Pippin 2020a: 24)[8]

One can detect in Pippin's reference to "the director" a lingering auteurism.[9] It could certainly be argued that Frampton's tendency to speak almost exclusively of what the *film*—rather than the director—does usefully sidesteps the kind of empirical questions about responsibility for different aspects of a film (exemplified, perhaps, by the often tetchy critical reception of *Citizen Kane*) that, fascinating as they are, are not directly relevant to how the finished film works *as a film* (recall the title of Perkins's most well-known book, *Film as Film*). Pippin does, in fact, appear to believe that the director is still, in most cases, the person *ultimately* responsible for the film as a whole, but he is very clear that we need to avoid any simplistic equation of intention with explicitly *conscious* intention:

> The "sense" embodied in the narrative and so the form's determinacy can be intuitively at work; for example, simply in seeing that such and such a narrational move would "make sense" in the context of the overall film, or that it wouldn't; that such and such an action

on the part of a character should be experienced as troubling; that a kind of self-blindness should be portrayed as destructive, not merely naive, and so forth.

(ibid.: 25, n. 2)[10]

Another way of putting what is essentially the same point is a remark about implication that Douglas Pye makes in his study of cinematic tone. Pye notes that although, speaking literally, "the film is not an entity that can itself imply anything ... the decisions that made it create for its viewers both a fictional world and implied ways of viewing it" (2007: 16). Films always imply *attitudes toward*—or *ways of seeing*—what they show; this is, fundamentally, because they must always show *in a specific way*. There is no such thing as "pure" showing, but this fact is a cinematic resource, not a limitation. Much of Pippin's work on film aims at exploring the complexities and subtleties of this resource. There will be a lot more to say about this particular kind of "self-consciousness," the intentions it embodies and reveals, and the notion of a cinematic "world," but it should at least be clear for now that Pippin thinks it is meaningful—albeit certainly metaphorical—to speak of films as being self-conscious. Film viewers are also self-conscious, which may appear too obvious to need saying, but Pippin is interested in a particular kind of self-consciousness, one we shall explore in more detail in the next chapter, at which he hints when he notes that when watching a film "we are in some sense aware that what we are seeing is being narrated" (2020a: 22).

In contrast, then, to a number of different strands within Film Studies that consider sustained attention to narrative, narration, and character inappropriate (representing, perhaps, a holdover from old-fashioned literary-critical thinking or a failure to absorb the insights of post-structuralist literary criticism in the wake of the author's much-discussed death) or simply uninteresting old hat (I once heard a senior academic express relief that Film Studies had largely moved away from a focus on "boring things like plot and character"), Pippin's notion of what it means to "think along" with a narrative fiction film, self-consciously to attend to the film's own self-consciousness, *requires* close attention to a film's narration and diegesis, to what its characters do and also to what they *think* they are doing. Pippin's account of *Rear Window* will serve to get a concrete example of this on the table. His chapter on the film explicitly focuses on the self-consciousness issue (it is entitled "Cinematic Self-Consciousness in Alfred Hitchcock's *Rear Window*"). It is the first chapter in *Filmed Thought* devoted to a specific film, and so its placement in the book, combined with the fact that it is one of the few chapters of that book that had not previously been published, suggests that Pippin intends it to serve as, in some ways, emblematic of his whole approach to film.

Pippin's choice of film for this purpose, however, might seem a little surprising. If self-consciousness has something to do with reflexivity—which it certainly does, although the two terms are by no means synonymous—then *Rear Window* might seem an overfamiliar, even a hackneyed, choice of film with which to explore the subject. The fact that there are deliberate parallels between the situation of the film viewer (and indeed, eventually, the film director) and that of Stewart's character Jefferies—a photographer temporarily immobilized by a broken leg, surveying the apartments and the courtyard visible from his own apartment window while voyeuristically piecing together what he sees into a series of interpretations and misinterpretations, crucially concerning a man's murder of his wife—has escaped nobody who has commented on the film. Pippin notes that "the striking similarity between the main character's immobile position watching the 'framed' dramas he sees in the windows of the apartments opposite his and the viewer's position in cinema" is "unquestionably the most commented-on feature of the film" (ibid.: 25). But it seems that Pippin feels that the undeniable aptness of the parallel also lays a trap for the film's interpreters, in that it has become *so* evident that there is a risk that we do not ponder its implications thoroughly enough (recall his remark, cited above, to the effect that assuming that it is obvious how to interpret Nietzsche's *Zarathustra* is as unhelpful as taking it to be uninterpretable). He refers, for example, to "the rather banal explanation of what attracts us to cinema, the possibility of seeing while unseen" (ibid.: 36).

So how *does* Pippin suggest we understand *Rear Window*'s "self-consciousness" and the ways we might "think along with" it? Without being able to do justice to the full subtlety of Pippin's interpretation—something that will, inevitably, be true of this book as a whole, lest it end up simply regurgitating Pippin's readings—some central strands are immediately clear. Chief among them is that a proper understanding of Jeff's voyeurism and the murder plot will not be achievable without paying attention to Jeff's relationship with his girlfriend Lisa (Grace Kelly). The latter is not simply color serving to "fill out" Jeff's character. Pippin claims that the film possesses "a triple plot" (first, "Jeff's growing obsession with voyeurism"; second, "the murder plot"; and, third, "what appears to be a long-standing resistance by Jeff to marrying Lisa"), and that the way all three are narrated "always raises the issue of the meaning of the interrelation of the three plots" (ibid.: 30–1). The voyeurism theme is, of course, made explicit by the film, when Jeff's nurse Stella (Thelma Ritter) observes that "we've become a nation of Peeping Toms." This is a historically specific observation, one concerning what—as we have seen—Pippin would call "historical subjectivity." Pippin takes it as a comment about specifically American subjectivity, referring to the fact that "we have … become a nation of moviegoers and, beginning around the time of the film, 1954, of television viewers" (ibid.: 31). But noting the parallels between Jeff and the viewer that Stella's remark suggests should be only the first stage in an interpretation; the connections between the various plots indicate this. Pippin states that there is obviously "something insufficient, deformed, about the way Jeff 'watches' his little films, and that has something to do with the deformation in his relations with others, paradigmatically with Lisa" (ibid.: 24, n. 1).

The film signals the inadequacy of Jeff's interpretations most clearly in the way he makes assumptions about Miss Torso (Georgine Darcy) that turn out to be inaccurate when her boyfriend finally returns and in his response to Miss Lonelyhearts's (Judith Evelyn) impending suicide. That Jeff is clearly inadequate both as an interpreter and a fellow human being is evident both in the way the goings-on in Lars Thorwald's (Raymond Burr) apartment distract him (and, to be fair, Lisa and Stella) from Miss Lonelyhearts, and in how he interprets what he does notice:

> Hitchcock seems concerned that we understand just how maladroit Jeff is at interpreting what he sees, saying what it means. At one point, he sees Miss Lonelyhearts get out a sheet of paper and starts to write, and he mutters that Stella was wrong; she is not preparing a suicide. But she certainly is; she is obviously writing a suicide note.
>
> (ibid.: 41, n. 30)[11]

As Valerie Orpen puts it, "if *Rear Window* were a tragedy, Jeff's tragic flaw would be his metaphorical blindness and not his voyeurism" (2003: 22). The film both maneuvers us into something like Jeff's position (in this paragraph I have, inevitably, been using Jeff's pet names for his neighbors, since the film gives us no alternatives) and, in places, carefully creates a distance that encourages us to evaluate his actions and to attempt to interpret things more successfully than him. Pippin concludes from this that Stella's remark is not intended merely "to suggest that filmed drama and comedy interest us because we like to be voyeurs, unobserved observers, but that we watch these screens *like Peeping Toms*. That is the *uninvolved spectatorial way* we watch them, as if what we see asks nothing of us, is simply there 'for us'" (ibid.: 31; emphases in original). Not everybody who watches without being seen is a Peeping Tom.

So, for Pippin, what he calls *Rear Window*'s "cinematic allegory" (ibid.: 36) is not merely a matter of how we watch films but how we *should* watch films. Though he does not discuss it, it does not seem that there is a great deal that he would disagree with in Laura Mulvey's paragraph on the film in her famous essay "Visual Pleasure and Narrative Cinema"—which itself draws on Jean Douchet's reading—as long as we conceive her claim that Jeff is "squarely in the fantasy position of the cinema audience" as working analogously with her subsequent remark that, in *Vertigo*, "the spectator, lulled into a false sense of security by the apparent legality of his surrogate, sees through his look and finds himself exposed as complicit, caught in the moral ambiguity of looking" (1989: 24). By this I mean that, for Pippin, the parallels between the audience in the cinema and Jeff (the immobile and ethically questionable viewer) serve as *starting points*—as ways of raising the question of how we might watch films and how that is connected to our relationships with others—rather than as *conclusions* or nonnegotiable discoveries, as if the film were to say, "The film viewer is a voyeur, and there's nothing we can do about it!" Psychoanalytic readings are therefore useful to Pippin insofar as they open up questions that are responsive to the fine interpretive details of the film in question, rather than imposing a grid of concepts that discovers the same thing in every film. In *Rear Window* he seems to find more of use in psychoanalytic readings of *character*, rather than of the film viewer, referring to what "in Freudian terms" we might call Jeff's "fear of his own desire for … feminization" (Pippin 2020a: 33).

The allegory that Pippin finds in *Rear Window* is not, then, a condemnation of the film viewer's ethically compromised situation so much as a way of putting that situation into question. It is not enough simply to attend to a film's self-consciousness, in the sense described above, which is to say the ways in which the film as an "aesthetic object bears a conception of itself, a source of unity and ultimately interpretive meaning" (ibid.: 24). We need also to consider *how* this is done, the specific ways in which a particular film is self-conscious. As Pippin puts it, in asking why a film shows us what it does in the way that it does, "such aesthetic attending already embodies a norm. It can be done well, or it can be done lazily, sloppily, indifferently, in a biased way, or self-righteously" (ibid.: 25). Though he is not entirely unambiguous about this, I take it to be Pippin's point both that *films* can show us things "well … lazily … or self-righteously," and that *viewers* can attend to what we are shown across a similar range of modes. The films that represent the greatest artistic achievements—and it is from among what he considers to be the set of such films that Pippin selects the films he writes about—are dangerous to underestimate. To watch *Rear Window* "voyeuristically" is, then, problematic not because it is to fail sufficiently to master the film by not being "clever" enough; it is, rather, a way of underestimating the film, of assuming that passive consumption is all that the film is worthy of.

Connecting these ideas to the notions of collectivity and intersubjectivity that are, perhaps, Pippin's central interests—whether philosophically or cinematically—raises questions about the relationship between insides and outsides. Stella suggests that "what people ought to do is get outside their own house and look in for a change," and Pippin is in complete agreement. In a remark that gets to the center of his understanding of subjectivity and agency (about which much more to come, particularly in Chapter 4), he notes that Jeff's tendency to treat Lisa as "a mere type, a Park Avenue, rich, spoiled girl" is connected to a refusal to "see himself from the outside," as he appears to Lisa, which "insulates him from others' view of him, a much more valuable potential source of self-knowledge than introspection" (ibid.: 36). The image of Jeff covering his eyes with his hand during the film's climax as he uses his flashbulbs to blind Thorwald is for Pippin an image of "blinded self-protection," one that makes the point "that his 'Peeping Tom,' external, spectatorial relation to the world has resulted in his own infirmity, a kind of willed self-blindness about others but especially to himself" (ibid.: 43). This is Pippin's summary of Jeff's attitude and the way that the plots intersect:

> Both [the Jeff-Lisa and the Thorwald plots] turn on Stella's inside-outside dialectic; on the one hand, Jeff's projective subjectivity, "looking" from inside his subjectivity out at everything else, never himself seen (least of all by himself), figured by his current position inside his apartment, but also evoked by the stasis, the immobility he suffers (so locked inside that everything outside is like a result of his projection), the effect of which keeps Lisa also "locked" into her position as fashion model, to be looked at from outside, not let in, treated as a surface; and on the other hand, Jeff's almost immediate suspicion of a neighborly murder, the result of a similar spectatorial position, likewise unable to see himself from the outside, in this case, to appreciate his own eagerness to figure a domestic life as nothing but whirring appliances, banal routine, and nagging wives.
> (ibid.: 35)

Pippin makes a distinction—but one that allows him to draw connections—between two things that can be either "lived" or "cinematic": *spectatorship* and *involvement*. There are real parallels between how we understand films and how we understand the other aspects of our lives: in both cases "we have to do some work, remembering past scenes, deciding which should not be remembered, interpreting how one past scene might or might not bear on a recent one" (ibid.: 27). But our involvement, and our attitude to it, is always at stake in this, as is indicated by the differing attitudes of Jeff and Lisa to Jeff's professional activities: "Jeff wants to photograph spectacles, events that require no deep interrogation of or involvement by the photographer. She wants him to become a fashion and portrait photographer, a job where, presumably, much more psychological investment in understanding the subject is required" (ibid.: 30, n. 16). In fact, we might see the irony in Jeff's position as operating a little more dialectically. Jeff doesn't only photograph motor races; the job that his editor refuses to send him on at the beginning of the film because his leg is still in plaster is in Kashmir, and later there is a reference to Pakistan. Presumably, Jeff is able to tell himself that the kind of physical discomfort and danger involved in photographing politically volatile situations *is* a kind of involvement. But that this involvement is still ultimately voyeuristic is demonstrated by the fact that Jeff shows no concern for whatever serious and presumably violent event is happening in Kashmir (which his editor tells him "is about to go up in smoke"), merely asking excitedly, "Didn't I tell you that's the next place to watch?" The verb—"watch"—is certainly not accidental.

Indeed, it has been said that nothing in Hitchcock is accidental; Murray Pomerance declares that "every nuance of his image is vital, no aspect decorative" (2011: 238). Although Pippin's readings are full of insight, and meticulously attentive to detail, they are not devoted to the kind of critical wizardry that pulls rabbits out of hats in order to reconfigure the film such that we see things in it that we could never have noticed otherwise. He works *with* the grain of the films he writes about, but attempts not to leave a thought half-developed. I suspect he would be very much in sympathy with Perkins's aspiration "to articulate in the medium of prose some aspects of what artists have made perfectly and precisely clear in the medium of film," and this because "interpretation is not an attempt to clarify what the picture has obscured" (2020: 248). Although Pippin points out that "Hitchcock was always so careful in his films to include visual details that repay multiple viewings" (2020a: 44), referring to D. A. Miller's *Hidden Hitchcock* as evidence, Miller's view of Hitchcock is rather different from Pippin's:

> Inevitably, we can't help sensing that there is more to meet the eye in Hitchcock than, in his viewer-friendly manner, he arranges to *greet* the eye. To put the point bluntly, everything we *are* asked to see in Hitchcock feels a bit disappointing: a façade that blocks

our view of all that we imagine we *might* see in the visual field. To watch a Hitchcock film is thus always to come under the spell of a *hidden* Hitchcock, and to want, somehow, to focus our attention on this imaginary thing or being.

(Miller 2016: 3; emphases in original)

It might help further to characterize Pippin's critical approach by considering a tiny detail in *Rear Window* that is not "perfectly and precisely clear."

Very early on, partway through the initial leftward pan across the courtyard, there is a blue flash in the central fourth-floor apartment of the building directly across from Jeff's apartment, presumably of a camera flashbulb, which is visible through the open windows (and also through the door onto the rooftop terrace onto which two women will later emerge in order to sunbathe, presumably in the nude, and get spied upon by a helicopter pilot). Are we "asked to see" this flash (see Figure 1)?[12] If we happen to be looking at the correct area of the screen it is impossible to miss; otherwise it is nearly impossible to see (I have had to point out its precise location to other people even when they were specifically looking for it). If we *do* see it, we can register some striped wallpaper and parts of a couple of framed pictures or photos, plus a chandelier, in the apartment from which it comes, but we can see no people therein. There are a few obvious possible interpretations of what is going on. Is there another photographer opposite Jeff, perhaps taking photos of the two women we see later? Are these fashion photos? Pornographic images? Later, when the dog is killed, four people appear in the window, two women—presumably the same two—and two men, perhaps the photographers. Or perhaps the women are taking photos of each other? Alternatively, of course, perhaps Jeff himself (or another of his neighbors) is being watched. (We have, after all, become a *nation* of Peeping Toms.) Could there even be another *Rear Window* taking place in another apartment, given that

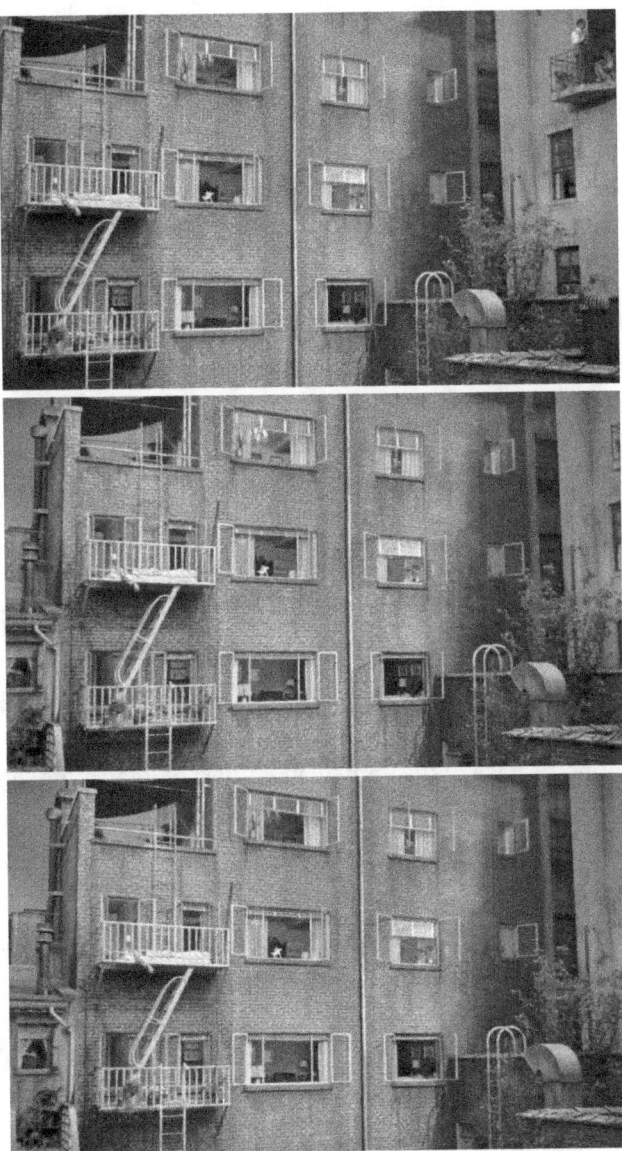

Figure 1 Blink and you (literally) miss it: the first flash in *Rear Window* (before, during, after).

(at least until Jeff gets hurled from the window) a series of flashes is all that an external observer would see of the film's climactic scene? But the early flash also indicates the limits of our—and Jeff's—voyeurism. We are likely to not even notice that there is something going on that we can't spy on; the indication that there is literally passes in a flash. There is always more to see, but realizing this may not in itself be enough to enable us to see it. (Wanting to see does not empower us to see, hence—presumably—the potency of the fantasies of power that voyeurism enables.) But even if we do spot it, we should not congratulate ourselves too much, because what we notice indicates the limitations of our observational powers—the barriers to involvement—much more than it confirms our panoptical potency.

Pippin's style of criticism is not the kind that focuses extended attention on this kind of tiny, ambiguous detail. And yet the preceding discussion is, I think, more Pippinian than Millerian because it "remains in thrall to the primacy of a film's narrative structure" (Miller 2016: 3). It seems most useful, at least in the first instance, to think about the flash in the immediate context of *Rear Window* rather than to explain it in terms of an economy of Hitchcockian trickery or suchlike (whether playful, sadistic, or otherwise). When Pomerance writes of another Hitchcock film, *Psycho*, that "the moment when Lila Crane (Vera Miles), opening the door to the Bates mansion with her left hand, trails her right hand behind her, pointing sweetly and in balletic gesture to the past (the past before motels existed), offers considerations on another order from the plot of the film" (2011: 237), Pippin would fully concur, as long as we do not thereby conclude that things of "another order" can have nothing to do with each other.[13] Pippin encourages us not to be like Jeff, who "can be said to have an impoverished notion of cinematic form, like a reader who reads 'only for plot'" (2020a: 44), but in so doing he does not propose that plot can be simply disregarded. Focusing only on plot can, curiously, have similar effects to ignoring the plot entirely, in that both risk interpretational cliché:

> He [Jeff] has *the plot* right, just as many viewers of Hitchcock watch and follow the plot successfully and take great pleasure in the technical brilliance of the editing, pacing, intersecting threads, and so forth. But they see nothing else, or they casually adopt some cliché about Hitchcock as the interpretive result, the meaning of the narrative: he is a perverse voyeur, a sadist, a cold, manipulative technician, a champion of the male gaze, a Catholic director convinced of universal and profound sinfulness, a cynic, or even the much more accurate cliché, but still a cliché, that he is a "humanist" at heart, and so forth. Many of his films, but especially *Rear Window* and *Vertigo* (above all, *Vertigo*), seem to me great protests against this.
>
> (ibid.: 39–40; emphasis in original)

Where, then, does *Rear Window*'s "great protest" leave us? Pippin's concluding remarks, uncharacteristically, seem to me not quite to pinpoint the intersubjective ironies with which Hitchcock leaves us. At the end of the film we see Jeff asleep once again, this time with both legs in plaster, while Lisa is reading a book called *Beyond the High Himalayas* which she discards for a *Harper's Bazaar* when she notices that Jeff is asleep. Pippin is certainly quite right that the surface impression that nothing has changed should give way to a sense that although "it is clear enough that managing the attempt at a new form of mutuality will still be quite difficult … Lisa seems confident that there will at least now be some measure of mutual respect and, better, mutual comprehension" (ibid.: 46), but his remark that, as a result, the tone "is upbeat, not ironic" (ibid.) needs qualification. Although diegetically the fact that the songwriter's finished composition is about a woman called Lisa is merely a coincidence, the way the sung name coincides with Jeff's sleeping face suggests that Lisa is still, for Jeff, something of a fantasy or a dream figure, just as she was in her very first appearance in the film. Doesn't the *Harper's Bazaar* suggest that Lisa has given up trying to adjust to Jeff and settled for merely *pretending* so to adjust? A possible response to this thought might begin by remembering that, previously, Jeff didn't *want* her to try to adjust, thinking that it would be futile. She seems, then, to be reading *Beyond the High Himalayas* precisely in order to facilitate a fantasy on Jeff's part that *he* is now willing to adjust to her adjustment. But the *Harper's Bazaar* then indicates that she is actually "managing the attempt at a new form of mutuality" precisely by *not* adjusting, not trying not to be herself. She *has* acquiesced to Jeff's earlier desires but pretends not to, for his sake. The ending is both upbeat—light and positive in tone—*and* ironic.[14] Although it certainly indicates that Jeff is now willing to imagine himself from the outside—from, for example, Lisa's point of view—when he does so we find ourselves in an extremely complicated tangle of self-images, images of other people's self-images, and images of images of self-images.

The richest cinematic exploration of such themes is, for Pippin, Hitchcock's *Vertigo*, to which he has devoted an entire book. We shall explore his reading of that film in Chapter 5. But having, I hope, given the flavor of Pippin's approach to film, we now need to fill in more of the details of the themes that have been introduced. I shall begin the process in the next chapter.

1

Modernism, Self-Consciousness, and Film

As the introduction to this book began to outline, a philosophical approach to film does not—for Pippin—necessarily involve the construction of theories about film but can be pursued by means of close, albeit highly self-aware, critical attention to individual films. The majority of *Robert Pippin and Film* will, therefore, pay close attention to Pippin's own close readings, something we began to do at the end of the introduction with *Rear Window*. But some further scene-setting will be helpful before we embark further on this project. This first chapter will, therefore, cover three subjects without which we will not be able fully to come to terms with Pippin's work on cinema. First is Pippin's understanding of modernity (which one could plausibly claim to be at the heart of his entire philosophical project) and the related notion of modernism. Second is the Kantian concept of "apperception," which has also been "a career-long preoccupation of Pippin's" (Suther 2020: 97). Hegel's appropriation of this concept is (argues Pippin) central to his philosophy; this Hegelian take on Kant underpins not only Pippin's understanding of cinematic narration but of what it is to watch a film philosophically. Finally, Pippin's lack of interest in constructing his own theories of film has not prevented him from occasionally producing theoretical writings about film—including (helpfully, and I think only apparently contradictorily) theoretical discussion of the non-theoretical nature of film-philosophy. This chapter, therefore, has a different relation both to films and to film theory than the remainder of the book. The first section and the first part of the second section barely mention films at all, while the second part of the second section and all of the third section are devoted exclusively to the theory of film. But having set forth this material, we will be much better placed to engage with the readings of classic Westerns that comprise Pippin's first book on film and are the subject of the next chapter. (Alternatively, if you're eager to get to some detailed readings of individual films, you might skip this chapter for now and return to it as and when you feel the need for a more thorough discussion of Pippin's philosophical stance.)

Modernity and Modernism

The first thing to say here is that Pippin tends to use "modernity" in what is probably its most expansive sense, to refer to something that began with the Enlightenment, the birth of modern science, the work of philosophers such as Descartes, Locke, and Hume, modern conceptions of the nation state, the family, and so forth—and that is still with us. In the words of Pippin's fellow Hegelian philosopher Terry Pinkard, "it is modern history—roughly that starting around 1687 or 1789, depending on whether one marks it at Newton's *Principia* or the French Revolution—that forms the most distinctive breaking point in history" (2017b: 157). Descartes was in some sense modern, and so—perhaps in a somewhat different sense, but one that is still part of the same story—are we. Pippin does not concur with the title of Bruno Latour's famous book *We Have Never Been Modern* (1993). On the contrary, he agrees with Hegel that the emergence of modernity was "the single most momentous event in, arguably, human history, certainly in Western history" (Pippin 2018a: 374). In the wake of such profoundly different anti-modernisms as those of, for example, Heidegger and Adorno, such a view is highly unfashionable in many quarters today and is often assumed to entail some kind of rationalist triumphalism that more or less effectively disguises a basically imperialist mindset (along the lines of "Western science dominates the world because it is The Truth"). Heidegger and Adorno both agree with Pippin about the fact of the "break" achieved by modernity, even while they often evaluate it differently. Thinkers like Latour and others who are often labeled as "postmodern," however, deny the very existence of the break. By taking the position he does, therefore, Pippin seems to have created for himself an extremely diverse set of ready-made philosophical opponents, not to mention a group of supposed allies he would prefer not to be associated with. What, then, does modernity mean for Pippin, and why does he insist on its importance?[1] This can be best shown, I think, by attending to two concepts: *normativity* and *autonomy*. I shall begin with the first and work toward a discussion of the second toward the end of this section.

In colloquial language, one frequently hears the word *normative* used more or less synonymously with "normal," so it is important to be clear that this is not what Pippin means by it. Something normative is something that can be done rightly or wrongly, something about which there is a way it *should* be done. It is, unsurprisingly, something that involves *norms*. Pippin describes normative considerations concisely as those "that invoke some sort of 'ought' claim" (2009: 36). Put another way, thinking about normativity involves thinking about *reasons* as opposed to *causes*.[2] If one snooker ball hits another it does not really make sense to talk about what the second ball "should" do, except quasi-metaphorically to express a prediction about what *will* happen or surprise about what *did* happen ("the blue ball shouldn't have moved that way; maybe the table isn't level"). But if, during a game of snooker, someone were to take a shot, as a result of which one of those balls flew off the table and smacked their opponent in the eye, we would enter the realm of the normative ("You shouldn't have done that!" "I promise I didn't mean to, my arm slipped!"). In her classic study of intention, originally published in 1957, Elizabeth Anscombe points out quite how diverse are the situations in which we use the language of normativity:

> That athletes should keep in training, pregnant women watch their weight, film stars their publicity, that one should brush one's teeth, that one should (not) be fastidious about one's pleasures, that one should (not) tell "necessary" lies, that chairmen in discussions should tactfully suppress irrelevancies, that someone learning arithmetic should practise a certain neatness, that machinery needs lubrication, that meals ought to be punctual, that we should (not) see the methods of "Linguistic Analysis" in Aristotle's philosophy; any fair selection of examples, if we care to summon them up, should convince us that "should" is a rather light word with unlimited contexts of application.
>
> (Anscombe 2000: 64)

This diversity might be seen to indicate that there is not much to be said about normativity in the abstract, but Anscombe also wryly indicates its ubiquity, indeed its inescapability, in the way she herself uses the term she is bringing into question ("should convince us").

It is no accident that discussion of the normative leads so readily to questions of agency and intention, of how subjects can meaningfully be said to *do things*. As we shall see in Chapter 4, Pippin believes that Hegel proposes an extremely interesting and promising account of agency; he proposes both that it can underpin the philosophical study of film and that such study of film can put it interestingly under philosophical pressure. For now, however, we need to be clear about the connection between normativity and Pippin's perception of the momentous break represented by modernity. Pippin stands between two opposed philosophical poles. For naturalists, one of the achievements that have followed in the wake of the birth of modernity is the ever-increasing dismantling or dissolution of the normative (what we ought to do) and its replacement by the causal (what the universe "tells us" to do).

One does not *really* do things because of reasons; these reasons are just by-products of fully material and mechanistic procedures, whether—say—neurological or evolutionary (or, of course, both). Other philosophers defend the existence of free will as something metaphysically distinct; our ability to make decisions must imply the existence of a faculty of uncaused causation that will never be fully describable by the physical sciences. These are two variants of what is known as incompatibilism; Pippin, however, defends a form of compatibilism. He agrees with the naturalists that there is no mysterious metaphysical free will, while simultaneously disagreeing with them that naturalistic explanations are all that we need. (David Macarthur gives an excellent and succinct account of the disagreement between those, like Pippin, who argue for "the explanatory priority of *sui generis* rational normativity" and the naturalists who deny this; see Macarthur 2019: 185–8.)

Pippin, then, thinks that first-personal accounts of agency are necessary—though certainly not sufficient—in order to explain why people (whether those people are real, historical people, or people in films like L. B. Jefferies) do what they do: "Normative questions … are irreducibly 'first-personal' questions, and these questions are practically unavoidable and necessarily linked to the social practice of giving and demanding reasons for what we do, especially when something someone does affects, changes, or limits what another would otherwise have been able to do" (2009: 38). Pippin has no wish to fend off the attacks on the supposed transparency of our notions of why we do things (attacks on, that is, the idea that I cannot be wrong about my own reasons) that are exemplified by the writings of the triad that Paul Ricoeur dubbed the "masters of suspicion," namely Nietzsche, Marx, and Freud—not to mention Charles Darwin or Benjamin Libet (whose experiments purported to demonstrate that the brain "makes decisions" before the subject is aware of it). But neither does Pippin think that naturalism fully recognizes the difficulty of responding to the challenge that this work and its implications collectively represents:

> Knowing something about the evolutionary benefits of altruistic behavior might give an interesting perspective on some particular altruistic act, but *for the agent*, first-personally, the question I must decide is whether I ought to act altruistically and, if so, why. I cannot simply stand by, waiting to see what my highly and complexly evolved neurobiological system will do.
>
> (ibid.: 38–9; emphasis in original)

Nor would we actually *accept* an evolutionary account in any actual situation where agency and responsibility were at issue:

> One imagines, with the proliferation of "evolutionary" accounts of behavior and mating rituals in particular, a wayward husband, having been caught philandering, protesting ... "What could I do? We now know that men are powerfully disposed to maximize the spread of their genetic information." It is a gullible spouse indeed who accepts such an excuse.
>
> (Pippin 2010b, response to Joshua Landy)

A non-gullible spouse who does not accept this excuse, however, is not committed to denying the truth of the claim about male evolutionary dispositions. If we really want to take on board the challenges to our self-understanding presented by the likes of Darwin, Marx, Nietzsche, and Freud, then the really difficult question is what *difference* their work should make to the way we act, even when their arguments are at their most convincing. Pippin believes that the interpretation of films can contribute to answering this question, in part because of the extreme complexity and diversity of the normative that we earlier saw Anscombe point out; only richly detailed specific examples are likely to offer any material for reflection that avoids banality or oversimplification.

It may still, however, not be entirely clear what all this has to do with modernity. One way of formulating the answer would be to say that it is with modernity that normativity becomes problematic in this way. The figure who represents the full birth of the modern for Pippin, in terms of the issues that most concern him, is Immanuel Kant (1724–1804). Robert Brandom describes the following as "perhaps Kant's deepest and most original idea":

> What distinguishes judging and intentional doing from the activities of non-sapient creatures is not that they involve some special sort of mental processes, but that they are things that knowers and agents are in a distinctive sense *responsible for*. Judging and acting involve commitments. They are endorsements. They are exercises of authority. Now responsibility, commitment, endorsement, authority—these are all *normative* notions.
> (Brandom 2013)

Responsibility is not a moral or ethical concept entirely separable from questions of rationality; to be rational *is* to commit oneself to claims for which one can be held responsible. Echoing the remarks above about compatibilism, Brandom goes on to argue that Kant realized that what distinguishes the realm of the mental is not something *ontological* (as in Descartes's dualism, in which mind and matter are two wholly distinct substances), but instead something *deontological* (i.e., something to do with duty, with—once again—what we *should* do). Kant believes this to be a discovery about what it is to be a rational agent, period, but Hegel believes that the insight is incomplete unless it is historicized. As Pinkard puts it, as history develops, "what seem to be constitutive of some social status turn out, as the shape of life develops itself, instead to be normative" (2017a: 18). Previously, say, a ruler who did not preferentially engage in warfare rather than diplomacy risked simply ceasing to be a ruler (if "rulers don't negotiate," then someone who negotiates cannot be a ruler). But as history proceeds such a view becomes less tenable, and the idea of preferentially engaging in warfare comes to appear as what a *good ruler* would do, rather than as part of *what it is* to be a ruler. Hegel, then, allies this view with the realization that these norms *themselves* change across history, which has the consequence that his account "bypasses the more usual hard and fast philosophical distinction between purely conceptual ... concerns and those of empirical matters" (ibid.: 19). Normative questions—just like interpretive questions—cannot be answered a priori.

There is, however, at least one immediately obvious objection to such a view. If social status is always, ultimately, normative, and if those norms are never absolute, it is hard to see how it can avoid relativism (in which we cannot, e.g., ever say that something—slavery, for example—is simply, whenever and wherever it occurs, *wrong*) or accommodationism (a philosophy reduced to special pleading to justify whatever happens to be the case). Hegel has often been accused of the latter, and less frequently of the former (or has been accused of a highly implausible account of historical progress precisely as a way of avoiding relativism). Pippin regards as a "starting-point" for contemporary Hegelianism "a commitment to the historicity of norms, but without a historical relativism, as if we were trapped inside specific assumptions and cannot think our way out of them" (2015a: 108). This is a very difficult issue that we cannot adequately address here, but one useful preliminary point would be to indicate the implausibility of the obvious alternative claim, namely that some practices are straightforwardly and timelessly right or wrong, irrespective of the existence of the societies in which they take place and are judged:

> For example, if we want to understand why gender-based division of labor became so much less credible a norm in the last third of the twentieth century, and exclusively in the technologically advanced commercial republics of the West, one begins to become a "Hegelian" with the simple realization of how implausible it would be to insist that the injustice of such a basis for the division of labor, the reasons for rejecting such a practice, were always in

principle available from the beginning of human attempts to justify their practices, and were "discovered" sometime in the early 1970s. And yet our commitment to such a rejection is far stronger than "a new development in how we go on." The practice is irrational and so unjust, however historically indexed the "grip" of such a claim clearly is.

(ibid.)

Our ability to effect changes such as the dismantling of gender-based division of labor (something that has surely begun to take place, even if in many instances it has not got very far) can serve to introduce the second theme I promised to deal with in this section, namely that of *autonomy*. In Hegelian terms, to say that "we" really have "done" something—such as begin to break down gendered work practices—and that to do so is something rational, is to make a claim about autonomy. This is another highly controversial claim, given the many good reasons there often are for seeing specific claims to autonomy as self-serving justifications. For Pippin:

> Hegel best realizes such a project [i.e. the originally Kantian project of determining 'whether such a subject can be so radically independent or self-determining, and especially whether such self-legislation can be said to be rational'] … and Nietzsche represents, in effect, Hegel's most problematic opponent, the thinker who best raises the question of the whole possibility and even desirability of such a "self-reassurance," a self-conscious justification.
>
> (Pippin 1999: 14)

For Kant as much as for Hegel, claims about autonomy are rooted in the fact that reasons can only *be* reasons for an agent if that agent *takes them as* reasons; we are all autonomous to that degree.[3] (This does not by any means imply that it is simply "up to me" which reasons *should* count as reasons—hence the irreducibly social, as well as historical, character of normativity. Later, we shall see that Hegel believes that individual subjectivity—and indeed, in many senses, even individual agency—is only possible because of the existence of other subjects.) If I go ahead and have that sixth beer, I haven't stopped being the kind of thing that makes decisions and turned instead into a being that is controlled by its immediate desires. I have *decided* to have the beer, however much the physiological effects that the preceding five have had on my body might be impairing the basis on which I make the decision, compared with my decision-making when sober. (Consider the differences between this and the situation in which what I thought was alcohol-free beer was in fact strong lager.) Hence the centrality to ethical reflection—and to our interpretation of films—of the distinctions between, say, a genuine excuse and an evasion of responsibility.

If we consider this issue in its broadest historical sweep, Pippin's position—recalling the narrative structure we have encountered more than once already in this section—is that

> modernity is ... not a hubristic, autochthonous will to autonomy and self-sufficiency, as Heidegger and others read it, but is itself irresistibly provoked by the growing, ever more plausible possibility that what had been taken to be absolute and transcendent was contingent and finite, since always self-determined, a contingent product of a human positing.
>
> (ibid.: 177)

But in contrast to the more triumphalist versions of its achievements, Pippin sees an interest in failure—in the breakdown of practices, the sheer difficulty of squaring the circle, of thinking in terms of reasons and of causes—as characteristic of modernity. He writes that for him, "and I think for Hegel, that is the most interesting and telling aspect of normative authority. It can fail" (Pippin 2015a: 89). Hence the title of the book from which the previous two long quotations have been taken, *Modernism as a Philosophical Problem*, and its subtitle, *On the Dissatisfactions of European High Culture*. In a later book, entitled *After the Beautiful*, Pippin makes this kind of account more concrete in an aesthetic context by means of a reading of the birth of modernist painting in the France of the late nineteenth and early twentieth centuries, chiefly in the work of Manet and Cézanne. The different applications and resonances of the words "modernity" and "modernism" are too complex to fully unpack here, but just as I have argued that, for Pippin, in modernity we see normativity becoming problematic "to itself," here he proposes that "perhaps the least (but by no means un-) controversial characterization would be simply to say that modernist art is art produced under the pressure of art having become a problem for itself, in a period when the point and significance of art could no longer be taken for granted" (2014: 1).

In *After the Beautiful*, Pippin argues that Hegel's sense of art as something that had once been—but no longer was—a central forum in which humans make themselves intelligible to themselves (or, to put it another way, that art had been superseded by philosophy) was mistaken. Pippin believes, on the contrary, that making ourselves mutually intelligible is still a crucial function of art, which includes the films he writes about. There is a sense, then, in which all of Pippin's work on film is written in *disagreement* with Hegel. But this is a disagreement that attempts to show the continuing relevance of Hegelian ways of thinking. As he writes about modernist painting:

> My hypothesis is that if one can understand the persistence of the kind of conflicting commitments in intellectual, cultural, and political life required by rapidly modernizing European societies, the kind Hegel thought had been overcome, one will be in a better position to begin to understand the aesthetic experimentation that seemed to begin with Manet.
>
> (ibid.: 38)

Pippin finds the aspects that contemporaries found so radical in paintings by Manet such as *Olympia* (1863–5)—for example, the way "the subjects in Manet's paintings often look out of the picture frame toward the beholder" (ibid.: 48)—as having the consequence that the image itself suggests that we think of the difference between seeing a painted surface in an artwork and seeing the object itself as like the difference between seeing a person, or a person's face, *as an object* like any other and seeing it as a *face* of a person, requiring a completely different relation between beholder and beheld.

(ibid.: 49; emphases in original)[4]

It is no coincidence that this difficulty echoes the difficulty of understanding ourselves and others in terms of both causes and reasons. In common with many who have discussed modernism in art, then, strangeness and difficulty are often central to Pippin's accounts. But he sees these features neither as simply a symptom of ethical and moral disorientation, or even pathology, nor as representing a turn away from content toward the purely formal (as in Clement Greenberg's narrative of modernist painting).[5] On the contrary, these aspects represent the way in which modern artworks and their audiences participate in historically grounded attempts at—or resistances to—mutual intelligibility, and this intelligibility need not be wholly conceptual but could quite properly be described as aesthetic, as unachievable in the absence of the experience *of* the artwork, *as* an artwork. Just as, Pippin believes, not all explanation of behavior needs to be naturalistic explaining-away, there is such a thing as *understanding* a painting, a sculpture, or a film that does not involve explaining it away, as would happen if we were to say something like, "the painter paints like this because of an imbalance in her nervous system and the consequences of the neglect she suffered as a child." Attempting to understand, say, a film *as a film* (to echo the title of V. F. Perkins's best-known book) need not involve "slicing off" its other dimensions (psychological, political, philosophical, etc.). There are psychological, political, and philosophical insights that can only be achieved *via* an aesthetic understanding—via the attempt to understand an artwork on its own terms—not by "applying" analytic techniques derived from other domains.

This helps to fill out the reasons why, as we saw in the introduction, Pippin does not believe that it is naive to interpret narrative films as if the characters they contain are human beings (something which, fictionally, they certainly are), but also that this does not prevent the critic from attending to the meaning of a film's form. Form and content may be distinguishable, but they are never separable. Unlike Pippin's work on film, *After the Beautiful* devotes more space to philosophical discussion than to attending closely to paintings. The issues discussed in this section are, however, beautifully compressed in his remarks in a later piece about Théodore Géricault's painting *Head of a White Horse* (see Figure 2) and the complex range of tonalities that it expresses. Pippin finds the painting "so arresting" because of

> the incontrovertible subjectivity or deep interiority of the horse, *literally visible*, even while mysterious, requiring interpretive work. There is something in the expression of the horse, even given the animals' exoticism and strangeness, with those huge nostrils, and its odd, almost carefully combed mane, all at once accusatory, wise, hesitant, both wary and knowing, uncertain if facing friend or foe, not to mention simply noble, in a pose of great dignity, in the expression of the horse, as if facing and seeking the "other" without which, for Hegel, it cannot be the subject it is, and unsure about finding such a realisation.
>
> (Pippin 2021b: 99; emphasis in original)

Following his reading of Hegel, Pippin's claim is that these things really are *visible* in the painting when it is properly attended to; these and other aspects of the painting are "not conceptually or discursively, but ... affectively intelligible" (ibid.: 101). Seeing this painting as, for example, simply an almost-successful quasi-photorealist representation of an animal would, in dismissing its strangenesses as straightforwardly evaluable lapses in technique, miss what is most remarkable about it. What is most worthy of note in this painting cannot be fully perceived without seeing the horse *as a horse*, while

Figure 2 *The Head of White Horse*, 1810–1812, by Théodore Géricault (1791–1824).

also simultaneously recognizing that it is in fact *a painting of a horse*.[6] There can be no simple spectrum between, on the one hand, being engrossed in a realistic world and, on the other, coolly judging an artwork as a manufactured object because, as the philosopher Richard Moran argues, "the very expressive qualities that disrupt any sense of a fictional world are in fact central for our psychological participation with artworks" (2017: 9).[7] As Pippin himself has written about film:

> We have no trouble remaining deeply engaged by a plot, thrilled by it, immersed, wholly absorbed in a fictional world at one level (a level at which we bring all our everyday experience of persons

and their motives to bear on trying to follow the plot and figure out the nature of the characters), while remaining at another level still attentive to … aesthetic [questions], attentive to the possible meaning of these elements shown in this way, to the point of the narration. I take this possibility as constitutive of being able to appreciate the cinematic narrative as a work of art.

(Pippin 2016a: 224)

To understand Géricault's painting in the way Pippin's description exemplifies it is to participate in questions of normativity (What makes a successful painting?) and autonomy (Who or what is responsible for the painting's qualities?) that, for Pippin, go to the heart of the distinctiveness of the modern. We could not give anything like the same answers to these questions with regard to this particular painted horse as we might give to the parallel questions concerning, say, an ancient Greek bronze horse without divorcing both of them from their historical circumstances. It might well be the case, however, that the corresponding answers we could give with regard to the painting and to, say, Béla Tarr and Ágnes Hranitzky's film *The Turin Horse* (2011) would be similar enough that pursuing their similarities could prove illuminating, and this because both painting and film are part of the larger story of modernity in a way that the bronze is not. Such an approach to the artwork—such a historically situated mode of aesthetic attention, we could say—involves a particular account of self-consciousness, which it is the task of the next section to elucidate.

Self-Conscious Seeing

Much of the radicality of Kant's philosophy—that which makes it so emblematic of modernity for Pippin—lies in the way it refuses either Descartes's rationalism (those ideas about which we can be absolutely clear without empirical assistance must be innate) or the empiricism of Locke (all our ideas must be, ultimately, derived from sensory experience; there is no such thing as an innate idea). Kant's complex alternative involves what he calls a "transcendental" investigation into the conditions of possibility of experience—those things which have to be true in order for an experience *to be an experience* at all. The details of this project would take us too far afield, but one aspect of it is very important because it is, so Pippin argues, central to Hegel's Kantian inheritance, and thus lies behind Pippin's Hegelian understanding of film viewing. As we shall see, this aspect has its most immediately obvious implications for our topic in Pippin's account of what we see when we watch a fiction film. But first, we need to get the most important philosophical details on the table.

The aspect to which I am referring is what Kant called—in a phrase that even Hegel, not known for the elegance of his style, called an "ugly monster" (Pippin 1999: 51)—"the transcendental unity of apperception." The essential idea is that it must be possible for a subject to be conscious of any of their experiences *as their experiences*.[8] If this were not the case, so Kant argued, we simply would not be having an *experience*; we would merely be buffeted by sensory information without the ability to experience the buffeting as such. This touches once again on questions of autonomy:

> In a claim that was to have far-reaching consequences for the rest of the German tradition, he [Kant] insisted that simply being "in" a mental state could not count as an experience at all, much less a foundational one. An object of consciousness, even a moment in the flow of my mental life, can count as a determinate moment or object, only if I construe it, or take it to be such a moment.
>
> (Pippin 1999: 53)

This means that consciousness can never be something that simply "happens" but must always be in some sense an activity, something that the subject is *doing*: "To experience is thus always to 'act' upon oneself in a certain way" (Pippin 1982: 169). But this might sound like it involves a two-stage process—that we, for example, see a tree, and then go on to think about the fact that we are seeing a tree. The most important aspect of Kant's argument, the one that Pippin thinks Hegel fully took on board (and indeed radically extended), is that to think of transcendental apperception as a two-stage process in this way would fundamentally misconstrue Kant's insight.[9]

This point can be elusive, but one way of thinking about it is as giving an "adjectival" account of consciousness. There is no such thing as pure, bare consciousness, *per se*. We must always be conscious *in a particular way*. Pippin explains it this way:

> Although it is true that when I, for example, perceive X, I also take myself to be perceiving, or apperceive, the latter is not only not an isolatable experience, it cannot be described in any way as an inference I draw or as a causal result of my perceiving. One could perhaps imagine an unusual situation where I do not know, say, whether I am perceiving or hallucinating, and where I try to infer from the evidence what I am doing or undergoing, but even in that case, what I *originally* experience already includes my perception of the state I am in *and* my implicit judgment of being in an unfamiliar state, and no later judgment about the case could be said to "add" apperception to my experience.
> (Pippin 1989: 23; emphases in original)

Even being unsure of whether or not I am hallucinating is a *particular* kind of awareness; it has, we could say, a certain "texture." All consciousness is textured in this way, and this texture is something we are always conscious of, even though we often—most of the time, in fact—do not explicitly *attend* to the fact that we are so conscious. (Terry Pinkard puts the point very nicely when he writes that we are not dealing with a situation in which a chef preparing a meal has to keep reminding themselves that they are "cooking and not, say, skydiving" [2017b: 117].) Whenever we are conscious, we are always self-conscious in this sense, which is very different from the colloquial usage; if I am self-conscious of my appearance at a party populated by famous people, that *is* much more like having an awareness of myself as if "from outside." Neither Kant nor Hegel want to deny that this experience is possible, or that we can—for example—think about our own experiences; they simply deny that this kind of self-consciousness is the kind that is involved in all experience, simply in order for it to be an experience.

Such an argument relates directly to the kind of phenomenological arguments we find in later philosophers such as Heidegger and Merleau-Ponty. Pippin himself makes the connection:

> Perception of course involves physiological processes that are species-identical across centuries and cultures, but perceptual knowledge also involves norms for attentiveness, discrimination, unification, exclusion, and conceptual organization that do not function like physiological laws. ... But while Hegel certainly accepts that the physiological components of perception are *distinguishable* from the norm-following or interpretive elements, he also insists that the physiological and the normative aspects are *inseparable* in perception itself. (As in Heidegger's phenomenology, there are not two stages to perception, as if a perception of a white rectangular solid is then "interpreted as" a refrigerator. What we *see* is a refrigerator.)
>
> (Pippin 2011: 25; emphases in original)[10]

Note that normativity (which we encountered so frequently in the previous section) again makes an appearance: even perception itself involves a normative dimension. This normativity is clearly apparent in skilled perception: an experienced ornithologist, for example, can consistently correctly *see* the difference between two kinds of hawk in a way that a beginner cannot. But, to reiterate once again, they do not do so by first ticking off a list of attributes and subsequently drawing the appropriate inference. There are really two very closely related points here. First, all consciousness takes a specific form, one that we always "apperceive," or are self-conscious of (are, that is, at least potentially aware of, such that we would agree or disagree with someone who described this form to us). Second, when the form that consciousness takes is perceptual it does not involve a two-stage process in which raw data is "interpreted" only at a later stage. We simply see a refrigerator and are self-conscious that what we are doing is seeing. (None of which is incompatible with finding out that we are, in fact, mistaken and were, in fact, looking at an unusual washing machine, or that we were not seeing at all but had had electrodes inserted directly into our brain.) From the first of these points, the one about apperception, it follows *a fortiori* that something similar must be true for the way we perceive and attend to works of art:

> Aesthetic experience … does not simply happen to one. It requires a particular mode of attending. … It is important to stress constantly that this knowing we-are-so-attending is nothing like a self-observation, an attending to ourselves as an object. It is a constituting aspect of aesthetic attending itself, not a separate noting of that fact.
> (Pippin 2019a: 533)[11]

Attending to a fiction film also involves something analogous to the second point. In his book *Seeing Fictions in Films*, the philosopher George Wilson presents an account of what happens when we attend to a fictional film. Extremely briefly put, the relevant aspect of Wilson's argument is as follows. When we watch a film, what literally passes before our eyes is a rapid succession of still images, often photographic representations of particular actors (say, Cary Grant). But we understand ourselves to be watching a fictional story, one in which, say, Roger Thornhill is mistaken for someone called George Kaplan (if we are watching *North by Northwest*). On Wilson's account, while we can be said to be literally seeing (a series of images of) Grant, we must be said to *imagine seeing* Thornhill: "Normal viewers of fiction films characteristically have an imaginative 'as if impression' of seeing the narrative objects and events of a fiction film. They have the continuing impression that it is as if they were witnessing segments of the fictional world" (2011: 73). This can happen, Wilson thinks, because they *imagine seeing* these "segments." Pippin is enthusiastic about Wilson's account (indeed, the importance of Wilson's work for Pippin is indicated by the fact that he is one of the dedicatees of *Filmed Thought*). But the terms in which he endorses Wilson's arguments subtly, but crucially, alter their implications. Pippin takes himself to be in agreement with Wilson that it would be a mistake to think that all that goes on when we watch a film is that we literally see the "projected, 30-feet-high images" that "are all there really is in front of us" and then do the rest of the work "inside our heads" (Pippin 2013a: 334). This appears to be Noël Carroll's position, expressed here in relation to Buster Keaton's *The General*: "We see images of Buster Keaton doing this and that, and imagine that Johnnie Gray is doing thus and so" (2006: 184, n. 7). No, both Wilson and Pippin want to say, in some sense we really do *see* Gray and not—in a two-stage process—only (images of) Keaton, about which we draw inferences that mandate us to imagine certain fictional goings-on.[12] For Pippin, this situation is analogous to the way we *see a refrigerator* (rather than drawing inferences from the appearance of a white rectangle) or the experienced birder *sees* a common black hawk and not a red-shouldered hawk. But specifying precisely in what sense we can be said to see Johnnie Gray is, of course, the tricky part.

Although he sees the possibility of avoiding one kind of two-step process (namely that, in watching films, we literally see some things—such as images of Buster Keaton—on the basis of which we go on to imagine other things—such as "that Johnnie Gray is doing thus and so") as one of the chief virtues of Wilson's account, Pippin concedes that Wilson's terminology sometimes gets too close for his liking to implying a different kind of two-step process, one that he wants to resist. Wilson's tendency to refer to viewers as *imagining seeing* risks doing so; things get even worse when, as sometimes happens, Wilson uses phrases such as "imagine yourself seeing" (see, e.g., 2011: 100). Pippin, on the other hand, prefers to use the phrase *imaginatively see* (see, e.g., 2013a: 336). I hope the connection with the idea of apperception is apparent. Recall the remark above about thinking adjectivally; for Pippin, we would do better to describe the way in which we see Roger Thornhill or Johnnie Gray as a kind of seeing (*imaginative* seeing), rather than it being a matter of us imagining a certain thing, namely "ourselves seeing." Pippin approvingly cites Richard Moran's remark that "to imagine something visually is not the same as to imagine seeing it" (2017: 15). The philosopher Bernard Williams makes a very similar point in his essay "Imagination and the self." Wilson refers to this piece early in his book as a "useful ... introduction to some of [its] central topics" (2011: 7). It seems to me, however, that he neglects the significance of one of the most interesting points Williams makes, one roughly equivalent to the remark of Moran's just cited, which provides a way of making the necessary distinctions in a way more compatible with the Kantian insight so important to Pippin.[13]

Williams makes the point that "it is misleading to say that straight visualizing is thinking of myself seeing something" (1973: 40). This is because to think of *oneself* seeing something requires an extra imaginative step, but one that is by no means required. I *could* imagine myself standing somewhere near the grassy knoll, watching Kennedy's motorcade approach, but it is equally possible to simply imagine it, visually, without paying any attention at all to "how" I am able to see what I am visualizing (this latter possibility echoes one of Wilson's central points about film viewing, that we do not need to imagine where we are located within the film world in order to be able to see what we see). The point is not restricted to visual imagination but extends much more generally. Williams goes on to point out that to imagine being Napoleon is a quite different thing from imagining *myself* being Napoleon, and that successfully achieving the former in no way requires that we also do the latter (ibid.: 42–5). Wilson believes that the predicament that Williams's article leaves us in is "deeply puzzling" because we seem to end up in close proximity to the claim that, "when viewers see a fiction X in a cinematic work W ... viewers do not *see* and do not *imagine seeing* X in W at all" (2011: 8); he calls this a "striking and implausible result" (ibid.: 9). But this situation only seems puzzling and implausible because Wilson assumes a dichotomy between two types of seeing, literal seeing and imagined seeing, whereas Williams could deny that viewers must either "literally see" or "imagine seeing" fictions in film and propose, instead, that viewers *imaginatively see* them. There are, that is, forms of "non-literal seeing" that are not best described as "imagining seeing" something, because the latter implies an extra step that is not necessary.

One of Wilson's objections to Carroll's position—denying that there is any "seeing imaginarily involved" (Carroll 2006: 184, n.7)—is that it seems to leave no room for distinguishing between what we see on the screen in a fiction film and events that happen in the fictional world but are not shown on screen. Wilson uses as an example a sequence from Fritz Lang's *M*, in which we see Peter Lorre's character buy a balloon for a little girl and are subsequently given to believe—but *not* shown—that he murders her: "The viewer 'sees' or (better) imagines seeing the purchase of the balloon (and perhaps the meeting), but, as the movie is constructed, the viewer does not 'see' or imagine seeing the murder of the little girl" (2011: 75). Using terminology derived from Pippin and Williams, we could say that we *imaginatively see* what is shown on screen (the purchase of the balloon), while we are free either to imagine the murder any way we like, or not to imagine it. (We could, if we so chose, imagine it visually, or even "imagine ourselves seeing it.") Visually imagining the (unshown) murder, should we choose to do so, *would* involve a two-step process, one of the first type (the type, i.e., that both Wilson and Pippin want to deny is involved in the normal way we watch fiction films). The film could be said to mandate such imaginings, in the sense that to imagine something that *does* take place in the fictional world is clearly a very different operation to imagining something that *does not* (such as if one were to imagine one of the reporters noticing the wooden sled in the furnace at the end of *Citizen Kane*). To refuse to take up this mandate, however, is not to fail to watch the film. As Pippin remarks, even though film "viewers are in some literal sense looking at celluloid (or digital) images, moving pictures, of actors on movie sets and location pretending to be characters in a made-up story ... anyone seeing simply *that* would not be 'watching the movie'" (2013a: 334; emphasis in original). In the case of *M*, we might simply acknowledge the fact that the little girl has been killed without feeling the need to imagine it at all (such has been, for what it is worth, my experience in watching this film).

Imaginative seeing is certainly a very complex procedure, but Pippin presents a compelling argument that, phenomenologically speaking, it is best understood as a one-step, rather than two-step, process. This is something it has in common with the Kantian sense in which *all* of our experiences, visual or otherwise, are self-conscious. This parallel might suggest at least one reason why we usually experience nothing strange about "seeing fictions in film." As Brian Price puts it, by resisting a "two steps approach," Pippin avoids creating "an impossible divide that stems from reason alone, which would leave us to make a leap of faith in order to understand why we experience fiction as we do" (2019: 504).

From Narration to Reflection: Film and Philosophy

If we grant the account just given, at least two questions immediately follow: *What* do we imaginatively see? And, what is philosophical *about that seeing* (rather than there simply being philosophical ideas underpinning our account of it)? Pippin has plenty to say about the second question, but rather less to say about the first. He is, though, very interested in *how* we see what we see in films, and so I shall address this before moving to Pippin's more general account of the relationship between philosophy and film.

The single most crucial point about Pippin's account of the epistemology of narrative film is that all such films presume a narrative agency. This is a very controversial topic, but it is important to be clear that although, for Pippin, such an agency is ineliminable, it is also necessary only in a strictly minimal sense. He by no means thinks that all films require us to conceive of a narrator that is even close to being a kind of "character," some sort of fictional human (or other) being. He does, however, think that since a film cannot help but show us what it shows us *in some particular way* or other, the way that we are shown things will always imply at least *some* kind of agency arranging the showing, or "running the show," we might say. This point is by no means limited to film. Pippin points out that the history of stage drama can be seen as having moved in a similar direction:

> When, later in the history of drama, we zip around in different scenes from place to place and time to time, the mimetic illusion is even harder to maintain, even if there is no directly mediating mechanism visible or assumable. We have at least some sense of selection, emphasis, control, direction, and so forth; something close to narration.
>
> (Pippin 2013a: 337)

Shakespeare would be a perfect example of this. This is not at all to say that Shakespeare is the narrator of his plays, but merely that, given the way *The Merchant of Venice*—say—"zips" back and forth between Venice and Belmont, we can ask what the dramatic effect of this "zipping" is, which is to say that we can ask *why* it happens. This means that—again only, in the first instance, in some very minimal and theoretical sense—there must be an agency to which we can attribute this organization. This argument should recall the discussion of intention in relation to *Rear Window*, at the end of the introduction. Pippin holds that there is something in common between the way that we might speak of a film having intentions and what we mean by saying that a human being has intentions, and that this by no means entails any kind of dubious anthropomorphism:

> Just in the way that a bodily movement in space can count as an action only by virtue of the self-understanding embodied in and expressed in it, an artwork, including any ambitious movie, embodies a formal unity, a self-understanding that it is always working to realize. ... In fact, the movie, one has to say in an ontological mode, *is the movie it is* only by means of this emerging, internal self-conception, a dimension we can miss if we too quickly apply some apparent formal unity, like a genre designation or a sociohistorical concept, or if we simply attend to the plot.
> (Pippin 2020a: 8; emphasis in original)

Making this claim more plausible will require a more thorough account of Pippin's Hegelian understanding of agency, which will have to wait until Chapter 4. For now, I hope it will suffice to point out the corollary of Pippin's understanding of cinematic narration that has the most practical consequences for his readings of films, which is his sensitivity to the *illocutionary force* of cinematic narration.

Illocutionary force is a term originating with the philosopher J. L. Austin, who we have already encountered extremely briefly as one of Stanley Cavell's most important influences. Speaking a sentence is one kind of act, which Austin dubbed *locutionary*, but one may also do something *by* speaking a sentence—such as promising, threatening, firing (an employee), marrying, and so forth. Austin distinguishes between locutionary acts and illocutionary acts; an instance of the latter is the "performance of an act *in* saying something as opposed to performance of an act *of* saying something" (1975: 99–100; emphases in original).[14] Similarly, Pippin declares of the narrational agent of a film, "Whoever that minimal agent, that agent does not *just* report, or narrate, or suggest, or imply, or remember; he or she also does something *by* narrating, remembering, etc." (Pippin 2013a: 339; emphases in original). The films that reward Pippin's kind of philosophical attention are those that respond interestingly to this kind of inquiry, the films in which pursuing the question of exactly *why* we are shown what we are shown, *in the way* we are shown it, leads to interesting and thought-provoking conclusions. Pippin acknowledges that "the analogy [between films and "speech-acts addressed to an audience"] is far from perfect," but he maintains that it is "serviceable in this context; it brings out the relation between seeing, and being shown what one sees" (2019a: 534).[15] The real usefulness of the analogy is that it allows us to distinguish between our understanding of what a film shows us and our understanding of *why* it shows us what it does, in the way it does, as Pippin brings out very clearly in the following passage:

> In the same way that we could say we understood perfectly some sentence said to us by someone, but that we cannot understand the point of his saying it now, here, in this context, given what we had been discussing, we could also say that we can understand some complex feature of a movie plot, but wonder what the point might have been in showing us this feature in such a way in that context.
> (Pippin 2017a: 5)

In Pippin's terms, this purposeful showing is an aspect of a film's *reflective form*: in the most philosophically interesting films, narration is not purely functional but is an aspect of reflection; as was cited earlier, for Pippin an ambitious film "embodies a formal unity, a self-understanding that it is always working to realize" (2020a: 8).[16]

The test of this claim is always in individual readings of films; it is not something that could be demonstrated by the kind of theoretical argument that operates only with generalities. But the objection could be raised that, without the kind of theoretical account that, as we saw in the introduction, Pippin explicitly rejects (rejects, i.e., in the sense that it is not what his work on film aims at, not in the sense that nobody should produce theories about films!), all one will be left with is a collection of more or less plausible interpretations of films with no means of drawing any conclusions that have wider significance. Pippin has two sorts of response to this accusation. The first concerns how it is that we should go about drawing wider conclusions or, more precisely, what it is that we might draw such conclusions about. Describing his own approach to film as "'immanentist' rather than contextualist," he goes on to say that "like most dualisms, this can be misleading," and that some "contextualist approaches presuppose a relatively unproblematic access to something like 'the movie,'" an assumption which—although it "can be valuable"—is problematic with respect to "movies that present us with a number of elements that are very hard to take in and process on a first viewing" (ibid.: 7). This is to say that one response to the "isolated readings" worry is that one cannot simply *assume* that one can easily tell what kind of film one is putting in context, and that therefore, in certain cases, any contextualizing work risks being misleading and even distorting if it makes too many such assumptions about *what it is* that is being contextualized, without the kind of patient interpretive work that Pippin advocates. The second response is simpler, and we have already encountered it. It is the claim that, for example, "the play *Othello* cannot be about, be a way of understanding, Othello's jealousy without also being about, showing us something about, jealousy in general" (Pippin 2021b: 241). The "isolated readings" worry may be a false worry; it all depends what it is that one wishes to draw generalizable insights about. If one wants to learn, say, in what ways the representation of African Americans in film is related to the development of the Civil Rights struggle, then this clearly cannot be achieved without "contextualist" research. But if a reading of *In the Heat of the Night*, say, convincingly demonstrates that the film shows us something about the specific prejudices it deals with, then it has *just thereby* shown us something about prejudice in general. Exactly how one might want to go on to build on—to *generalize*—what it has shown is a further question, but nothing beyond producing the reading itself (which, as I say, we are assuming to be convincing) is necessary for it to have *generalizable* significance.

When we are dealing with normatively rich "thick" concepts—which would include concepts such as jealousy or prejudice—or with questions of a similar level of complexity that are always deeply embedded in the specifics of their context (such as, e.g., "When rightly blaming someone, when is it wrong to *keep* blaming him or her?" or "Can the same action be said to be at the same time both good and evil, noble and ignoble, loving and self-interested?" [Pippin 2017a: 8; emphasis in original]), Pippin's view is that "there is no better, perhaps no other, way to understand such phenomena than through … guided but not regulated imaginative reflection" (ibid.: 9, n. 15). And the greatest narrative films are, for Pippin, some of the best guides for just such reflection. As he puts it at greater length:

> So much philosophy is so unavoidably guided by intuitions, and such intuitions are so formed by examples, and such examples must of necessity present so cropped and abstract a picture of an instance or event or decision, that, left to its traditional methods, philosophy might be ill-equipped on its own to answer a question like one about the true *content* of an historical ideal like "autonomy," or authenticity or "leading a free life." One needs to bring so many factors into play at once that one non-traditional but more promising path might be through reflection on the modern novel (or modern drama or poetry or film or even modern painting).
>
> (Pippin 2006: 89; emphasis in original)

Generalization is not necessarily illuminating, precisely because these kinds of concerns "do not seem to admit of anything like Socratic definitions, or necessary and sufficient conditions for their having the determinate meaning they do" (ibid.: 8); it would be philosophically distorting, rather than illuminating, simply to assume that "the abstraction of some common set of features and so the postulation of some vague principle" (Pippin 2020a: 7) *must* be a productive way of approaching the understanding of them. Clearly, then, Pippin sees a continuity between the kind of philosophically informed interpretations of films that he produces and ordinary moral reflection. This is, for him, a positive quality rather than something that reduces the philosophical distinctiveness of his readings. He disagrees explicitly with Noël Carroll's account of the philosophical significance of *Vertigo*, for whom any philosophical insight that the film might occasion could only be revelatory for "the general public," not for "the graduate seminar room of a research university" (2007: 113). But Pippin disagrees not so much because he thinks that only trained philosophers can appreciate *Vertigo*'s philosophical significance, although he does acknowledge that "some awareness of the philosophical tradition" cannot but be helpful (2017a: 11, n. 17). On the contrary, Pippin's point is that although "a good deal of the film's philosophical revelation is certainly accessible to 'the general public' … a very great deal more depends on multiple viewings [and] extremely close attention" (ibid.). Philosophical reflection is available to almost anybody, but most people do not engage in it. Rather than a distinction between the philosophically untrained "general public" and a group of erudite specialists, the most important distinction for Pippin is between those who are willing to spend time and energy on "multiple viewings" and "extremely close attention" and those who prefer not to. The "general public"—as a whole—are not willing to do so, but those members of that public who do spend their time in that way are—at least potentially—engaging in philosophical reflection. Pippin's claim that much of what goes on in *Vertigo* "would indeed be a fit subject for a graduate research seminar, if the seminar were about the nature of the human struggle for mutual intelligibility" (ibid.) in no way entails that it is *only* in such a seminar that these questions might be addressed in a genuinely philosophical manner. Indeed, given that "changes in the technology of film viewing have made possible a studied attention to film without great expense and investment of time" (Pippin 2020a: 3, n. 1), it must be easier than ever before for such philosophical reflection on film to at least have a chance of taking place, in any number of different situations.

Let us reiterate the core of Pippin's philosophical approach to film one last time. First, it is important to be absolutely clear that he does not think that his approach is the *only* approach to the study of film that is properly called philosophical. On the contrary, he believes that such a position would be indefensible: "No one can deny that interesting philosophical questions can be raised about film, such as questions about the nature of the medium, its distinctness as an art form, the nature of cinematic experience, its relation to theater or painting, and so forth" (Pippin 2017a: 3). But he still wishes to defend the more controversial position according to which "a film (or a novel or a poem) itself can be understood as a form of thought" (ibid.). Indeed, Pippin's first extended foray into such a philosophical treatment of aesthetic objects was a book about the novels of Henry James in relation to the questions of historical subjectivity with which we began this chapter. Something that he says there applies equally well to his work on film.[17] In response to the charge that "the application of philosophical categories, especially moral evaluation" to literature is inappropriate, for various reasons, such as "the density and complexity of psychological experiences and meaning … the uniqueness of aesthetic experience itself … [or] the contrary reliance of philosophy on argument and proof" (Pippin 2000a: 18), Pippin replies that working with such generalities seems to him to be the wrong level on which to construct a response: "Such a general charge is almost unmanageably abstract … and I mention it here only to say that I have no general answer to it. I think it can only be answered in small details, and from the side rather than head on" (ibid.: 19).[18]

It is high time for us to leave the rather frontal attack that this chapter represents and start to approach things more obliquely, but just one final remark before we do so. We have already encountered what we might call the "deflationary" aspect of Pippin's approach to film in his remark about "just trying to understand the film." It should, I hope, be abundantly clear by now that this in no way indicates hostility towards philosophically ambitious approaches to film. But it does indicate, once again, something about Pippin's attitude to the relationship between the general and the specific. Just as films do not, for Pippin, serve us best philosophically as illustrations of preexisting philosophical concepts or dilemmas, neither is Deleuze's strategy of using films to help produce *new* philosophical concepts Pippin's way. He has a wariness towards philosophical novelty for its own sake and would, I think, agree with the philosopher Charles Travis about the need to be wary of being seduced "into philosophically exciting, but unsupported, theses" (2006: 34). This does not, of course, mean that Pippin wants actively to *avoid* philosophical excitement! But it does mean that excitement in and of itself cannot be a philosophical criterion. Pippin sets out very well the stakes of his writing on film, the criteria according to which it *should* be assessed—which this book aims continually to keep in mind—when he writes the following: "Writing that does justice to the specificity of the film experience and to its philosophical stakes is not one that has any rules or even, as of yet, many paradigmatic examples. And that *writing* is the test of whether there is such a thing as film philosophy" (2019a: 536).

2

The Political Psychology of the Wild West

The first book on film by Pippin to be published emerged from his Castle Lectures, delivered at Yale University in 2008, appearing in 2010 under the title *Hollywood Westerns and American Myth: The Importance of Howard Hawks and John Ford for Political Philosophy*. The book contains chapter-length analyses of Hawks's film *Red River* (1948) and Ford's films *The Man Who Shot Liberty Valance* (1962) and *The Searchers* (1956). It also contains shorter discussions of Ford's *Stagecoach* (1939) and Nicholas Ray's *The Lusty Men* (1952). The subtitle already indicates the quietly provocative nature of the book's argument. What possible contribution (to say nothing of its "importance") could any mainstream Hollywood director—let alone directors such as Howard Hawks and John Ford, both of whose politics have tended to be either dismissed as irrelevant or denigrated as reactionary—have to make to such an august and venerable field of study as "political philosophy"? A rejected version of the title gives, in fact, a clearer indication of the nature of the political concerns that lie at the heart of the book. In a footnote of an earlier book, Pippin refers to a then-forthcoming work called *Political Psychology and American Myth: Violence and Order in Hollywood Westerns* (2008: 280, n. 5). Although he obviously decided that an adjusted title would be more elegant, this version very clearly indicates the three aspects that one needs to be clear about in order to grasp his project: what he understands by "political psychology" and "American myth," and how the treatment of "violence and order" in Western movies helps us explore these notions.

First, then, "political psychology." Different kinds of psychology are of great importance to much of Pippin's work on film; in Chapter 5 we will encounter what he calls "moral psychology." These terms do not, however, refer to the kind of psychology usually found in psychology departments. Instead, they are intended to emphasize the irreducibly first-personal dimension of experience (Pippin's philosophical interest in which was touched on in the introduction), something which—in this context—is explored primarily in terms of the fictional characters involved, rather than the experience of the film viewer. This kind of psychology "cannot be properly understood as an empirical social science" (Pippin 2010a: 15), because the self-understanding of human agents is not something that can be comprehended simply by observation. It also requires interpretation, an act of putting oneself imaginatively in the shoes of the agents in question. Pippin claims that in many cases, if we do not seriously take into account the self-understandings of a film's characters we will miss much that is of philosophical consequence. Political philosophy as a whole is not merely impoverished but distorted if we assume that human beings are best conceived as wholly rational: "There is something amiss in addressing the political question as if human beings were exclusively rational calculators or creatures of pure practical reason" (ibid.: 13). But this is not simply to say that political philosophy needs to make allowance for irrationality. The situation is more complex than that, because "it need not always be the case that the lack of fit between a proposed ideal or rational structure and a dissatisfying experience of such demands in a life is a result of irrationality or evil. ... it might be evidence that such a scheme is not desirable" (ibid.: 14).

These self-understandings must be seen in a decidedly anti-Cartesian way: there is no possibility of incorrigible access to one's own subjectivity. To put it another way, characters in films are—just like us—not transparent to themselves. (Pippin is fond of referring to Bernard Williams's distinction between what we think and what we *think* we think; see, e.g., Pippin 2012: 18; Pippin 2016b; and Williams 1993: 7, 91.) One immediate consequence of this is that it is frequently important to pay attention not only to characters' sense of themselves, but also to their sense of other people and to other people's sense of them. This territory very quickly becomes extremely complicated (and is often easier to grasp in watching a film than it is to put into prose without inducing headaches). It is, for example, often important to pay attention to one character's sense of another character's sense of that first character's sense of themselves, as when Pippin writes of a scene in *The Man Who Shot Liberty Valance* between Link (Andy Devine) and Hallie (Vera Miles), that "he (alone) knows what she gave up for the world she wanted. ... He knows this; she clearly knows he knows; and he knows that she knows he knows" (2010a: 93). George Butte calls this phenomenon "deep intersubjectivity": "the story of subjectivities experiencing or not experiencing or partially experiencing or mis-experiencing or believing they experience themselves by way of the other's similar perception or misperception or both" (2017: 3–4). It is, precisely, both the *sociality* of such phenomena and the preponderance of possible *errors* or *misunderstandings* which render them, for Pippin, ideal sites for the exploration of a political psychology, of what kinds of first-personal experiences and understandings make different kinds of politics either possible or impossible. (Pippin notes that the very existence of something properly called politics cannot be assumed but needs to be demonstrated; for thinkers such as Marx and Nietzsche, all politics is essentially just a cover for the exercise of pure power, whereas for Hannah Arendt, modern technological bureaucracy renders politics no longer possible; see Pippin 2010a: 11–12.)

In pursuing the political psychology they dramatize, Pippin aims to read canonical Hollywood films with—not against—their grain, but precisely in order to discover material that disturbs the possibility of excessively neat readings. Thus his investigations into the politics of certain Westerns result in, rather than avoid or dismiss, aesthetic claims; the seriousness of the politics of *Red River*, *The Man Who Shot Liberty Valance*, and *The Searchers* is, for Pippin, part of their aesthetic greatness—which is to say their greatness as films. In a recent interview, Pippin lucidly sums up his general approach to the relationship between film viewing and philosophical thought, echoing ideas we have already touched on in the introduction:

> The issue of what the relationship is between the aesthetic experiential dynamic of watching a film and the reflective dynamic is something I think is quite interesting and not terribly well understood, because the usual assumption is that the latter, the reflective dynamic, ruins the former. It just clouds and complicates the pure experiential dimension of the film. But ... thinking has a kind of affective dimension as well, and to be intrigued or puzzled or challenged or inspired to think by a film is not a bad thing, it's just part of what it is for the aesthetic experience to be aesthetic. It's not the intrusion of an alien form of thought ... If you can show someone, anyway, that it's what the film itself demands of you, then you've made your case ... that the film *as a film* is asking you to do something beyond just receiving it, beyond just being passively entertained.
>
> (Pippin 2020b)

The specific "reflective dynamic" that Pippin explores in the Westerns and discusses in his book is political; he claims to discover political thinking at work in the films themselves, that each of these films calls for some kind of political thinking simply, in the first place, in order to be understood. Well aware that this approach sets him at something of a remove from many other investigations into the ideology of film, he refers wryly at one point to the "unmistakable air ... of 'ideology critique' (to use a term I doubt has been used before in discussions of Ford)" that he perceives in *The Man Who Shot Liberty Valance* (Pippin 2010a: 98). Elsewhere he writes of "the fact that the origin of the territorial United States rests on a virulent racism and genocidal war against aboriginal peoples" but claims that we find in *The Searchers* a "direct confrontation" with this fact: this war "would not have been possible and perhaps would not have been won without the racist hatred of characters like the John Wayne character" (ibid.: 104). Any reading of *The Searchers* that thinks it is simply obvious that the film excuses or papers over such attitudes rather than attempting seriously to wrestle with them is, Pippin thinks, not looking closely enough or thinking hard enough.

The claim that "there are few documents of American self-understanding in which the issues are posed in a more gripping and compelling way than in Westerns" (ibid.: 155) indicates that Pippin thinks that the choice between neutrally setting forth a film's "explicit" political position without judgment and interrogating or dismantling its "implicit" political commitments is a false dichotomy. The most interesting Westerns display political thinking—ideology—at work at a particular time, which is revealing in itself (they are "documents of American self-understanding"), but they also put this thinking to work. Westerns are not merely exciting ("gripping") yarns that portray (or betray) political mythologies; they also put these mythologies under pressure. The thinking about politics and political myth to be found in these films is itself worth taking seriously, because it is itself "compelling."

The Westerns that most interest Pippin, then, subvert any simplistic understanding of the genre as consisting mainly of (supposedly) apolitical adventure stories or of regressively bombastic affirmations of Manifest Destiny and American triumphalism. In the richest and most interesting Westerns, so Pippin argues, the relationship between violence and order, in particular, figures contradiction and uncertainty as much as it does heroism and the successful founding of American self-identity. Here is a summary remark to this effect:

> If we treat Westerns as a reflection on the possibility of modern, bourgeois domestic societies to sustain themselves, command

allegiance and sacrifice, defend themselves from enemies, inspire admiration and loyalty (that is, to command and form the politically relevant passions in some successful way, to shape the "characters" distinctly needed for this form of life), then one surprising aspect of many Westerns (often criticized in the 1960s for their supposed chauvinism, patriarchy, celebration of violence, and so forth) is a profound *doubt* about the ability of modern societies (supposedly committed to peace and law) to do just that.

(ibid.: 24; emphasis in original)

Westerns are often a kind of origin story about the coming-into-being of the society within which they were made, a society where the rule of law is now established and violence, if by no means eliminated, is at least regulated—or *supposedly* regulated—by that very law.

This was not originally the case; as the United States expanded westward, which it often did with extreme violence, law had to be *introduced*. Thus, the transition from one kind of relationship between violence and order—or force of arms and force of law—to another had to be negotiated. Pippin argues that

> there are many great Westerns about the painful and even tragic transition from a frontier form of life, often lawless, requiring the heroic and martial virtues, to a modern, bourgeois, capitalist form of domestic life: *Shane, Man of the West, The Gunfighter, The Man Who Shot Liberty Valance, Ride the High Country, The Wild Bunch, The Lusty Men, The Shootist*, virtually all of Budd Boetticher's Westerns. The issue obviously touches an American nerve, probably because we are not quite convinced that the transition has been made, or that we want to make it.
>
> (Pippin 2010b, response to Mark Wrathall)

Note Pippin's emphasis on the kind of "virtues" these different forms of life involve: a different way of relating to the world is required in each form of life, a different way of evaluating situations and actions, and thus a different form of political psychology: a crucial question is "how the bourgeois virtues, especially the domestic virtues, *can be said to get a psychological grip in an environment where the heroic and martial virtues are so important*" (2010a: 20; emphasis in original). Pippin is clearly thinking in terms of the ideas about historical subjectivity that we encountered in the introduction and in Chapter 1. It is not merely a question of which kinds of acts are considered virtuous and which villainous, but one of what it is really to *live* according to a particular morality, to see the world in terms of it. (To do something simply because *others* think it virtuous is very different from doing so because *you* believe it to be virtuous.) In conflicted situations, such as those frequently depicted in Westerns, these questions are frequently very far from straightforward. In exploring mythologized versions of historical examples of such conflicts, Pippin believes that many great Westerns are also reflecting on the conflicts involved in living in America during the times in which the films were made, because a reflection on the conflicted origins of a society can help reveal the conflict that still remains, perhaps concealed, in that society; hence Pippin's reference to "ideology critique." In a passage that, he tells us, is directly influenced by *Hollywood Westerns*, Terry Pinkard helpfully summarizes the broader philosophical and historical assumptions that underlie Pippin's position:

> Orders of thought are, when practical, concrete constellations of passions, principles, and practices that fit into one order. For such orders of thoughts, the issue is always more than whether that order is consistent, that is, more than merely the issue of whether the principles do not contradict each other. It has to do with whether the order itself generates a kind of moral psychology that can be successfully lived or put into practice or with whether the principles generate passions that in turn undermine the authority of the principles.
> (Pinkard 2017a: 40)

To come, finally, to the third of the three central aspects of Pippin's *Hollywood Westerns*, after "political psychology" and "violence and order": stories about the founding of the very society that is telling those stories are aptly described as mythic. For Pippin, "mythic accounts are about events in the remote past of decisive significance for the present (often about foundings), and they assume that the course of these events is the result of actions undertaken by heroes of superhuman abilities" (2010a: 19). The self-reflexive quality of myth (that for a myth to be a myth it must be able to be understood as a story that a society tells *about itself*) means that "mythic self-consciousness is an attempt at a form of collective self-knowledge" (ibid.: 102). The ideas about self-consciousness that we encountered in the previous chapter are therefore highly relevant both to the political psychology that Pippin sees as expressed and interrogated in the greatest Westerns, and to their mythic dimensions. It is worth underlining how different this understanding of myth is from many structuralist-inflected accounts in which, thanks ultimately to the influence of Claude Lévi-Strauss, myths are thought to be structured by timeless archetypal oppositions.[1] For those influenced by this tradition, to call something "mythic" is to move in the direction of abstraction. The primary such opposition in Westerns is usually seen to be that between wilderness and civilization (see the helpful list of oppositions laid out in terms of this fundamental opposition in Jim Kitses's *Horizons West* [1969: 11]). We should also, however, bear in mind the knack such oppositions have for inverting themselves so that, for example, *representations* of wilderness can come to represent the height of civilization. David W. Teague notes how the deserts of the American southwest were, until roughly the mid-1890s, "powerful icons of howling wilderness," but that by 1910, in the likes of "the nature writing of Mary Austin, the art of Georgia O'Keeffe, the photographs of Alfred Stieglitz, and the essays of Joseph Wood Krutch," the very same deserts became "associated with the very height of American culture" (1997: 3). Western movies were made in the wake of the latter perspective but also look back to the former; we might say that, for example, John Ford's Monument Valley frequently represents "howling wilderness" to many of the characters in his films, but signifies something much closer to "the very height of American culture" to many viewers.

Transformations are, however, difficult to grasp from within a strictly structuralist understanding of mythic opposition. Consider, for example, this remark by Suzanne Liandrat-Guigues about a sequence in *Red River* in which Tom Dunson (John Wayne) pursues his adopted son Matthew Garth (Montgomery Clift), who he considers to have betrayed him:

> Because there is not even the slightest instance of parallel editing, the usual suspense created by showing pursuers and pursued is denied. What we have is a more cyclical time, distinct from the normal temporality of the advancing herd, a mythical time during which beings are disclosed and reassembled by virtue of this new modality of movement to-and-fro.
> (Liandrat-Guigues 2000: 24)

For Liandrat-Guigues, the introduction of "mythical time" seems to involve an interpretational mode which moves away from narrative or diegetic issues ("suspense ... is denied") and focuses instead on more purely abstract patterns ("this new modality of movement to-and-fro"); the two dimensions represent two incompatible "orders." Pippin insists that he has "no particular ax to grind in the debates about structuralist, psychoanalytic, and various comparativist methodologies" (2010a: 160, n. 17), but nevertheless his tendency is to explore the ways in which myth is operational in psychological terms, rather than seeing psychological and mythic readings as two different strategies (whether complementary or contradictory). Pippin proposes that André Bazin's suggestion that Westerns be regarded as forms of American myth needs qualifying, at least with regard to some of the richest and most complex instances of the genre. He suggests that, rather than following Bazin in seeing Westerns as instances of "modern mythology," in many instances we would do well to reverse the order of the terms. The films discussed in *Hollywood Westerns* "might better be called examples of mythological modernism, for the level of reflection, self-consciousness, self-thematization, and even irony is much higher than is usually attributed to Westerns or to myths" (ibid.: 96). As one simple example, consider the irony of what is almost the final line in *Stagecoach*, Doc Boone's (Thomas Mitchell) famous remark to the Marshal (George Bancroft) after Dallas (Claire Trevor) and the Ringo Kid (John Wayne) have departed for a life together in Mexico: "Well, they're saved from the blessings of civilization" (see ibid.: 10).[2]

The sense of myth that Pippin finds relevant to the Western is not, therefore, one in which myth is a way of simplifying and clarifying meanings, of reducing ambiguity for the viewer. On the contrary, he wants to show that the Westerns he discusses dramatize what it means to live one's life according to forms of mythic thought; sensitivity to the complexities of doing so *increases* the ambiguity of these films, indicating what Pippin calls their "mythological modernism." In keeping with this approach, Pippin does not tend to read the symbolic aspects of these films as if they directly encode meanings for the benefit of the viewer; instead he embeds them in his readings of the films' narratives and the ways that these narratives invite us to understand the experience and psychology of the characters. As a small example of this kind of approach—one not drawn from Pippin but, I think, in the spirit of his readings—one might consider the different treatment of the "dead man's hand" in poker (the black aces and black eights that, according to legend, Wild Bill Hickok was holding when he was shot dead in 1876) in *Stagecoach* and *The Man Who Shot Liberty Valance*. Luke Plummer (Tom Tyler) in the former film and Liberty Valance (Lee Marvin) in the latter are both shown with the dead man's hand. Valance (Lee Marvin) proudly displays it before he goes out to his confrontation with Ransom Stoddard (James Stewart), oblivious to any negative connotation; the hand seems to serve mainly to tip the wink to the viewer who recognizes the symbolism. In *Stagecoach*, however, things are more complicated (see Figure 3). Plummer has the dead man's hand before he goes to meet his death at the hands of the Ringo Kid. Having just been told that the Kid is in town, Plummer stands up. Before departing, he looks down at the cards in his hand, and hesitates. Prompted by his look, his female companion also looks at the cards. We are then shown the hand in close-up, after which we return to the two-shot of Plummer and the woman. He begins to head off, his face in shadow, but she continues to stare at the cards, giving a clear, if subtle, sense that they have both recognized the symbolism.

The shadow that obscures Plummer's face does, however, introduce an ambiguity as to whether or not he has recognized it. Might his hesitation instead indicate irritation at having to interrupt the game when on a winning streak? (He looks down at the cards one final time before departing and barks, "Cash in!") If this is the case, there would be a distinct irony in his reaction, given that he's about to "cash in" his life. Once again, however, it is an irony recognizable *within* the film, and not merely by the film's viewers. We might say that the woman's reaction indicates that at the very least, from the perspective of the inhabitants of the film's world, Plummer *should* have recognized the significance of the hand.[3] Plummer's death is not merely symbolized for the viewer, but Plummer himself—or at least those around him—may be assumed to be thinking of Hickok's death, and therefore to be disconcerted by Plummer's poker hand; as Barry Keith Grant puts it, "fate permeates the film and is accepted by the characters within the story as part of nature, much like the landscape" (2003: 16). This fatalism is a part of a mythic dimension that is the richer for being active *in* the film's world. This sequence is not mythic merely for the viewer; instead, a sense of negotiation with mythic symbolism is part of the way the film's characters understand their relationship to their own actions.

Figure 3 Living myth in *Stagecoach*.

Having said this, Pippin by no means assumes that Westerns are always best read in terms of the complex kinds of psychology that most interest him. He fully admits, for example, that properly understanding *Stagecoach* involves appreciating "how archetypal rather than merely individual are the treatment of character and the theme of justice" (ibid.: 3). But he has been accused of allowing his interest in political psychology to seduce him at times into reading Westerns *too* psychologically. Gilberto Perez, for example, charges aspects of Pippin's interpretation of *The Man Who Shot Liberty Valance* with precisely this mistake (2019: 38). This film, told mostly in flashback, tells the backstory of the illustrious senator Ransom Stoddard. His fame is predicated on the confrontation in which, as a young lawyer, he shot and killed the villainous Liberty Valance, who had been terrorizing the town of Shinbone. In point of fact, however, as Stoddard reveals towards the end of the film, Valance had actually been shot from the shadows by the now long-forgotten Tom Doniphon (John Wayne). Famously, Shinbone's newspaper editor (Carleton Young) declines to print the true story: "When the legend becomes fact, print the legend."

Stoddard's wife Hallie (Vera Miles) was originally assumed by everyone (including the parties involved) to be destined to marry Tom. The film's final scene shows Stoddard and Hallie departing Shinbone in the train. "Nothing's too good for the man who shot Liberty Valance," the conductor (Willis Bouchey) tells them. Pippin is clear that the return to Shinbone has involved, for Hallie, a confrontation with what her life as Stoddard's wife has involved, specifically "that she perhaps gave up the love of her life" (2010a: 93). But this does not, Pippin thinks, involve any knowledge on her behalf of the truth about Valance's death:

> When he [Stoddard] parts from Hallie to talk with the journalists he tells Hallie only that he is going to "mend some political fences." … [T]here is no sign on the face of the impassive, sad Hallie that

she realizes what he is actually proposing to do. In fact, there is
no sign that she knows at all that the Valance myth is a lie. At the
conductor's last words on the train, she registers no reaction.

(ibid.: 94)

Perez quite rightly points out that this is mistaken, because "when the newspaper editor presses the senator to talk about the friend he and his wife have come to bury, Hallie looks at her husband and indicates her approval" (2019: 38–9). When the editor demands an explanation of why Doniphon's death has brought the senator back to Shinbone, Hallie looks intently at Ranse. He stands up and eventually meets her gaze, at which point she gives him a little series of nods of the head that diminish in size. It is then that he concedes the editor's point; Perez's remark that "that look is an unmistakable sign that Hallie knows the truth and wants Ranse to let it be known" is persuasive (ibid.: 39). But Perez is unpersuaded that her love for Tom Doniphon is relevant:

> At the end of the movie, on the train leaving Shinbone, Hallie tells Ranse that her heart is there. She doesn't mean that she has always loved Tom rather than the husband she rejected him for: she means that she enduringly loves the West, the West of her youth, the dead West. *Liberty Valance* isn't the psychological story of a love triangle; it is a national allegory.

(ibid.)

Pippin is also incorrect about the end of the film, when he claims that Hallie "registers no reaction" to the conductor's remark. Her reaction is subtle and easily missed, but it is very definitely present. (See Figure 4, noting the position of Hallie's head; her mouth and eyes; the difference between her shoulders in the second and third images.) At the beginning of the jovial and rather pompous exchange between the conductor and Ranse, she looks at the conductor, but soon turns away, eyes half closed and head bowed in what seems to be a fairly

The Political Psychology of the Wild West

Figure 4 Hallie's reaction at the end of *The Man Who Shot Liberty Valance*.

blank reverie, her expression unchanging. Clearly she hears this kind of thing all the time and it's of no interest to her. As he utters the film's final line ("Nothing's too good for the man that shot Liberty Valance"), the conductor walks past Ranse and Hallie, blocking our view of them, but as he passes she is lifting her head, her eyes widening and lips parting ever so slightly, after which her mouth closes again. But her eyes remain open, looking directly ahead of her, both blankly and sadly. Then her shoulders slump—just a tiny amount—in resignation, after which (the camera tracking in to frame the two of them slightly more closely) Ranse extinguishes his match and doesn't light his pipe, though he still holds it up, distractedly. Then we cut to an external shot of the train departing, and the film ends.

One train of thought following from this reaction of Hallie's that we could trace further than Pippin does is the idea that, rather than seeing Hallie as having sacrificed a life with the man she really loved, it is only later that she realized exactly what she gave up. She *was* enamored by Ranse's learning and sophistication and vulnerability; she *chose* him. It is only with the passage of time that she—just as much as Ranse—has had the opportunity to reflect on what the conflict between "fact" and "legend" really signifies. This is true whether she learned who really shot Liberty Valance at the time, or later. (If at the time, then at that time she presumably saw Tom's action as freeing her up to marry Ranse and leave with him, which is precisely how Tom understands it; if later, then whenever she learned the truth she learned that she did not marry the man she thought she married.)[4] But if observing Hallie closely at the end of the film challenges Pippin's account of this moment, it serves only to reinforce his claim (which he makes in the passage, already quoted from earlier, that connects Ford with "ideology critique") that although the film gives us no sense that "our political world can simply dispense with legends and instead institutionalize more prosaic and more morally complicated narratives," it also indicates that there is a blindness involved in living one's political life according to legend, and "suggests that the cost of continuing such blindness is too high," and that "Hallie is the figure for that price" (Pippin 2010a: 98). Perez's charge that *The Man Who Shot Liberty Valance* is a "national allegory" *rather than* "the psychological story of a love triangle" sees a dichotomy that does not exist for Pippin. It is precisely the psychology of the film's love triangle, and the ways that the three components of that triangle (Hallie, Ranse, Tom) negotiate the legends and deceptions of the West, that *constitute* the film's political allegory. We explore the film's "national allegory" *by* reading the characters psychologically, as far as this will go, not by assuming at the outset something about the way that myths or allegories work. Perez's claim that what Hallie "enduringly loves" is "the West," not Tom Doniphon, is *itself* a psychological reading. But the sadness and resignation that are perceptible in Hallie's reaction at the end of the film suggests that her love of the West is inseparable from her love for Tom. Pippin's account implies, rightly I believe, that *Liberty Valance* is more interesting if read in terms of depth psychology, and that to deny this would not be to read allegorically *rather than* psychologically but rather to hamstring interpretation by deciding in advance what kind of psychology has any business appearing in an allegory.

It is not, of course, the case that all Westerns, even all great Westerns, allegorize the West in the same way. Pippin claims that *Liberty Valance* "is not a mythological treatment of a founding. It is rather about mythological accounts of foundings" (ibid.: 96). As an example of a Western that *can* be seen as the former, we might consider *The Virginian* (Victor Fleming, 1929), which is more of "a mythological treatment of a founding," but one that can still be understood in terms of political psychology, as an exploration both of the society being founded and of the subjectivity required for this founding to succeed. When the Virginian (Gary Cooper) discovers that his friend Steve (Richard Arlen) is stealing cattle, he doesn't turn him in, which would be dishonorable. But they have a discussion about civilization and seriousness. The Virginian says: "This whole country's taking things more seriously," to which Steve replies, a little later: "This county's getting too civilized, too solemn." Steve equates swapping babies lined up for christening (a prank initiated by the Virginian that he and Steve pulled off earlier, with the Virginian pinning the blame entirely on Steve) with cattle rustling—they're both just harmless pranks—while the Virginian does not, which of course means that he has to have Steve hanged when the posse eventually catches him and the other rustlers. (The film plays a lot with notions of maturity, clearly allegorizing the youthful status of the nation, for which Cooper's mixture of grace and gangliness is ideal: sometimes he seems as if he hasn't quite grown into his body yet.) But Steve does not object to the consequences of his actions. Instead he reveals himself, ultimately, to subscribe to the same worldview as the Virginian, and so—quite consistently—he goes to his death cheerfully and says nothing to the Virginian (because otherwise he would have cried). It is all a matter of saving face, of being able to look one another in the eye, to—in other words—*exist* as a society.

Later an older woman named Mrs. "Ma" Taylor (Helen Ware) tells Molly (Mary Brian), a schoolteacher who has come to Wyoming from Vermont, that the lynching is "our kind of law." Molly eventually finds that she can—just about—understand the first killing ("I forced myself to think of it as you did, a public duty, law and order"), but tells the Virginian that to kill Trampas (Walter Huston), the villainous leader of the rustlers, would simply be murder (in "cold blood," a charge he interestingly does not deny). But the Virginian explains that it is a matter of honor, explicitly in terms of his reputation among the others. He denies her claim that this is just a matter of pride, claiming that the specific label doesn't matter that much: "I don't know what you call it, but it's something in the feelings of a man, down deep inside." It is, perhaps, only apparently inconsistent that the Virginian moves very quickly from saying that "If folks came to think me a coward,

I couldn't look them straight in the eye ever again" to declaring that "It wouldn't matter what other people thought, but I'd have to know inside of me that I thought enough of my own honesty to fight for it." Sociality and subjectivity are utterly entwined. Molly reasonably points out that then the killing will just carry on, which the Virginian accepts: "There'll always be killing to do, until this country ain't a meeting place for men like Trampas." For now, that time can itself only exist as an almost mythic notion, albeit one located in the future rather than the past.

The Virginian, then, seems aimed at bringing us, like Molly, to an understanding both of what this kind of society was like and of what it *felt* like, what kind of passions—what kind of subjectivity— were necessary for it to be sustainable; precisely the questions that are at the heart of *Hollywood Westerns*. It demonstrates considerable complexity, but it also portrays the political psychology it dramatizes as sustainable, if people can learn to act rightly (which often involves acting heroically, one reason why its account is mythic). In contrast, *Liberty Valance* is *about* mythological foundings, rather than presenting a mythological account of a founding, precisely because it attempts to explore the transition from a country that is "a meeting place for men like Trampas" (or like Liberty Valance), to one that isn't. And this necessitates an altered relation to myth: "Apparently a victory over Liberty Valance (over unconstrained 'liberty' as an absolute 'value') by Tom Doniphon would be just one more episode in a cycle of violence, revenge, and intimidation. Valance must be killed by a representative of a new order; his death must *mean* that" (ibid.: 81). One cannot, it seems, escape myth without *using* myth, without a mythic escape from one form of society to another.

Pippin has, however, somewhat revised his interpretation of the film's depiction of this transition. In *Hollywood Westerns*, he claims that "Ranse, for all his high-mindedness, is willing, without much visible struggle with his conscience, to build his life on a lie," and that "this is dishonorable, and there is no question that Ford wants us to see that it is dishonorable, even if it is also partly excusable" (ibid.: 93). But more recently Pippin has come to believe that such a view "is too extreme" (2016a: 227). His interpretation of the editor's famous line—"When the legend becomes fact, print the legend"—is now as follows:

> At the beginning of his legendary status, the legend is not "yet" fact. The defeat of Valance and *all that he stands for* is a mere legend. But over time, with statehood, the railroad, schools, and with Ranse's role as governor and senator in making that possible, the legend has *become* fact, Ranse has "become" the man who shot, who defeated, who finally overcame Valance, and all that he represents.
> (ibid.: 228; emphases in original)

He couldn't, of course, have done any of this if Valance had killed him! Once again, it is not simply a question of a filmic allegory but of an allegory that is active, that is wrestled with, *within* the film's world. Stoddard has not straightforwardly been living a lie because the defeat of Valance has come to operate quasi-allegorically for those who see Ranse as a hero. (They see his activities as a senator as allegorically related to the original act of heroism and violence, the defeat of Valance.) This is something that takes time. Tom is clear about what his killing of Valance has rendered impossible: immediately, his own future with Hallie and, implicitly, the life that he, Tom, represents (as opposed to that which Ranse represents). This is why he burns down the house he was building for himself and Hallie. But despite the aptness of Douglas Pye's observation that the "change of world is mimed in one of the most obviously expressive pieces of editing in Ford, from Tom's burning house to the raucous but spurious animation of the political convention," this transition does not actually take place instantaneously (1996: 121). For it to be achieved, Ranse needed to live out his life as the man who shot Liberty Valance. One could say that by behaving in a manner so contrary to the values of the old West, shooting a man from the shadows in a profoundly unheroic manner ("Cold-blooded murder, but I can live with it. Hallie's happy. She wanted you alive"), Tom killed the old West. But it still took Ranse, and others like him, to give birth to the new United States.

The melancholy of the final scene indicates the cost of doing so. Perez believes the following:

> What should trouble Ranse's conscience is not the lie he has lived with—nor the fact that he wasn't the man who pulled the trigger—but that the law and order he eloquently advocated entailed the violence that killed the West; so that, in effect, he was the man who shot Liberty Valance.
>
> (Perez 2019: 39)

This view, however, seems to equate the West with Valance in a way that is not wholly convincing, and in this regard Pippin is more precise: it was in defeating what Valance stood for that the West came to an end. It is not that Ranse should feel guilty for having destroyed "the West"; it is that destroying Valance also entailed destroying the lively old Shinbone and producing the antiseptic, less diverse, modern version we see at the beginning and end of the film. What is upsetting is that there seems to be no way of destroying the one without destroying the other. Although one can feel nostalgic for the old version, and even regret its passing, given how ghastly it was to live with the constant threat of Valance, it is not clear that Ranse could feel straightforwardly *guilty* for having helped do away with it; he arrived in Shinbone precisely to do away with such men, even if he was wrong that this could be achieved simply with lawbooks and without guns.[5] So Ranse can regret what reality turned out to require, but to think it could have been otherwise would be sheer fantasy. But realizing this does not provide Ranse with a straightforward way of reconciling himself with "the lie he has lived with," because—even if to call it "dishonorable" is to go too far—it remains, in some senses at least, a lie. And Ranse is quite right to be troubled by this; for Pippin, this represents genuine historical insight into political psychology, not a self-indulgent hand-wringing. There simply is no straightforward choice available between a fully justified lie (the lie brought about civilization, hence Ranse *no longer* has any reason to trouble his conscience) and an unjustified one (whatever the good consequences, the lie remains a lie; the ends do not justify the means).[6] This is why, despite having revised his opinion about the dishonorableness of Ranse's actions, Pippin still describes the film's closing lines as suffused with "bitter absurdity" (2016a: 227).

The Man Who Shot Liberty Valance ends, then, with something of a dying fall, albeit one that is complicated and disconcerting. Another of the Westerns that Pippin discusses at length, Howard Hawks's *Red River*, also has a complicated ending, one that Pippin reads as deliberately bathetic. Rather than focusing on the introduction of law, *Red River* is more concerned with the birth of American capitalism and the kind of society—of authority—that this necessitates:

> There are no sheriffs or judges or gunfighters in this movie, so it is not a classic Western about the inauguration of the law or its psychological grip. Rather, it is about the transition between an autocratic, charismatic, largely pre-modern or feudal form of authority to a much more humanistic, consensus-oriented, prudent, more recognizably modern mode of rule and civil order.
> (Pippin 2010a: 40)

Hawks's film tells a mythologized version of the founding of the Chisholm Trail in terms of the developing rivalry between Tom Dunson and his adopted son Matthew Garth. As Dunson and Garth lead their herd of cattle from Texas towards Missouri (the Civil War having caused beef prices in Texas to collapse), Dunson becomes increasingly tyrannical, verging even on madness. When he threatens to hang a group of deserters, Matt takes over the leadership, banishes Dunson, and decides to head for Abilene, Kansas, rather than Missouri. Dunson chases him, promising to kill him, but their final battle proves bathetic. Neither man is killed; instead they tumble into a cart filled with domestic goods and rapidly make friends again.

For Pippin, this bathos is not an artistic failing but brings out a demythologizing strand at the heart of the film that, while very different, parallels that of *Liberty Valance*. Pippin argues that the fact that there is no fight to the death "suggests that this transition of power from Dunson to Matt *is not inherently revolutionary*" (ibid.: 53; emphasis in original). In *Liberty Valance* we are dealing with a situation of real, fundamental, transition. Dunson's tyrannical side, compared with Matt's personable reasonableness, suggests that the same will be true about *Red River*. But what the men's reconciliation demonstrates is that

> Matt does not really threaten Dunson, he just represents a more efficient, reliable way to preserve what Dunson stands for. … I suggest that this is disturbing (dramatically and for what it says about the American imaginary), not redemptive or progressive, and that this is what is bothersome about the ending, not its dramatic limitations.
>
> (ibid.: 56)

Much of the drama of the film concerns the two men's perceptions of each other: there is a division between "Tom's worry that Matt is too soft, too civilized or too feminine to rule" and Matt's "justifiable sense that Tom has wildly exaggerated the dangers of anarchy (as conservatives often do) and so has established an unnecessarily violent tyranny" (ibid.: 41). There is much to encourage the viewer to side with Matt, and certainly Tom's inflexibility is his undoing, but Matt is also lucky. He calls it right, in that there does turn out to be a railway at Abilene, but it's a case of a calculated risk rather than rationality winning out against irrationality. Tom is not *simply* foolish not wanting to risk the venture on hearsay (none of the men who tell the ranchers about the railway has actually seen it for themselves; they have only heard of its existence from still other people); his reluctance to believe the rumors about the railway being at Abilene is not sheer hubris but could also seem like a rational calculation about the risk of wagering everything on a rumor.[7] Hence, precisely, Matt's increasing tension as they get closer to Abilene (note Matt's remark, "He was wrong; I hope I'm right"; i.e., they could *both* be wrong, which is not a politically reassuring realization). But there is a further irony here: "Since the film is actually about financial speculation, risk taking, and the new world of commerce, one could easily make the case that Matt's decision to try for Abilene is actually the 'tough' one" (ibid.: 56). Matt is the more successful (the more *natural*) capitalist; Tom is something else, representing something more like Marx's stage of "primitive accumulation." Tom's mythologizing of his own qualities—chiefly his hard work—operates in accordance with Marx's claim that "primitive accumulation plays approximately the same role in political economy as original sin does in theology," using a narrative about "two sorts of people; one, the diligent, intelligent and above all frugal élite; the other, lazy rascals" to obscure the fact that we are really dealing with a history in which "conquest, enslavement, robbery, murder, in short, force, play the greatest part" (1976: 873–4).

Perez once again provides a usefully dissenting voice: "Father and son stand for the same thing—the rule of capitalism—and the son manages democratically to hold on to the power that the people were going to take away from the autocratic father. That's why it all comes down to comedy in the end" (2019: 37). Perez finds comedy in the ending but not mockery; Pippin would quite agree with his first sentence, but sees it as having dark implications for what we call democracy that Perez does not accept. Perez seems to assume that the son tempers the father, but Pippin emphasizes the fact that Matt and Dunson end up ruling *together*. The film reveals "that the great mission of the massive drive ('good beef for hungry people') had all along been just another banal for-profit commercial venture. This is the stuff of bathos, not heroism" (Pippin 2016a: 227). The fact that

Dunson's tyranny is not obliterated but rehabilitated is disconcerting in itself. The ending is thus simultaneously comically bathetic and rather disturbing: "the vague unease we are left with is one of the film's great achievements" (Pippin 2010a: 59). It would be fair to say, however, that Pippin's reading feels more "against the grain" of the film than is the case with the John Ford films he discusses. Perez's skepticism as to whether "*Red River* qualifies its epic mode by imputing it to Dunson's—or to Texan, or to American—self-aggrandizement," given that it "achieves an epic grandeur unsurpassed among Westerns," is understandable and, for what it is worth, tallies better than Pippin's account with what we know of Hawks's own views (Perez 2019: 37). But, once seen, Pippin's sense of the "mock-heroic" is hard to unsee (2016a: 226).

Not all critics are convinced that Dunson really does intend to kill Matt right up until the last moment. Hubert I. Cohen thinks that, during his conversation with Tess (Joanne Dru), with whom Matt has fallen in love, and vice versa, Tom decides not to kill Matt, but *pretends* still to intend to. Part of his evidence is what Tess shouts at Tom during their final bathetic fight: "You Dunson, pretending you're gonna kill him!" Cohen does not give a detailed account of why Dunson would wish to engage in such a pretense, besides implying that it helps him to "save face" (2010: 91). (Certainly, the film gives us plenty of indications that Tom finds changing his mind very hard indeed.) Cohen argues that this aspect of Hawks's film inspired one very famous aspect of Ford's *The Searchers*—the third film that Pippin discusses in detail in *Hollywood Westerns*—namely Ethan Edwards's (John Wayne) decision not to kill Debbie (Natalie Wood). *The Searchers* is a famously complex and ambiguous film that tells the story of Ethan's quest for his niece Debbie, accompanied by Martin Pawley (Jeffrey Hunter), his adoptive nephew. Debbie is abducted by the group of Comanche, led by a chief named Scar (Henry Brandon), who rapes and murders the rest of her family, including Ethan's brother Aaron (Walter Coy) and his wife Martha (Dorothy Jordan), the object of Ethan's illicit desire. Martin initially assumes that their goal is to rescue Debbie, but soon realizes that Ethan (who is a racist of pathological proportions) in fact intends to kill her because to live as an "Indian" is worse than death. Martin intends to prevent Ethan from succeeding in this goal, but in the end does not need to, because Ethan changes his mind.

This seems to happen at the very last moment, but Cohen thinks otherwise. He argues that Ethan changes his mind in the scene in which he gets Martin to read his will aloud. Ethan has, previously, constantly denigrated Martin, refusing to let him address him as "uncle," because as one-eighth Cherokee, he sees Martin as a "half-breed." But he leaves everything to Martin in his will, declaring him his last surviving relative, and this despite the fact that, as Martin points out, Debbie is still alive. Cohen claims that "no matter what Ethan now *says*, he knows that he dare not kill his niece lest he lose his son as well," and that after this scene Ethan merely *pretends* to still intend to kill Debbie (ibid.: 89; emphasis in original).[8] Pippin would have, I think, a number of reasons for finding Cohen's accounts of both films interesting but ultimately unpersuasive, chief among them that Cohen's psychology is insufficiently complex. Cohen works with a clear distinction between *intending* to do something and *pretending* so to intend. But in his analysis, Pippin works through a number of possible accounts of the reason that Ethan does not kill Debbie and comes to the conclusion that the most satisfactory is that Ethan doesn't understand himself: "Of what significance is it if Ethan's own expectations *about himself* turn out to be wrong?" (2010a: 129; emphasis in original) This has complex implications for what it is that Ethan can be described as *wanting to do*, or even as *having done*. I won't go into this in much detail here because the self-knowledge and self-deceit themes tie directly into the questions of agency most fully treated in Pippin's book on film noir, to which we shall turn in Chapter 4. But his summary is this:

I would suggest that Ethan has not acted impulsively nor revealed that he is weak-willed with respect to deeply held beliefs, nor that he has been transformed by the quest, nor that the scalping of Scar has shamed or humanized him. What we and he discover is that he did not know his own mind, that he avowed principles that were partly confabulations and fantasy. We (and he) find out the depth and extent of his own commitments only when he finally must act.

(ibid.: 131)

Most relevant to the wider questions of political psychology addressed by *The Searchers* is the way that Ethan's racism is connected to the society in which he lives. As Pippin remarks, "There is one stunning scene that establishes the generality of the problem of Ethan, and which suggests that Ethan is not the crazy outsider or the dark and repressed side of this white American society. He is its representative" (ibid.: 119). The scene in question includes an outburst that Laurie (Vera Miles), Martin's future wife, comes out with when he announces his continuing intention to rescue Debbie from Ethan's murderous quest:

> "Fetch what home? The leavings of Comanche bucks, sold time and again to the highest bidder, with savage brats of her own? Do you know what Ethan will do if he has a chance? He'll put a bullet in her brain! I tell you Martha would want it that way."

Pippin calls this "the most shocking scene in the movie" (ibid.: 140), and notes that it takes place while she is wearing her wedding dress, Martin having interrupted her wedding to Charlie McCorry (Ken Curtis): "Clad in such virginal white, Laurie also seems to hold the most innocent, unreflectively held and common views from her world" (ibid.: 120). The combination of symbolic purity and race hatred is striking and clearly significant, but Pippin's account doesn't reckon with other aspects of Laurie's character, such as the earlier business with Martin in the bathtub. She berates him for being "bashful," given that she has brothers, but it is clear that this is a form of sexual play, and that she is much more sexually confident than Martin. (See ibid.: 175, n. 16 on Martin's passivity and femininity.) Laurie uses pragmatism and down-to-earthness as a pretext for flirting. She clearly thinks of herself as hardheaded rather than innocent; presumably she thinks her racism is also a form of worldly-wise realism.

Pippin writes, convincingly, of the importance of the way that Ethan is treated at the end of the film:

> The community does not reject Ethan. ... They pretend he does not exist; no one speaks to him, says goodbye, tells him he can or cannot come in ... I take this as Ford's indicating some aspect of their own willful ignorance of their own racism ... and their own (unacknowledged) need for a character like Ethan.
>
> (ibid.: 139)

Perez's account of the ending is compatible but puts the emphasis slightly differently:

> The Debbie that comes home brings with her if not Indian blood then an experience of Indian life, an admixture of Indian culture, a tolerance of difference; and Laurie and Martin will marry and consummate their mixture of races. American society hasn't overcome its racism, but it now lives in the house of miscegenation.
>
> (Perez 2019: 43)

And yet Laurie's confidence in her own maturity suggests yet another possible reading. At the beginning of the film the part-Cherokee Martin is perfectly well accepted by everybody apart from Ethan; the film cannot straightforwardly represent a journey towards "the house of miscegenation" because Aaron and Martha's house was *already* such a house at the beginning. In ignoring Ethan, the community is not only refusing to acknowledge their need for his racism, but also avoiding an exploration of the fact that he changed his mind. They can welcome Debbie back without confronting the fact that

Laurie didn't want her back, can continue to treat Martin and Debbie straightforwardly as white, while the man who "also identifies with what he hates," as is indicated by the many parallels between Ethan and Scar, as well as by details such as "the Indian rifle scabbard that Ethan always carries" and "his intimate knowledge and apparent acceptance of Comanche religion," is banished (Pippin 2010a: 112).

Pippin claims that Ethan is

> a kind of walking manifestation of the costs incurred by the repression necessary for civilized life, and his eruptions of hatred, revenge, racism, and blind fury are tied to these inner dynamics as much as they are to the external threats and projects of the "official" or conscious civilized world.
>
> (ibid.: 115)

This is borne out by his exclusion, which represents the continuation of "the repression necessary for civilized life" rather than a move to a state beyond racism. It is as true today as it was for the Civil Rights era in which *The Searchers* was made that the United States has not reached such a state, and Ford's film neither pretends that it has, that it will ever be easy for it to do so, or that doing so is likely to take the form of the steadily progressive expansion of "the house of miscegenation."

3

Worlds Apart: Polanski and Malick

This chapter serves as a bridge between the longer chapters that precede and follow it. Using Pippin's readings of Roman Polanski's *Chinatown* (1974) and Terrence Malick's *The Thin Red Line* (1998), it develops more explicitly his understanding of what it means for a narrative film to have a "world." It will be helpful to get this as clear as possible before we turn, in the next chapter, to Pippin's account of agency and the challenges that some films—and certain film noirs in particular—pose to many of our commonsense assumptions about it.

Films and Their Worlds

At the end of *Hollywood Westerns* Pippin briefly discusses Nicholas Ray's (1952) film *The Lusty Men*, which he describes as a film that could "be said to be about the 'end of the Western' itself, the waning power of these narrative myths in our collective imaginary" (2010a: 142). In the film, former rodeo rider Jeff (Robert Mitchum) coaches a younger, ambitious rider called Wes (Arthur Kennedy) who over the course of the film becomes ever more greedy and reckless, despite the protestations of his wife Louise (Susan Hayward). At the film's conclusion, despite not having ridden for years, Jeff enters the rodeo again and is grievously injured:

> We get the impression that Jeff has done all this for Louise to show Wes the folly of continuing on the rodeo circuit (of indulging the

fantasies about an independent and wilder life) and so to shock some sense into him. We hear the doctor caution Jeff to lie very still, and he tells him that he has broken a rib and punctured a lung. But instead of lying still he rolls awkwardly and forcefully onto his left side, seems to embrace Louise and thereby, we infer, punctures his heart too, or at least deliberately causes a mortal internal wound, and he dies.

(ibid.: 153)

Pippin argues that in "the way that gesture is treated ... there is a kind of affirmation by Ray that Jeff's sacrifice was worth it, that there is nothing petty or small-minded or cowardly about what Louise wants," which is to say an "unexciting," settled bourgeois domestic life: "It is what the various foundings depicted by Westerns were *for*" (ibid.: 154). These foundings brought about, we could say, the possibility of a bourgeois world on the North American continent. It is still common to hear "bourgeois" used as an entirely pejorative adjective, and Hegel is frequently seen—and not only in radical circles—as both the theorist and the prophet of the historical inevitability of the dominance of market-based bourgeois societies (the role claimed for him by Francis Fukuyama and his ideas about the "end of history").[1] Given this, the fact that Pippin is happy to declare himself a Hegelian, combined with remarks such as that just cited about *The Lusty Men* (that "the various foundings depicted by Westerns" brought about the possibility of a settled bourgeois existence, and that this might be a dignified possibility, worthy of approval), might seem to imply that Pippin himself is a "bourgeois apologist," an advocate for the form of modern democratic societies as the best possible form of society who sees the bourgeois world as the proverbial "best of all possible worlds," or even as that toward which all of history directs itself. To conclude this would, however, be profoundly mistaken, and therefore it will be worth quickly presenting a small collection of passages that indicate this.

One reason, largely outside the scope of this book, that such a view would be a caricature of Pippin is that he believes that the views of Hegel mentioned above are themselves caricatures:

> Although it is often forgotten in the usual rush to condemn Hegel's triumphalism, reconciliationism, Prussian accommodationism, and so forth, all of his major works express varying degrees of anxiety about the major norms and institutions, that basic form of life, emerging in Western Europe in the first third of the nineteenth century: "modernity" for want of a more precise word.
> (Pippin 2018a: 380)

Hegel did, however, certainly think "that the rule of law, basic rights protection, especially property rights, a market economy and a representative state, the satisfactions of romantic love and the modern or nuclear family, the protection of a zone of genuine privacy and real individuality were all, in effect, *satisfaction enough*"; but, just as certainly, in thinking this, according to Pippin,

> Hegel was, understood historically, wrong ("psychologically wrong," let us say), and a good deal of later European high culture has to do with in just *what* sense he was wrong ... This sort of a world, Hegel's world, both disguises itself from itself, in massive strategies of self-deceit, its own hidden brutality (think, for example, of the films of Claude Chabrol) and must end in an erotic failure, boring.
> (Pippin 2010c: 122–3; emphases in original)

At the end of Chabrol's *La Cérémonie* (1995), for example, the viewer feels almost no sympathy for the slaughtered family—even though their cruelties were, "rationally" speaking, relatively trivial—largely because of the stultifying banality and hypocritical self-absorption of their lives.[2] So while Pippin is not willing to discard or dismiss all of the achievements of bourgeois society, neither does he by any means think that it represents the fullest achievement of human society, or an unimprovable form of human life: "The basic 'bourgeois' picture is not false, a mistake, or 'ideological': in Hegel's terms, it is simply 'incomplete'" (2005a: 2). Pippin's—admittedly unfashionable—position seems, then, to be that it is possible for bourgeois modernity to involve "massive strategies of self-deceit," for Hegel's account of it to be in many ways "psychologically wrong," and yet still to see it as based on a fundamental picture of the world that "is not false," and that Hegel's philosophy can help us to understand. (As we shall very shortly see, Pippin reads *Chinatown* as an exploration of what a world would be like in which this picture *were* false.) The crucial political question, then, is what kind of world might be able to remedy its deficiencies, to make itself more complete, to address its "hidden brutality"—if any, given the melancholy fact that "there may be no such possibility, consistent with modernity itself" (Pippin 1997: 127, n. 74).

How might we explore whether or not such a world is possible, and what does it have to do with how we understand fiction films? It is common to speak of the "world" of such films; film-critical and film-theoretical texts relevant to Pippin that do so include V. F. Perkins's essay "Where Is the World?" (2020: 270–300) and Daniel Yacavone's book *Film Worlds* (2015). Pippin writes:

> One very useful [way of putting the issue of the relation of plot to a film's "emerging, internal self-conception"] is that sketched by Yacavone 2015 in terms of the duality between the "world in the movie," on the one hand, and the "world of the movie," on the other, what we see and attend to as depicted, and our sense of it being depicted in a way, or the "movie world" as a selection, highlighting, focusing, and, in its cinematic way, commenting.
>
> (Pippin 2020a: 8, n. 6)

Characteristically, however—as we have seen him do with George Wilson's work on cinematic narration—Pippin's discussion of Yacavone's work puts the emphasis in a slightly different place from the original. For Yacavone, the distinction between *world-in* and *world-of* usually operates as one between fictional, diegetic "facts" (Where does Bruce Wayne live? What motivated him to become Batman?) and "stylistic" issues of aesthetic intentionality (Why do Tim Burton and Christopher Nolan—not to mention Leslie H. Martinson—choose the color schemes or editing patterns they employ in their various *Batman* films?). To quote Yacavone, "most theoretical treatments of cinematic worlds ... are largely self-limited to what films are *about* in terms of a story [i.e., the *world-in*] rather than what they also *are*, as created, unified works—together with what they *mean* in nonnarrative (or extranarrative) and nonfictional ways [i.e., the *world-of*]" (2015: 3–4; emphases in original).

Pippin, however, indicates a slightly different way of putting the distinction to work, one that is cognate with the emphasis we have seen in his work on Westerns with the way that their mythic and symbolic dimensions can be active *within* the fictional world of the film (the *world-in*). For Pippin, in Roman Polanski's (1974) neo-noir film, "Chinatown" is "a world in the movie"; it is not simply "that area of Los Angeles" but is instead "what the characters feel and believe about what they call Chinatown" (2020a: 8, n. 6). On top of this "there is Polanski's filmic world, *Chinatown*," which "he ultimately lets us see ... *is much worse* than even the most cynical characters can appreciate" (ibid.; emphasis in original). For Pippin, then, understanding the *world-in* a film is not simply a matter of narrative comprehension but also involves attention to the film's world *as seen by the characters* (where "world" means something similar to what Wittgenstein meant in his famous remark in his *Tractatus*, 6.43, that "the world of the happy man is a different one from that of the unhappy man" [2001: 87]), while the *world-of* is not confined to a film's "nonnarrative (or extranarrative)" dimension but includes what we might call a film's attitude to, or perspective on, the fictional characters and events that it depicts. Both of these aspects can involve political psychology in the sense that we have seen Pippin claim to be active in some of the greatest Westerns. This is true even in films that might be charged with downplaying or evading political questions by treating them allegorically, as emblematic of unchanging aspects of the human soul; I am thinking specifically of *Chinatown* and of Terrence Malick's *The Thin Red Line*.

Social Pathologies and Bourgeois Metaphysics

Pippin argues that there is an aspect of political existence, broadly conceived, that "is not a feature representable discursively" (2020a: 108), and that, therefore, matters of cinematic tone and affect—Yacavone's *world-of* the film—can have profound political significance:

> A film ... can have a mood suffused through it, something not quite the same as a signature style, but an effect of a consistent, controlled style. Ford's Westerns, the great ones, create a mood of historical fundamentality, that matters of great political and social significance are at stake (the place of violence in a civilized life, for example).
>
> (ibid.: 107)[3]

One of Pippin's terms for a state of being in which something is fundamentally awry is "social pathology," a term that resists any simplistic division of wrongdoing into its individual and collective aspects.[4] In *Chinatown*, for example, "Polanski creates and sustains a constant, uneasy mood among all the unknowing characters, that *something is not at all right here*" (ibid.; emphasis in original), a feeling that Pippin puts in dialogue with Theodor Adorno's claim in his book *Minima Moralia* (1951) that something is fundamentally wrong with life itself in late capitalist bourgeois society: "Wrong life cannot be lived rightly," or even (in the epigram to the book's first section, from the nineteenth-century Austrian writer Ferdinand Kürnberger) "life does not live" (2005: 19, 39).[5] Pippin notes that pronouncements such as this might seem rather "vatic" but observes that they are clearly intended to refer to "a normative, not physical breakdown" (2020a: 113). He uses the example of an elephant in a circus, which is obviously alive in the strict sense, but also completely unable to live the real life of an elephant: "there is no 'right' way to be an elephant in a circus" (ibid.). So it is, according to Adorno, for human beings in modern postindustrial society.

As difficult as such an idea might be to grasp, and as highly contestable as it remains even should we manage to do so, Pippin's point is that *Chinatown* gives us an image of what a world in which it was true might *look* and *feel* like. In Robert Towne's screenplay and Polanski's film, two narratives about great evil are intertwined with one another, one concerning the private manipulation and exploitation of Los Angeles's water supply (something based on a fictionalized account of historical realities, albeit shifted forward a couple of decades; the film takes place in 1937 but the sources of the "water plot" took place in the teens), and another concerning incest. Both plots center around the character of the significantly-named Noah Cross (his first name referring ironically to the first of the double plots and his surname to the other), memorably played by John Huston. Pippin notes that "the structure of the film forces us to ask what the two plots, the water swindle plot and the incest plot, have to do with each other, if anything," but that for critics with either a heavily sociohistorical or, alternatively, psychoanalytic focus a satisfactory answer has not been forthcoming: "for many in each camp, the other plot is a digression, diversion, or distraction" (2020a: 108–9). Pippin asks how, if we do not want to take this kind of way out, we might read the film.[6]

There is clearly something emblematic or even allegorical at work. As Mike Davis notes, in works such as *Chinatown* "Los Angeles is ... a stand-in for capitalism in general. The ultimate world-historical significance—and oddity—of Los Angeles is that it has come to play the double role of utopia *and* dystopia for advanced capitalism" (1990: 18; emphasis in original). But given that this is so, what does Los Angeles's Chinatown represent in the film? As we have already seen, Pippin argues that what it signifies is crucial not only for viewers of *Chinatown* but for the film's characters; in fact, understanding what it means for characters in the film (as part of the *world-in*) is crucial to understanding its more general significance (as part of the *world-of*). He gives short shrift to any notion that it is a racist signifier for "inscrutability"; this is precisely how it is *used* by the characters in the film: "Polanski is ironizing, or making fun of, the idea that all the evil in Los Angeles could be located in an ethnic ghetto" (Pippin 2020b). Ultimately, the film demonstrates precisely that "the distinction between Chinatown and Los Angeles is an illusion, that we (the bourgeois world and its rule of law) are *in* such an unfathomable world and can never escape" (Pippin 2020a: 102; emphasis in original). We might recall the famous remark by Mephistopheles in a play by a playwright who shares a surname with the most famous detective in noir cinema: "Why this is hell, nor am I out of it" (Christopher Marlowe, *Dr. Faustus*, scene 3, l. 77).

Vernon Shetley's (1999) article on the film is "far and away the best discussion of the double plot" Pippin has encountered (2020a: 109, n. 14). In that article, Shetley detects a generic hybridity in the film:

> *Chinatown* is a film noir, a detective film, but also, through the character Noah Cross, a Western. Cross, in his appearance and his history, invokes a distinctive myth, the crusty, determined, plain-spoken pioneer, whose gruff manner is the outward sign of the quintessentially American qualities of self-reliance, independence, and enterprise. ... Noah Cross is a form of the pioneer hero, who gravitates toward the west to enjoy its promise of freedom, and whose energy and fortitude tame nature, making the desert bloom. ... [But] Noah Cross himself acknowledges that it is Hollis Mulwray [Darrell Zwerling], the bespectacled public servant, who "made this town," and that the city's founding had more to do with engineering than conquest.
>
> (Shetley 1999: 1096)

Chinatown is, therefore, connected to the issues concerning foundings and transitions from one set of values to another that Pippin discusses in his book on the Western. (Cross's remark about the fact that all sorts of things—he specifically mentions "politicians, ugly buildings, and whores"—get respectable if they "last long enough" might even suggest a parallel-world variant on *Liberty Valance*, in which Valance himself becomes the senator simply by not dying, his past being conveniently forgotten.) Both plots are connected to this issue; Shetley notes, in remarks that Pippin calls "illuminating," that for Lévi-Strauss "the incest taboo marks the dividing line between nature and culture, in its establishment of a principle of affiliation that goes beyond mere biology" (ibid.: 1099).

One might also note that the former partners Cross and Mulwray used to own Los Angeles's water, but that Mulwray came to believe that water was not the kind of thing that ought to be privately owned. Cross never came to that realization, and still thinks that both water and daughters can—and *should*—be owned, as long as the owner is himself. So there is also a kind of founding myth in the background of the film concerning the move from "primitive accumulation" to a legally-regulated state in which water is not owned, except that this move fails because the state—the water board, the police—is entirely corrupt. (Elected politicians are interestingly almost entirely absent from the film, apart from the Mayor [Roy Roberts], whom we see briefly early on. In a parallel *Chinatown* Cross would be a senior politician; it seems even darker or more cynical to say that he doesn't even need to be, that he doesn't even need to produce a public face in order to manufacture consent.) It is not clear if the film proposes that the ownership of things such as water was a state that needed to be passed through, but this is at least plausible: as we hear from the Mayor, "beneath our streets is a desert." A habitable world had to be *created*; we aren't dealing with somewhere that was inhabitable in any kind of "state of nature."

But *what*, precisely, has been created? As Pippin observes:

> The idea that there can be a collective allegiance to a common good is also the idea that the state's monopoly on the use of legitimate coercive violence cannot be understood as at the service of whatever private interests are predominant at the time. In such a case there would be no state, no genuinely public sphere, no politics, just some (putative) collective means to insure that the use of public power be consistent with some sort of like use for all, always subject to manipulation by anyone with wealth enough to manipulate without penalty.
>
> (Pippin 2020a: 112–13)

That is what *Chinatown* offers us: not an apolitical study of evil, but a picture of a world *without politics*. We discover that "in any such world, one is morally complicit with such wrongness just by surviving, by existing at all" (ibid.: 108). Pippin notes that there is a rational objection to such an interpretation, that "there seems a clear center of responsibility for what is so wrong about Los Angeles: Cross and those who serve him" (ibid.). But the problem with such a response (that we can deal with evil simply by dealing appropriately with evil people when they crop up, as they always will, evil being a perennial possibility within the human soul), is that it does not explain "what Cross [has] to do with 'Chinatown'" (ibid.).[7] For this we need to recognize two things. The first is that the world of *Chinatown* is historically specific:

> We are finite beings who depend on others for the achievement of our ends, and in a world of highly divided labor, this dependence is more and more unavoidable. The most significant arena in which this tension must play out is the political world, and that means especially the state's assumption of a monopoly on the legitimate use of violence. ... So there is something almost pathetic in the final scene when Jake [Jack Nicholson], of all people, encourages Evelyn, "Let the police handle this," a plaintive expression of hope

that is immediately, and, by this point, compellingly for most viewers, countered by Evelyn [Faye Dunaway; Cross's daughter and the victim of the incest plot]: "He *owns* the police."

(ibid.: 114–15; emphasis in original)

The police *cannot* be owned, if we take the word in a normative sense; an owned police force is *not* a police force (it is a private army, or something similar). (One difficult question that the film then raises is whether or not an owned daughter ceases to be a daughter.) Secondly, we need to pay attention to what Pippin calls "'tonality' or a cinematic representation of a mood or common 'attunement' in the narration," the "undercurrent of futility, confusion, and paranoia" that the film cumulatively generates (ibid.: 108, 115). Avoiding the kind of two-step account that we saw Pippin criticize in Chapter 1, we do not so much infer this mood *from* the film as experience it *in* our viewing.

It is, for Pippin, in this mood that *Chinatown* most powerfully demonstrates what it might be for life, in Adorno's terms, to be "false." The world of *Chinatown* is not fully intelligible; rational planning simply does not allow one to work confidently toward the desired outcomes. "Good intentions and commitment to others" must be seen to

> assume what moral action always does: that one knows one's own motives, that one understands what is happening, and that one can predict safely what a course of action will bring about. Since none of these assumptions is true, doing "as little as possible" seems the safest choice. Assuming these conditions have been met is not only naive, but very dangerous.
>
> (ibid.: 105)

Chinatown is therefore, like *The Searchers*, another example of extreme cinematic pressure being exerted on our usual assumptions about intentionality and agency, a phenomenon whose quintessential exemplars are the classic film noirs (see the next chapter for discussion of this). Therefore,

> it is appropriate that we too, the viewers of the film, are left so confused about such things as Cross's motives, the police's intentions, the fate of Katherine [Belinda Palmer; Cross's daughter *and* granddaughter], or what it means to suggest that Jake should just "forget" about the fact that a vast water swindle is succeeding, and that a sexual predator has got his hands on a new young victim.
>
> (ibid.: 114)

Jake, the private detective, tells Evelyn that when he used to work in Chinatown he learned to try to do "as little as possible," because his efforts to protect somebody had exactly the opposite effect, a plot that repeats itself identically with Evelyn. When looking down at her dead body at the end of the film he murmurs the same line to himself. It would have been better for Evelyn had he managed to do "as little as possible" in this situation; but he failed, because—as his partner Walsh (Joe Mantell) famously tells him—"this is Chinatown"; nor is he out of it.

A possible difficulty with Pippin's reading, however, is that its fatalism might seem to excuse Jake, at least to some extent, for his failures, because nothing he could have done would have led to a better outcome, given the inescapability and irrationality of "Chinatown." Chief among these failings is his eagerness to assume that Evelyn is a murderer and kidnapper, "as if," Pippin notes, he "has seen to many noirs" (ibid.: 100, n. 1). He clearly didn't pay enough attention to Howard Hawks's *The Big Sleep* (1946), however, in which the detective also thinks the worst of a female protagonist who turns out simply to be trying to protect a female relative. Shetley observes that

> what differentiates *Chinatown* from *The Big Sleep* is that Bogart's Marlowe bears no moral judgment for his distrust of Bacall's Vivian Rutledge, while the whole tragedy of *Chinatown* turns on

Jake's refusal to trust Evelyn, a refusal for which the film asks us, in
the end, to hold Jake to account.

(Shetley 1999: 1102)

Does Pippin's reading fail sufficiently "to hold Jake to account"? Francey Russell reads *Chinatown* in terms inspired by Stanley Cavell in which Jake's obsession with knowledge, with *knowing* Evelyn, prevents him from *acknowledging* her, in a way that also implicates the viewer: "In our fixation on the promise of knowledge, we, along with the protagonist, miss the opportunity for acknowledgment. Hence its tragic ending" (2018: 8). The point is excellent but perhaps the even darker reading, one that is more consistent with Pippin's, is that it would have been better if Jake had tried *neither* to know *nor* to acknowledge Evelyn, but simply to do nothing—to *ignore* her. And, in that sense, he is quite right that "as little as possible" would have been the correct option, except that the film also indicates that it is not a viable option; one can no more forget something, or somebody, because one wants to any more than one can believe something simply because one wants to. Ultimately, Pippin notes that he does not agree with what he takes "to be the 'conclusion' the film seems to leave us with" and that he "would prefer to take it as a prophetic warning about the world of late capitalism" (2020a: 115, n 21). But that the world of "false life," we discover in *Chinatown*, is not ultimately persuasive—given, as we saw at the beginning of this chapter, Pippin's reluctance simply to dismiss the bourgeois vision—does not make it any less compelling, nor the social pathologies that it dramatizes any less real.[8]

If *Chinatown* is about living, then *The Thin Red Line* is much more concerned with (the prospect of) dying. It is the second film adaptation of James Jones's (1962) novel of the same name, covering the fighting on the Solomon Island of Guadalcanal, and—argues Pippin—asks an important question concerning political psychology, namely "how ordinary citizens of commercial republics can both come to participate in acts of extreme violence and come to understand in some way what they are doing" (ibid.: 207). And yet its treatment of this question, and the way in which it answers it, are extremely unusual. In fact, the film "is not an 'antiwar' film at all. Or even a political film for that matter. The national mission in fighting the Japanese, the 'cause of freedom,' and so forth are never mentioned" (ibid.: 216, n. 25). Just as with *Chinatown*, Pippin finds the way *The Thin Red Line* disorientates its viewer to be crucial to an understanding of the film, because although

> *The Thin Red Line* ... has many of the elements of a Hollywood World War II movie ... as in [Malick's] other films, these genre conventions create expectations and suggest explanations that are then undermined, refused, left open, made to seem irrelevant, made mysterious, or even ironized. ... especially in this war movie, Malick's two quite dramatic technical innovations—his almost devout concentration on the visual beauty, magisterial indifference, and sublimity of the natural world, and the unusual meditative interior monologue voice-overs by individual characters—violate not only genre conventions but many narrative, dramatic, and psychological elements of realist fiction films.
>
> (ibid.: 205)

The Thin Red Line's affinities to more familiarly generic war films set up certain expectations—such as, for example, that the film will explore "the psychological bases of political and thereby military authority" or "the idea that war creates an emotional bond of love that takes over in critical situations, that the men fight, even to the death, for each other"—that it is very hard for the viewer not to bring to mind but that turn out to be irrelevant (ibid.: 221).

This means that the film lays certain traps for the viewer unless they are very careful. Pippin writes very well about the complications and ironies of the relationship between Lt. Col. Tall (Nick Nolte) and Capt. Staros (Elias Koteas), in which Staros disobeys Tall's order to make a direct assault on the Japanese on Hill 210, only for Tall to insist and the attack to succeed, with the result that "we end up unsure what to think" (ibid.: 219); Pippin (2020b) calls this "the most interesting irony" in the film. Pippin demonstrates that a number of critics think that Tall ends up learning from Staros and uses his flanking move, which would be a fairly straightforward reconciliationist solution to the conflict between them. This is in fact *not* what happens in the film; instead, Tall turns out to be *right* (Pippin 2020a: 218, n. 19). Malick's subversive use of conventions warns us against using them as shortcuts toward interpretation; we need to constantly ask ourselves whether we are seeing what we want to see, rather than what we should be seeing. Or indeed hearing—another subtle point that Pippin notices is that the first and last voice we hear in voice-over does not belong to one of the film's obviously central characters, but to Pvt. Train (John Dee Smith), a character we see only a few times, although many viewers, and indeed critics (see Chion 2004) assume that the first and last voice we hear belongs to Jim Caviezel's Pvt. Witt (see Pippin 2020a: 214).

So what is the purpose of all this confusion, beyond mimicking the fact that war is disorientating? Pippin argues that it should sensitize us to small details and put issues of perspective continually in question, so that we are always asking ourselves whose point of view we are seeing, hearing, or both. Pippin claims that all the questions raised by *The Thin Red Line* are determinedly kept open ("Nothing in this film is dispositive about anything" [2020a: 201, n. 15]), so much so that "no one speaks for the movie, for the auteur; the characters speak for themselves" (ibid.: 213). Pippin convincingly shows, for example, that the difference between the idyllic Melanesian village at the beginning and the one we see at the end, "now with violent arguments among the tribe members, suspicious, wary children, disease, [and] stacks of human skulls," does not have anything to do with any changes wrought by the war but by Witt's change of perspective; the differences testify "to how much of what *we originally see* depends on *what Witt thinks he sees* (or wants to see)" (ibid.: 215; emphases in original). From this follows Pippin's interpretation of the answer he finds the film providing to the question raised above—that is, "how ordinary citizens of commercial republics can both come to participate in acts of extreme violence and come to understand in some way what they are doing" (ibid.: 207). The answer is that this can happen if those so engaged in war can themselves come to achieve something more fundamental than a political psychology, something on which such a psychology could be based or—as most happens in this film—that can render one unnecessary. It can happen, that is, if these soldiers can manage to have some kind of philosophical perspective on the prospect of their own deaths; this requires what Pippin calls in the title of this chapter a "vernacular metaphysics," on the understanding of "something Stanley Cavell sometimes says: that there can be no real virtuosity for true philosophy as there is for mathematics and music. It must be something that in some way anyone does, can do" (ibid.: 224).

As we have already seen, maintaining this position requires Pippin to insist that the film does not identify itself with any particular perspective within it, that its "reflective form" asks questions rather than endorsing answers. So, for example, the treatment of light in the film's many images of nature is to be understood as suggesting "that we are seeing not mere objects but objects *in their being illuminated* by this basic ontological question [that of "what it is for them to be at all, especially to be alive"], prompted by their being at all" (ibid.: 225; emphasis in original). On Pippin's reading, the film does not even identify itself with the content of Train's voice-overs (even the final lyrical affirmation of "all things shining"), because elsewhere in the film we hear "the imagined voice of [a] dead Japanese soldier, addressed to Witt as if a kind of indictment," and whose "strange, imagined dialogue ["Do you imagine your sufferings will be less because you loved goodness? Truth?"] in effect rejects the whole premise of Train's speculative questions and makes it even less likely that Train's monologues ... are in any way representative of the film's point of view" (ibid.: 227). This kind of gesture, in which something that a viewer might assume can be unproblematically taken as "the film's point of view" turns out to be relative to the perspective of a character, is very common in Pippin, and has been challenged. One example is his claim that the main flashback in *The Man Who Shot Liberty Valance* represents Ranse's narration—or at least view—of the events: "this is *Stoddard's* narration, and there are signs that this fact might be coloring what we are seeing" (ibid.: 78; emphasis in original). Pippin points to details such the casting and the comparison between the characters as we see them in the flashback and the film's "present" to support this point (see 2010a: 78–9, 168, n. 16). Perez, however, objects that "Ranse is neither exactly the narrator nor unreliable," and cites as evidence the fact that we see things that "the presumed narrator couldn't have seen" which tell us "something crucial to the story" (2019: 38). But I think this relies on an excluded middle that Pippin would deny. Films can play very fast and loose with narration, and there is no reason why a narration cannot be consistently colored by a certain character's perspective and still show us things which that character couldn't know; "the requirements of fictional credibility are rather loosey-goosey" (Pippin 2013a: 335).[9]

Granted this point, whether or not an aspect of a film can be said to relate more to the dramatization of a character's viewpoint (to the *world-in*, considered in the expanded sense we have seen Pippin recommend) rather than the film's own sense of itself (the *world-of* the film in question) has to be demonstrated anew in each instance. I am not sure that I am entirely convinced by Pippin's arguments about *The Thin Red Line* in this regard. Pippin argues, for example, that Pvt. Bell's (Ben Chaplin) memories of his wife (Miranda Otto) "may be imaginative projections, romantic fantasies," given that Bell eventually "gets a devastating letter from his wife, suddenly asking for a divorce" (2020a: 216). As plausible as this seems at times, there are also images of her playing worriedly with the curtains while a man—who may or may not be Bell—sleeps, and then standing, arms folded, with a troubled expression, her back to a man who is approaching from the middle distance. The range of interpretational possibilities here is very large. These images could well also be Bell's fantasies (they cannot be his memories); they could even be his wife's fantasies (perhaps the image with the approaching man represents her anxious projection of what Bell's return would be like if she didn't tell him about her infidelity). But, however we read them, they are not stylistically differentiated from the film's other images of her. We see these images after we see and hear Bell talking about how he hasn't even looked at another woman since the war started. Immediately after this he receives the letter asking for a divorce. If the images of his troubled wife are also Bell's fantasies, then he is not as confident in her as he seems. This is a possible reading but the more likely, it seems to me, is that the film intends an irony in the juxtaposition of his declaration of fidelity with images of a reality that is unknown to him, representing either her doubts about her own fidelity or her actual infidelity. If so, this irony doesn't appear to extend to the film's style, in that Miranda Otto looks just as delicate and beautiful as she does in all the film's images of her (see Figure 5).

Similarly, on Pippin's reading, the idea that "maybe all men got one big soul who everybody's a part of—all faces are the same man, one big self," which we hear in one of Witt's monologues, must be seen as part of the film's enquiry into the "vernacular metaphysics" of the film's characters, the psychological underpinnings of their acceptance of the death and killing that their participation in the war requires. (Requires, that is, if they are not to be broken by it, as is Jon Savage's Sgt. McCron.) The fact, however, that Train also asks, at the end of the film, "Are they the workings of one mind? The features

Figure 5 "Romantic fantasies" in *The Thin Red Line*?

of the same face?" suggests to me at least a qualified endorsement of such ideas by the film; the irony is that the viewer is permitted to perceive the rhymes between the different monologues that the characters cannot. We are part of one soul without knowing it, being vouchsafed only occasional glimpses of this truth: "All things shining." The final three images of the film show three Melanesians in canoes, two brightly colored parrots, and one coconut sprouting on a lonely beach. Both Michel Chion (2004: 72) and Pippin (2020a: 229) refer to the transition at the end from human to animal to vegetable, but they do not explicitly note that the film ends by counting down (three humans, two birds, one coconut). Granted, it is ambiguous whether this is a move toward isolation or toward unity, just as it is unclear whether this movement is better read as "'regressive' on the evolutionary ladder" (Chion 2004: 72), or as a concentration on the fundamentals of life (the coconut, after all, is a kind of "kernel"), but mysteriously transcendent wholeness seems to me to win out over meaningless isolation.[10] Ultimately, as Stanley Cavell remarks about a very different film, "this is just something further each viewer must try out on his or her own" (2005: 49).

So, although I may not be fully persuaded by Pippin's account of *The Thin Red Line*—I would be very happy for the film to be as he presents it, but I cannot make this fully tally with my experience of it[11]—his insistence that we should be wary of assuming too quickly that a film endorses not only *what* it presents but *how* it presents it is a very valuable lesson. As Pippin notes of the worlds of—and in—all the films he discusses in *Filmed Thought* (in words that are equally applicable to all of the films he has written about at length):

> Our attention is also drawn in these films, more prominently that in many others, to *the way* that world is cinematically depicted; what is cinematically highlighted, ignored; why the camera moves and frames events one way rather than another; to what end a musical score signals something sad or ominous; and above all, in many of the films discussed, various figurative and expressionistic means are invoked to suggest that everything we see depicted is not as it seems, must be interrogated, thought about.
>
> (Pippin 2020a: 11; emphasis in original)

Films that demand to be approached in this way make any straightforward division into plot and style—where either (1) the style, essentially, merely dresses up the plot or (2) the plot provides a convenient skeleton on which to hang the stylistic activity which is the real focus of interest—ultimately incoherent. (Which is not to say that there are not films for which one or other of these approaches might not be perfectly adequate.) Pippin constantly encourages us to think about how and why *this world is shown*, something we cannot do without attending both to the world (as a *world*) and the showing (as a *showing*); this is, ultimately, the whole point of distinguishing between *world-in* and *world-of*. But to develop these ideas further, we need to think more about the relationship between how characters *see* their world and what they *do* within it. In much of his work Pippin aims to shake up our understanding of what it is for a character to act *at all*—and this is nowhere truer than in his work on film noir.

4

Film Noir and Agency: Do We Know What We're Doing?

This chapter will argue that Pippin's studies of agency—of how we go about applying the appropriate act descriptions to the behavior of ourselves and others—are fundamental to his investigations of film and represent probably his most important and original contributions to Film Studies. After establishing the centrality of this idea to the broad sweep of Pippin's career—it is very important to the interpretation of Hegel to which he has devoted much of his career—the chapter will center on Pippin's second book on film, *Fatalism in American Film Noir: Some Cinematic Philosophy*, showing how films by directors including Jacques Tourneur, Orson Welles, and Fritz Lang have developed his philosophical thought on these topics rather than serving as sites for illustrating a preestablished theory. The chapter ends by covering Pippin's more recent studies of action in the films of the Dardenne brothers.

"Rational Agency as Ethical Life"

Coming across what is one of the earliest references to cinema in Robert Pippin's published writings is rather surprising for someone already familiar with his books on film. In *Hegel's Practical Philosophy: Rational Agency as Ethical Life*—which, alongside *Hegel's Idealism*, is, to date, probably Pippin's most influential and frequently discussed book—we find the following passage:

And there is the classic Western or civil war movie scenario. Tex has been shot in the leg and will die if the leg is not amputated. As his comrades prepare to amputate, Tex begs them, in agony and fear, not to amputate. But we, and his comrades, do not take such protestations as what he genuinely wills.

(Pippin 2008: 80–1)

Here a film—and not even a specific film, but merely any number of films belonging to a certain category, or even an imaginary film, involving this supposedly "classic ... movie scenario"—is pressed into service in order to serve as an illustration for the purposes of furthering a philosophical argument. This, it should be abundantly clear by now, is not what Pippin considers the most interesting or fruitful way that film and philosophy might intersect. In fact, however, Tex is not Pippin's invention; his discussion here is engaging with (and in fact disagreeing with) an example used by the philosopher Christine Korsgaard. Nevertheless, the example is useful both because it addresses something that lies right at the heart of Pippin's philosophical interests and also because, given the ways that Pippin believes that films relate to this "something," it is not at all inappropriate that Korsgaard frames her example in terms of film.

Korsgaard argues about Tex's situation that

> the right thing to say is that fear is making Tex irrational. After all, the judgement that someone is irrational doesn't have to be a criticism. The government of reason, like any other, requires certain background conditions in order to maintain its authority. Faced with the prospect of having his leg sawed off, Tex's sensible nature is quite understandably in revolt.
>
> (Korsgaard 1997: 238)[1]

Pippin disputes this account because it seems that, according to Korsgaard, Tex has a rational self which his fear somehow prevents from coming to the fore in this particular situation. This is, argues

Pippin, to misrepresent the way rationality, intention, and personal character actually operate. Before his injury, Tex might have believed himself to be the kind of person who would bravely and stoically accept the prospect of having his leg amputated. The fact that he turns out *not* to be has nothing to do with his fear "overriding" his rationality:

> In resisting the amputation, Tex is not "too weak" to be the "Real Tex." He expresses and discovers something about this real Tex in such resistance, something about the nature of his commitment to life, the weight of his fear of pain, his ability (or lack of it) to invoke and rely on an ideal picture of himself, and so on. He is not, in resisting, "weakly" the Real Tex. He is just Tex.
> (Pippin 2008: 83, n. 34)

Pippin thinks that Hegel's philosophy can help us to break out of an extremely deep-seated—but nonetheless inaccurate and unhelpful—picture of intentionality and agency which sees intentions as something that occur "within" an agent, and that then may or may not end up being successfully actualized. He wants to replace this picture with one less tied to individual moments in time ("When you picked up the knife, did you intend to kill her?"), one that instead sees intention as having to do with a subject's continuing, and developing, relation to their actions ("I thought I didn't, but I've come to realize that I *really did* want to kill her"). Pippin quotes with approval Elizabeth Anscombe's observation that "if you want to say at least some true things about a man's intentions, you will have a strong chance of success if you mention what he actually did or is doing" (Anscombe 2000: 8; cited in Pippin 2008: 80, n. 26).[2] To argue this is not to say that what we intend to do, before we act, is irrelevant or uninteresting, but it is to argue that we have no uniquely privileged access to our own intentions (we can be wrong about what we intend), that it may well be only *in* acting that we find out what we actually intended, and that this will often involve consideration of the actions and reactions of other people (my intentions are not a wholly private matter).

The Kantian (and Hegelian) ideas about apperception that we encountered in Chapter 1 are again relevant: intentionality is largely a question of self-consciousness, but only if by that term "we mean not what we intend when we turn our attention to ourselves, but in what relation to ourselves we are when we claim something or act" (Pippin 2019b: 113). Pippin argues that Hegel asks us

> that we in effect widen our focus when considering what a rational and thereby free agent looks like, widening it so as to include *in* the picture of agency itself a contextual and temporal field stretching out "backwards" from or prior to, one might say, the familiar resolving and acting subject, and stretching "forward," one might also say, such that the unfolding of the deed and the reception and reaction to it are considered a *constitutive element* of the deed, of what fixes ultimately *what was done* and *what turned out to be* a subject's intention. (The ultimate goal is to break the hold altogether of the notion of "a moment" of resolve or a moment of causal efficacy.)[3]
>
> (Pippin 2008: 152; emphases in original)

To make this more concrete, Pippin again uses an example drawn from film, only this time—much more characteristically—he refers to a specific film, albeit one about which he draws conclusions very comparable to those he drew concerning poor old Tex:

> When Marlon Brando's character says to his brother in *On the Waterfront*: "I could have been somebody, a contender," a Hegelian brother might have said: "You *are* somebody. The somebody who wasted his boxing talent by listening to me and taking a fall for a pay off. You have become wholly, explicitly, what you were implicitly. You may regret that you are (were) not someone else, especially not the person you thought you were, but you *have become* the person you are."
>
> (ibid.: 162; emphases in original)[4]

These can be difficult ideas, entailing, as they do, the idea that to be a "rational agent" is ultimately "a kind of collective social construct, an achieved state" that has much more in common with a status like "being a speaker of a natural language"—because "vocalisations count as speaking the language only within a language community that takes such vocalisations to commit the speaker to various proprieties and entitlements"—than it does to classes or statuses like "'featherless biped,' or 'being a female'" (Pippin 2000b: 162–3).[5] Agency, according to Pippin's Hegel, is best seen as *normative*, as something that we achieve or fail to achieve, which is only possible within a community. In isolation, I could no more, say, insult someone—or fail to do so—than a hermit could be a traffic warden (without ceasing to be a hermit). Despite the complexity of these ideas, Pippin's readings of specific films demonstrate that films can make them vivid and graspable, as well as showing that exploring them by means of the interpretation of film is by no means a question of concretely illustrating separable philosophical arguments, or merely of helping us to get our heads round them. Rather, getting our heads round them in concrete instances *involves* philosophical reflection about agency and responsibility.

This does, however, mean that Pippin is required to do something that many different strands of Film Studies, and studies of fictional narrative in general, have long attempted to dismantle or expose as naive; namely, to treat fictional characters as real people. But Pippin, while accepting that to do so with regard to some kinds of characters would be foolish or at least inappropriate—"Henry James, say, is not a model for how the novels of, say, Flaubert or Musil or Kafka or Beckett should be read, just as Tourneur or Welles or Ford is no model for how to interpret Godard or Bresson" (2012: 108, n. 4)[6]— also believes that in many cases it *is* possible to do so without fallacy or simplemindedness, because in investigating agency in these terms we are involved in the search for the appropriate act descriptions in each case, which is something that is required both in our "real lives" and in the interpretation of fictions:

> While screen images are not persons, and film narration is sui generis, there cannot be two *completely* different modalities of such sense making [i.e. between 'what we do when we try to understand what we and others normally do and what we do in trying to understand moving pictures of actions'] ... Motion pictures of characters, whatever else they are, are still representative, actually, since the complex, imputed "author" of the film ... is representing actors who are ... themselves representing a person's life and action, all in ways they think will be understood.
>
> (ibid.: 2–3; emphasis in original)[7]

Film characters are, very often, constructed—by screenwriters and directors—and performed—by actors—on the understanding that viewers will try to understand them as, in some sense, persons. In such instances, if one wants (to use the phrase once more) "to understand the goddamn film" it cannot be inappropriate to try to do so in terms that relate to the ways we try to understand the extra-filmic reality we share with those screenwriters, directors, and actors; and this precisely because those creators have made the creative decisions they have on the presumption that we will do exactly that. As Pippin says, "we have to 'make sense of what characters do,' and for classic Hollywood realist narrative, we bring to bear on that question the ways we attempt to make sense of our own and others' actions" (ibid.: 2). Where things become particularly interesting to Pippin is when this process of understanding proves to be *difficult*; and there are no more paradigmatic examples of this than can be found in some of the great film noirs. Pippin is willing to make some very bold claims about these films, such as the following, which outline the ways that Pippin's interests in historical subjectivity, in the intelligibility of agency, and in Hollywood film all come together in his studies of film noir:

It might even happen that the degree of *confidence* with which I could expect that what I intend to happen will happen, and happen just because of my intending it, could, at least in the most significant cases, begin to collapse, and this in ways having to do with ... socio-historically varied possibilities ... There might then be a question to pose: in the face of a world-historically significant collapse of such confidence, is there an art form uniquely suited to the exploration of the uniquely temporal dimensions of action in such a critical situation (call it "late modernity")? ... Perhaps that art form would be a cinema ever more self-conscious of its unique potential, its historical moment, and its distinctive temporal mode of rendering intelligible. And, if that is so, perhaps we should amend Bazin's famous claim that the essence of the cinema is the Western and suggest that film reaches its distinct potential as an art with *film noir*.

(Pippin 2016a: 222; emphasis in original)

Fatalism and Film Noir: Tourneur, Welles, Lang

In 1946, Nino Frank, a French journalist who was one of the very first people to refer to something called a "film noir" wrote that "after films like these, the characters of ordinary detective films will seem like puppets" (quoted in Dimendberg 2004: 5). Frank means to applaud the newly-found realism he discovered in noir, but his reference to puppets is suggestive. The tension that Pippin finds at the heart of many great film noirs is between the ways that the protagonists of these films see themselves as the puppets of circumstance, or of fate, and the fact that their own attempts to direct the course of their actions reveals them to be something like failed puppet *masters*, so that "characters deliberating and initiating various deeds come to look like pathetic figures frantically pulling various wires and pushing various buttons not connected to some moving machine they are riding, on a course completely indifferent to anything such characters pretend to do" (2012: 15–16). This is of course a kind of limit case; noirs do not show characters having *no* control over the consequences of what they do, but no *significant* control, no control concerning what really matters. Just as a lousy puppeteer might be able to make a certain puppet move, and even to successfully move, say, either their arms or their legs, but to have no finer control than this, so Pippin argues that the noirs he studies can serve "as a way of shedding some light on how agency might be said to have such a thing as degrees" (ibid.: 18).

This can be counterintuitive, because it comes so naturally to us to consider agency as a kind of on/off capacity—do we, for example, have free will or not? Film noirs are compelling because of the evidence they provide "about the differences between *what we think we 'still' think* (about individual causal agency, self-knowledge, moral responsibility, and our reflective access to ourselves), and *what we actually think*—and so respond to, are moved by, find credible, and so forth," something which will thereby "raise obvious questions about *what we ought to think* about the issues" (ibid.: 19; emphases in original). So although Frank's discovery of realism in the films he christened "noir" can seem a little quaint, in the wake of so many subsequent movements towards cinematic realism or naturalism, his insight is not, for Pippin, irrelevant, because the question of *credibility* is key to the philosophical significance he finds in the noirs he discusses. The fact that much of what we see in those films *does* seem in some way recognizable "just by itself puts a great deal of pressure on the conventional, modern account of agency (what we think we think)," and given that this "arises naturally on an attentive viewing of the films," it must be the case that this pressure is, at the very least, "credible" (ibid.: 25).

This focus requires Pippin to spend time considering narrative detail, searching for the best way simply of describing what the characters *do* in films such as *Out of the Past* (Jacques Tourneur, 1947), *The Lady from Shanghai* (Orson Welles, 1947), or *Scarlet*

Street (Fritz Lang, 1945), to name the three films that have a chapter dedicated to them in *Fatalism in American Film Noir*. This is at odds with many approaches to noir that focus more intently on, say, visual mood, sociological symptomatology, or psychoanalytic diagnosis. Even some broadly sympathetic commentators are skeptical of its value; Eliot Bessette writes that "Pippin spends much time untangling the films' baffling plots, but this accomplishes little" because the chief goal of these plots is to generate a texture of disorientation; the films are much more "interested in creating the impression of a labyrinthine underworld than in composing a perfect, logical system of interactions," making any attempt fully to disentangle them a fool's errand (Bessette 2013: 159). But Pippin's claim is that because providing act descriptions proves so difficult in many noirs, it is not a task that can be sidestepped. We can't (or at least shouldn't) shift directly to questions of mood, say, because to do so would be to prejudge aspects of interpretation. The *specific* difficulties involved in following the plot or describing what the characters do and why contribute to the *specific* mood a film generates—to, for example, exactly what kind of "labyrinthine underworld" we are given an "impression of." Nor can we replace narrative investigations with studies of visual style. *Something* must be making us feel a certain way, and if we are at all engaging with the film as a fiction, then that something can't purely be a matter of—say—chiaroscuro lighting and weird camera angles.

But neither is it simply a matter of plot. It is quite true that working out who killed the chauffeur in *The Big Sleep*, the question that, according to legend, even Raymond Chandler couldn't answer, doesn't contribute much to our understanding of Howard Hawks's film. (For what it's worth, I think it was Joe Brody.) This is not the kind of "disentangling" that Pippin finds both necessary and illuminating. What is at issue is the discovery, in attempting accurately to describe what happens in these films, that we often think that we understand much, much better than we do the normative notions "closest to us" in everyday life, and the thinness of that understanding can have consequences for the sustainability and vitality of the social practices subject to such norms. "Loyalty," "moralism," "self-righteousness," "freedom," "self-deceit," "honor," "justice," "betrayal," selfishness," and so many related notions are what have come to be called "thick" concepts, the meanings of which are very hard to identify in classical Socratic definitions.

(Pippin 2012: 24)[8]

There are what we might call "global" and "local" aspects to this discovery. The "global" aspects relate to a world in which our usual understandings of agency have turned out to be false, or at the very best inadequate. The problem is that in the world portrayed in the film noirs that Pippin discusses—a world sharing much with the modernity we, the viewers, inhabit—there is often a profound dislocation between knowledge and action. This is so both because characters cannot control what will result from their actions—"how little of the future they can actually effect as individuals" (ibid.: 4)—and because of how little they can even control what they *do*, let alone its consequences, precisely because they are not transparent to themselves, because of "how absurd it is to expect them to be able to 'step back,' as it is said, from their commitments and desires and goals and reflectively deliberate about what they ought to do" (ibid.).[9]

In the introduction I referred to Pippin's insistence that to really take on board the challenges to our self-understanding presented by the likes of Darwin, Marx, Nietzsche, and Freud involves the extremely difficult question of what *difference* their work should make to the way we act, one he thinks contemporary philosophy has tended to shirk. Let us say I am fully committed to the notion that all agency is an illusion, that human action is fully described by entirely determinate physical procedures. It remains the case that

"I, qua agent, cannot simply 'wait' to see what my neuro-chemical processes will result in" (Pippin 2005a: 115). Christine Korsgaard makes a similar point when she asks, "Having discovered that my conduct is predictable, will I now sit quietly in my chair, waiting to see what I will do? Then I will not do anything but sit quietly in my chair" (1996: 95).[10] The great philosophical interest of film noirs, for Pippin, lies in the way they represent "a shared world not wedded to the notions of reflective individuals formulating plans for avowed purposes and then enacting causal powers to effect them" and offer us "what is, in effect, a partially worked-out picture of what it would be to live in such a world" (2012: 12). These films can be read, Pippin argues, as answers to the question raised above—what difference *would* it make?

Of course, even given the historical account of subjectivity that Pippin defends, if Darwin, Marx, Nietzsche, Freud et al. are right, there is a sense in which they were always right. (Human beings *never did* have a metaphysical property called "free will.") So the issue is not merely what it would be like to live in a world in which thinking in terms of "reflective individuals formulating plans for avowed purposes and then enacting causal powers to effect them" is highly limiting and often misleading; it is also what it is like to live in a world that has begun, even if only in limited and distorted ways, to *recognize* or *acknowledge* that this is the case. It is this—the fact that "the experience of our own agency has begun to shift"—which means that according to "the Hegelian assumptions" on which Pippin operates, we are led toward "a radical claim: that what it is *to be* an agent has begun to shift as well" (ibid.: 22–3; emphasis in original). And this is where what I suggested we could call the "local" dimension comes in. Much of the irony in film noirs derives from the idea that, even if the "global" picture of agency is such as described above, that does not prevent its invocation in specific, "local" instances from becoming, for example, a self-serving excuse or an evasion of responsibility. As

Pippin puts it, "the complexity in many noirs stems from the fact that, while much *does* seem fated and beyond control, appeal to such a fate is also clearly *also* an act of self-deceit or a willful evasion of a responsibility one clearly bears" (ibid.: 49; emphases in original).

The explanations for action, or inaction, given *within* the noirs Pippin studies very often display such acts of self-deceit or evasions of responsibility. Michael O'Hara's (Orson Welles) voice-over narration in *The Lady from Shanghai*, for example, begins with "three exculpations, qualifications on the strength of his agency" (ibid.: 55). First he says that "when I start out to make a fool of myself, there's very little that can stop me," which is itself a very difficult notion—that one can be, as Michael says later, "a deliberate, intentional fool"—but he then immediately claims ignorance as a cause of his calamities (that if he had known how things would turn out, he wouldn't have got involved in the first place), and finally that after seeing Elsa Bannister (Rita Hayworth) he was not in his "right mind." The whole film begins by plunging the audience into a collection of "what appear to be damning and philosophically problematic self-characterizations, all of which in reality already seem self-protective and, suspiciously, to some degree morally exculpatory ('I was foolish, ignorant, crazy, etc.; I couldn't help myself')" (ibid.: 56). Michael's three explanations, or excuses, follow one another in very close, even bewilderingly close, succession. Pippin notes that part of the reason that film noirs show up the inadequacy of reflective models of agency is that they dramatize situations where there simply isn't *time* for reflection: "events come at characters much too fast and too confusingly to allow such reflection or reliance on the already reflected" (ibid.: 39). He makes this remark specifically concerning *Out of the Past*, in which

> many of the situations Jeff [Bailey; Robert Mitchum] faces require such immediate, creative improvisations: what to do after Kathie [Moffat; Jane Greer] shoots his partner, after he discovers Kathie

back at Whit's [Kirk Douglas] mansion, after he discovers Whit shot dead, none of which he is "reflectively" prepared for or has much if any time to consider before he must act.

(ibid.: 40)

Pippin observes that in such moments Jacques Tourneur, the film's director, makes "typical" use of "a kind of half profile from behind [Mitchum], and so a withholding of vital information about his reactions and attitudes" (ibid.: 33). The viewer can see that Jeff has to improvise, but is denied access to the evidence of the process of deliberation we might find in his face, obscuring our sense of his reflective agency.

In the two situations mentioned above as requiring "immediate, creative improvisations," however, we *do* see Jeff's face, in ways that are equally "typical" of the film (see Figure 6). In these shots, almost mirror images of one another, Jeff appears in shallow focus, seen from slightly below, one side of his face in shadow, his lips parted in puzzlement about what he has seen—or is seeing. The first image is more dramatic than the second (his partner has suddenly been shot in the middle of a fistfight by a woman he trusted), whereas in the second, the discovery of Whit's body more "gently" interrupts—if we can say that—his previously rather surprisingly nonchalant confidence that his plan is working out, but the visuals underline the connections between the two moments. Both images convey a sense that Jeff is not only puzzled about what confronts him, but is also somehow puzzled about *his own reactions*, or at least about what had been his assumptions about what was going on, about *what it was* that he was doing, or was involved in.[11]

So, in a structure that Pippin finds echoed in other noirs, Jeff is not only taken aback by what the people around him do; he also puzzles *himself*. Pippin writes very interestingly about a number of moments in *Out of the Past* in which Jeff apparently acts inconsistently, showing

Figure 6 Considering the need for "immediate, creative improvisations" in *Out of the Past*.

how credible these moments are, rather than writing them off to genre convention, or using them as evidence that reading for psychological depth in this kind of film is misguided. In characteristic noir style, the plot of the film is very involved, but central to it is the triangle between Jeff, formerly a private detective who is hired by the powerful gambler Whit to find Kathie, the woman who has shot him and stolen $40,000 from him. Jeff finds Kathie, but—apparently not believing that she stole the money—doesn't return her to Whit, only for Jeff's partner Fisher (Steve Brodie) to discover them and get shot by Kathie for his pains, after which she flees. Jeff tries to get "out of the past," setting up a small-town gas station and taking up with a local girl called Ann Miller (Virginia Huston), but subsequently discovers that Kathie has returned to Whit of her own accord. Eventually a complicated series of crosses and double-crosses leaves all three of them dead. At one crucial juncture, Jeff finds himself with Kathie in the office of a man named Baylord (John Kellogg), who is working for Whit, after Jeff has been double-crossed (in a complex maneuver involving the murder of a lawyer named Eels [Ken Niles] and some files incriminating to Whit) by Kathie and another of Whit's agents, a woman named Meta Carson (Rhonda Fleming):

> Jeff knew the files were in Eels's safe because *Kathie* told him, but after a knowing look exchanged between them, he lies for her. *Immediately* thereafter, though, when the gangster Baylord wants to know who told him about the affidavit (a document signed by Kathie saying that he, Jeff, killed Fischer [sic]), it seems that the very act of explaining the document pulls him in another direction. He lets the question hang without answering, and when Kathie, understandably counting on his continued loyalty, says, "Did Meta tell you?" this time he simply says no, and so allows the only possible inference—that Kathie told him—all with all with a quiet "Sorry" to Kathie (and no explanation for this sudden shift).
>
> (ibid.: 44; emphases in original)

Pippin tries out a variety of ways of describing this sudden change of direction, whether as the result of Jeff being "inconsistent" and so "irrational," or that "after calculating that he can and should protect Kathie, [Jeff] simply change[s] his mind, realize[s] that he has nothing to fear since he holds all the important cards, and seize[s] the opportunity to make a point to Kathie" (ibid.: 44–5). Crucially, however, if—as we have already seen Pippin suggest—we think of Jeff

> as in a way improvising responses on the fly … it might be a while before it is clear, even to him, what his overall commitments to Ann, to Kathie, his fears of Whit, and so forth, all mean in this context (what they mean especially in terms of what he ought to do).
>
> (ibid.: 45)

The crucial point, Pippin wants to make here, is that if we assume that in such a situation "what happens must count as so impulsive as not to count as an action … that assumption is question-begging, simply defines out of existence what Jeff does as 'not a doing'" (ibid.: 45–6), rather than allowing it to prompt us to reconsider what might count as an action; it would be similarly question-begging simply to assert that these inconsistencies are evidence that noirs are not available for this kind of psychological reading.

The disparity between Jeff's own, "local" perspective on such rapid changes of course and our more "global" view of his actions is highlighted in a number of ironies that Pippin emphasizes. When, for example, Jeff discovers that Kathie has been working with Whit to frame him for Eels's murder, and then agrees to run away with her again:

> We notice again (1) how bitter is Jeff's condemnation of Kathie for "changing sides" so quickly; and (2) *how quickly Jeff himself changes sides* at the end of the scene. (He thinks she is acting in a way completely inconsistent with any way he would act; *then he acts that way.*)
>
> (ibid.: 34; emphases in original)

In fact, the speed that Pippin refers to runs in parallel with an emphasis on languor and inaction, especially in the sequences set in Acapulco. The film at times generates a sense of drawling listlessness for which Mitchum's delivery is perfect, one that is summed up in his line "all I had to do was wait"; the only action required was *in*action. Action in the film proves both too fast *and* too slow. One frequently available self-justificatory position, for example, is that *events* were too fast, which is equivalent to *my* being too slow (in the sense of not being *able* to act any faster, rather than culpably failing to act fast enough). Jeff heads to the telegraph office the day he discovers Kathie in Acapulco to wire Whit that he has found her, but finds the office closed. This, however, only serves to clarify his desires and intentions, because he fails to wire Whit on any subsequent day, which he could very well have done; thus I do not think it is quite accurate to say that "Jeff gets involved with Kathie largely because the telegraph office was closed," which seems too close to Jeff's own fatalistic interpretation of contingency (ibid.: 47).

Out of the Past vividly demonstrates the ways that contingency can be treated as more or less equivalent to fate—things just turned out this way, there's nothing I could have done about it—but also shows that denying that this is the case (that we can do nothing about the way things turn out) need not involve denying the role contingency has in shaping our lives. It appears (to me at least) that it is genuinely accidental when Jeff drops the coin that rolls towards Kathie in the bar at Acapulco, which leads to the guide Jose Rodriguez (Tony Roux) mistaking them for a couple and so gives Jeff the chance to talk to her. And yet, when Jeff says to her, right at the end of the film, that "we owe it all to Jose Rodriguez," this is obviously untrue. Theirs was not a chance meeting, as they both well know. But this means that Jeff cannot actually mean to say that everything that happened to them turned on a contingency they had no control over. It seems more accurate to say that he is saying that there is no binary choice between being buffeted by chance and being in complete control of one's life, as Kathie acknowledges by saying that they've been both "wrong a lot" and "unlucky a long time." Contingency will run through everything and luck will always play a role. In this sense they do "owe it all to Jose Rodriguez": the *specific* way things turned out is always colored by the contingencies that he stands for. If Rodriguez hadn't mistaken them for a couple Jeff might, for example, have had to come right out at the beginning and tell her that he was working for Whit. But their responses to the vagaries of luck are still *their responses*, and in this sense Jeff's remark is sarcastic; the dryness of his delivery is perfect in allowing him to equivocate on this point, to seem simultaneously sarcastic and sincere. It is also crucial that Jeff's line is delivered *after* we have seen him make the phone call that we will, retrospectively, be able to interpret as to the police, alerting them to his and Kathie's flight, and leading to both of their deaths. As Pippin puts it, concluding his chapter on the film,

> when Jeff refuses to accept Kathie's fatalistic characterization that both of them simply *are* "no good" … and calls the police, he has not discovered a power Kathie thought he lacked. … He ends up an agent, however restricted and compromised, in the only way one can be. He acts like one.
>
> (ibid.: 49; emphasis in original)[12]

One very prominent aspect of *Out of the Past* that I have not mentioned thus far, and that it shares with a great many other film noirs, is that a good proportion of it unfolds as a flashback. Characteristically, Pippin is very sensitive to the fact that the flashback represents *Jeff's* narration, which means that "it and the events narrated *both* require interpreting. This is a story Jeff is telling *Ann*" (ibid.: 38; emphases in original). As we saw in the previous chapter with respect to *The Man Who Shot Liberty Valance*, Pippin believes that such a structure can color the majority of a film. In the case of Orson Welles's *The Lady *from Shanghai*, he argues that it colors the *entire* film, and in ways that relate directly to his central questions of agency, its limits, and the relationship between the retrospective dimensions of the ascription of intention and the temptations of self-exculpation. We are told that Michael O'Hara plans to write a novel; Pippin notes that early in the film "we even see him in a sailors' hiring hall scribbling away at what is probably his novel" and argues that "what we are hearing as the voice-over appears to be the novel he has written after all these events are over" (ibid.: 54).[13] Reading the film this way means that Pippin sees a fundamentally ironic relationship between the reflective form the film, we could say, *purports* to have, and that which it *actually* has. Pippin thus comes to an interpretation of *The Lady of Shanghai* that is in important aspects diametrically opposed to that of Andrew Britton, who argues that

> O'Hara is a "big boob," Tiresian sage or besotted lover at Welles's convenience, and, when the film wishes to make desultory critical gestures in the direction of American capitalism, he is even passed off as some kind of working-class hero; the only thing these roles have in common is that they define the hero as an outsider in a wicked world.
>
> (Britton 1992: 221)

Pippin would reply that all these things are Welles's representations of *Michael's* view of himself. Such a claim indicates once again the importance of an attention to tone and to what each viewer finds credible when watching a film with a critic's interpretations in mind. I am not sure if it would be possible to *prove* that the film ironizes O'Hara. The argument that it does turns, once again, on credibility, but not of plot, nor even exclusively of character; instead it turns on what one might call *aesthetic* plausibility. Britton claims that "the entire conception of O'Hara's character is impenetrably anomalous and contradictory" (ibid.), to which Pippin's response is, more or less, "that's just the point!" It is sufficiently unlikely that this is simply an aesthetic mistake by Orson Welles to warrant, at least in the first instance, a charitable attempt to account for Michael's "anomalous and contradictory" character. In general, of course, this kind of "that's the point!" answer will only sometimes represent a helpful insight; at other times offering such a response would simply be special pleading, but this is, once again, not something for which any kind of general or theoretical criteria are possible. It all comes down to individual cases.

In the case of *The Lady from Shanghai*, Pippin is able to demonstrate how open to the charge of self-justification Michael's various self-interpretations are. Although it would be possible to suggest that Michael's readiness to condemn himself, at least in certain respects, argues against viewing the film as his evasive self-justification, Pippin points out how to be viewed as "innocent" or "stupid" is "much preferable to his political self-image than 'just as corrupt as everyone else'" (ibid.: 59–60). Even though Pippin argues that successful ascription of intention often needs to be retrospective, Michael expresses this idea in formulations that are odd enough to raise suspicions that the film might not be said straightforwardly to endorse his point of view: "Faith, Mr. Bannister, I've already told your wife—I never make up my mind about anything at all until it's over and done with." This is just as implausible as the claim that one could set out intentionally to make oneself a fool. Michael is clearly attempting to distance himself from himself *as an agent*: "this form of narration allows Michael to narrate what he is guilty of without being *guiltily aware* of those deeds" (ibid.: 62; emphasis in original).[14]

If Michael's view of his agency were to be borne out, one would be able to *be* a certain kind of person independently of what one actually *does*. The complicated relationship between one's *actions* and one's *nature* runs through *The Lady from Shanghai*. The film's plot is, if anything, even more convoluted than that of *Out of the Past*. It involves Elsa Bannister; her husband, the criminal lawyer Arthur

Bannister (Everett Sloane); Bannister's partner George Grisby (Glenn Anders), and their various schemes to kill one another—schemes in which they involve Michael O'Hara. Two motifs crucial to the film are those of an "edge," and of stories and storytelling. When Michael first meets Bannister, one of his sailor friends paints the world as one in which everyone needs an "edge," but where gaining an edge is simply a matter of sheer force, of power and luck; one man simply happens to have "a gun, a nightstick, or a razor" while the other doesn't, so the first will win any fight between them. Later, in what is probably the film's most famous scene, aside from the culminating shoot-out in the hall of mirrors, Michael looks down at the picnicking Grisby, Bannister, and Elsa and tells the story of a group of sharks that became so frenzied with bloodlust that they ate one another; "there wasn't one of them sharks in the whole crazy pack that survived."[15] This scene brings together the notion of an "edge" with that of a story, because it is emphasized that stories *themselves* can be the "edge" that somebody has on somebody else. Bannister tells Michael that he "should know what George knows about me," and Elsa asks him whether he wants her to tell Michael "what you've got on me." (The viewer never finds out the details of these stories.) It is this that prompts Michael to tell his story of the sharks. Bannister compares physical and social power with his reference to the need to give Michael "a handicap," ironically recalling his, Bannister's, own status as a physical cripple. Clearly, the darker and more potent forms of power are *not* physical, presumably precisely because a man who "just happens" to have a blackjack will beat one who just happens not to; innate physical difference has very limited power to affect the outcomes of any contest in the real world. In the earlier conversation about having an edge, however, although it is suggested that a singer has the advantage over a sailor because he has a microphone to make his voice louder, the question of what makes him "sing prettier" in the first place remains unanswered. The conjunction of "edges" and stories at the picnic thus also relates to the theme about one's relationship to one's nature, expressed in Elsa's supposedly Chinese proverb that "one who follows his nature keeps his original nature in the end." Does Grisby just *happen* to have something on Bannister, and Bannister just *happen* to have something on Grisby?[16] Or is there in fact something in their natures which determines the power relationships between them, just as no microphone could supply the "something in here" which makes the singer sing better than the sailor in the first place? Something like this seems to be indicated by the fact that even though Bannister has employed a detective, Broome (Ted de Corsia) in order to find things out—to tell him stories that will supply him with an edge—when Broome informs Bannister that Elsa and Grisby are plotting to murder him, Bannister irritably replies that he *already knows* what Broome, quite reasonably, assumes is the exactly kind of thing he was hired to discover.

In Michael's story, all the sharks end up killing one another. Michael knows he cannot be a shark, simply because he survives, which none of Elsa, Bannister, or Grisby manages to do. Which is a terribly convenient solution; in fact, says Pippin, Michael "is one of the sharks and cannot admit that about himself"; he is "just as corrupt as everyone else" (ibid.: 119, n. 27, 60). Nevertheless, this does not mean that Michael is a hypocrite: "The pose he presents, the example of the maxim that 'everybody is somebody's fool,' is not a hypocritical attempt to deceive the audience, viewers, readers. He believes it and by believing it accepts a kind of diminished status and so *is* diminished" (ibid.: 73; emphasis in original). In this regard Jeff Bailey and Michael O'Hara are opposites. Even if only at the very end, Jeff manages to achieve the status of an agent by "acting like one" (ibid.: 49), whereas Michael compromises his agency simply by accepting that it is compromised. They are also broadly similar, in that both are "endlessly reluctant to act, and when they do, they are mostly responsive and often halfhearted" (ibid.: 11). Pippin offers these qualities as characteristic of noir heroes in general, but it is clear that he is talking about a subset of film noir that particularly interests him. We might, for example, contrast these passive protagonists with Humphrey Bogart's portrayals of two quintessential noir protagonists, namely Sam Spade in John Huston's *The Maltese Falcon* (1941), and Philip Marlowe, in *The Big Sleep*. Although Spade says, early in *The Maltese Falcon*, that "it's not always easy to know what to do," hesitancy does not characterize either man. In fact, both of them are very good, and rapid, judges of character; Marlowe takes an instant liking to the unlucky Harry Jones (Elisha Cook Jr.), and an instant dislike to the malevolent Canino (Bob Steele). If we think of another noir that Pippin discusses briefly, Billy Wilder's *Double Indemnity* (1944), Spade and Marlowe have a lot more in common with Edward G. Robinson's Barton Keyes (and the "little man" inside him that helps him judge character) than they do with Fred MacMurray's Walter Neff and the tangle he gets himself into precisely as a result of the way he lurches from passivity to activity and back. It is another character played by Edward G. Robinson, however, that provides one of the most extreme portrayals of film noir's paradoxes of passivity, namely Christopher Cross in Fritz Lang's *Scarlet Street* (1945), which is the third film to get a close examination in *Fatalism in American Film Noir*.

In their very different ways, Pippin thinks that *The Lady from Shanghai* and *Scarlet Street* offer particularly interesting perspectives on the sociality of agency. In the former film, it is

> almost as if *all* action is shown to be some kind of collective action, requiring a coordination that involves a shared act description and some reliable assessment of others' motives and intentions, all of which have to be achieved and sustained, is somewhat fragile and the source of much possible confusion.
>
> (ibid.: 74; emphasis in original)

The confusions and difficulties that result when "reliable assessment" breaks down are figured by the film's hall-of-mirrors conclusion: "since each cannot determine where each is in relation to the other, they cannot effectively maneuver, they cannot distinguish their true position, *themselves*, from the multiple reflections either" (ibid.: 71; emphasis in original). *Scarlet Street* offers another perspective on the difficulty of comprehending individual action in the absence of a reliable grasp on the "motives and intentions" of those around one. But it uses some very surprising and interesting strategies to achieve this; Pippin says the film "might more properly be called a variation on the genre" of noir (ibid.: 75). Rather than offering the kind of perplexing narrative filled with mysterious agents that we find in *The Lady from Shanghai*, we have a relatively straight-forward narrative; rather than a richly drawn and naturalistic world, one filled with the kind of "deep intersubjectivity" we find in the novels of Henry James or the films of Jean Renoir, the film is instead "filmed indoors, on a studio sound stage, and it looks it. There is very little urban liveliness or spontaneity; the very air seems dead and stale" (ibid.: 76). In the hands of many critics, such a description would be clearly pejorative. For Pippin, however, this is an achievement of the film, part of the way it manages (in a manner diametrically opposed to what we found in the last chapter to be the case with Nicholas Ray's *The Lusty Men*) to portray "bourgeois domestic life—the peaceful, secure, commercial, and domestic activity many heroes in Hollywood Westerns were desperately trying to establish" as something "so stultifying and banal that even crime began to look attractive to those trapped in it" (ibid.: 7).[17] Similarly, when we hear that, as a painter, Chris "has a problem with 'perspective,'" that "his world and the film world are without 'depth,'" the implication is "not that this is due to Chris's amateurish lack of talent, but that his primitive style has actually captured the artificial and depthless reality around him" (ibid.: 76).

Scarlet Street tells the story of an utterly conventional henpecked bank clerk, Chris Cross, one of whose few pleasures is painting on Sundays, and the way he falls for a "manipulative prostitute" (ibid.: 65) called Kitty March (Joan Bennett)—though he believes her to be an up-and-coming actress—who is herself controlled by her pimp boyfriend, Johnny Prince (a particularly unpleasant turn by Dan Duryea, almost a match for his role as Waco Johnnie Dean in Anthony Mann's *Winchester '73*). Johnny passes some of Chris's paintings off as Kitty's, which leads to her fame. This does not distress Chris, but when he discovers that she does not love him and has been seeing Johnny all along, he murders her. Johnny, not Chris, is convicted of the crime, and Chris ends up homeless, perpetually tormented—but not by guilt. He ends up "trapped permanently in the moment he most cannot understand or even admit to himself: the moment when he heard Kitty tell Johnny she was crazy about him" (ibid.: 92). The dialectical intricacies and ironies of Chris's self-understanding revolve around the fact that "Chris wanted to become something 'in the eyes of Kitty' and, given who Kitty was, the person he could not acknowledge as Kitty, he has become that person, the pathetic old man, capable only of being acted upon, never truly capable of acting; the man Kitty thought he was" (ibid.: 94). Pippin notes that although his infatuation with Kitty makes Chris behave in a way he never has before ("I never saw a woman without any clothes!" he tells his wife), he does not experience his passion for Kitty as "an alien force"; on the contrary, "it makes profound sense to him," and is deeply connected to what he thinks is her respect for his art: "The link between art and sexuality, or the aesthetic liberation and sexual liberation themes, are a focus throughout the film" (ibid.: 78). The art critic Janeway (Jess Barker) is surprised to be told that Chris's paintings are the work of a woman, because they have a "masculine energy"; although this might seem to buy into a shallow stereotype of gendered expression, the notion that anything to do with Chris could express such an energy, something that would very much be news to him, further complicates the ironies at play.[18] All of this reaches its most condensed point in Chris's portrait of Kitty, which is entitled

"Self-Portrait" but is, of course, signed with *her* name. The film achieves all these intersubjective complexities, however, via a focus on Chris that, at climactic moments, becomes Expressionist in its exclusivity and its technique. After Johnny's execution, for example, he hears the voices of the dead Kitty and Johnny, and at the end of the film all the other inhabitants of the city vanish apart from Chris's desolate figure, retreating from the camera. Pippin points out that this tendency begins when Chris first meets Kitty: "the normal, realistic film sound track shuts off and we hear only the roaring, rushing sound of, apparently, the elevated train overhead" (ibid.: 81). This not only evokes Chris's experience but also suggests "some kind of force is rushing along, sweeping Chris up and beginning to 'carry' him to a destiny he will not be able to escape" (ibid.).

A little oddly, Pippin does not once mention—not even in the footnotes—Renoir's *La Chienne*, of which Lang's film is a remake, following the plot very closely (at least until the conclusion). Chris corresponds to Maurice Legrand (Michel Simon), Kitty to Lulu (Janie Marèse), and Johnny to Dédé (Georges Flamant). At first glance, Renoir's film seems much more richly "worlded" than does Lang's.[19] The photography gives a real sense of a solid world; the three main characters are more fully and more plausibly drawn (Renoir was particularly proud of his attention to the way they speak, the nuances of accent, slang, tone of voice; see Welsch [2000: 55]); and the surrounding world is darker and more realistically corrupt than in Lang's film (see, e.g., the way Legrand's colleagues are cruel to him, or the way the art market—literally—pimps out Lulu just as much as Dédé ever did). But a comparison with between the two films and what Tom Gunning calls their "antithetical fictional and stylistic worlds" (2000: 309) helps to further clarify what it means to Pippin for a film to have a world, something we discussed extensively in the previous chapter. *Scarlet Street* demonstrates that, even if, to have a "world," a film needs to generate a certain amount of credibility, this by no means necessitates any particular form of naturalism or realism, and is perfectly compatible with a situation where, as here, "all of the other characters in the film are fairly one-dimensional as Lang concentrates almost the entirety of his attention on Chris" (Pippin 2012: 75). It is this which helps generate the film's intensity, as it concentrates with an almost hallucinatory closeness on the paradoxes of agency and self-knowledge that Chris's situation generates.

Although it is highly reductive to reduce the rich attention to detail of Pippin's readings of these three noirs to a one-line summary, he himself offers this distillation:

> If one had to summarize the most general *Denkbild* that emerges from *noir*, one would do well to paraphrase Pascal on skepticism: there is too much of our own destiny that we can control for us to be fatalists, but there is too little self-knowledge and control for us to be, say, Kantian moralists.
>
> (Pippin 2016a: 233)

Is this perhaps a disappointing conclusion? Some, certainly, have found Pippin's work on noir to be disappointing. Bessette claims that "despite its philosophical merits, however, the film components of this volume disappoint. Many of Pippin's interpretations are standard readings borrowed from prior film scholarship" (2013: 159). This is not, I think, a fair criticism; the discussions of, say, the rapidity with which Jeff changes his mind in *Out of the Past*, or of the consequences of seeing *The Lady of Shanghai* as Michael's novel, or of the way that the Christmas setting of the ending of *Scarlet Street* juxtaposes, with savage irony, the "melancholy baby" of the song with the infant Jesus (Pippin 2012: 93), are all fresh and original. Although Bessette feels that the "minor insights" he grants that Pippin affords "cannot adequately support the larger philosophical claims," his counterclaim that "Chris Cross murders because his beloved scorned him, not because of some metaphysical point about the nature of habits" (2013: 159) disputes nothing in Pippin's book. Pippin's point is that even though, in murdering Kitty, Chris could be said to act "out of character," this is *not* because he suddenly "loses his mind." He indeed murders Kitty because of her scorn for him; what is remarkable is that "none of us, least of all Chris, could have anticipated this way of finally acting rather than constantly being acted upon," but that we nonetheless experience it as credible (Pippin 2012: 89). This bears out the book's central contention, that agency "is far more significantly linked to self-knowledge than any causal power" (ibid.: 94).[20]

Bessette suggests that Pippin's work risks falling between two stools, ending up unsatisfying either to film scholars or to philosophers:

> Knowing the degree to which free action requires prior deliberation scarcely improves our understanding of what *Out of the Past* might *mean*, or how industrial conditions influenced its production, or how it embodies Tourneur's style, or other typical questions of this field. In turn, Pippin acknowledges he has another problem with his philosophical audience. Since they have no scholarly way to reply—fellow philosophers will not reinterpret *The Lady from Shanghai*—his perspective on action theory may not get a hearing.
>
> (Bessette 2013: 159; emphasis in original)

The first clause in this passage makes it seem as if Pippin is *applying* a philosophical theory, whereas his point is that it is, precisely, in trying to understand what *Out of the Past* means that we come to understand something more about the relation between agency and deliberation. The second and third clauses are certainly true, but no approach needs to do everything at once. Bessette's final point, at least, can be empirically disconfirmed. In *Notre Dame Philosophical Reviews*, the philosopher Jerrold Levinson (2013), despite having a number of philosophical differences with Pippin, locates his "main disagreement" with the book in the interpretation of *Scarlet Street*. It may be true that philosophers are willing to give Pippin more attention than Film Studies scholars, but the thesis of, and the motivation behind, this book is the claim that Film Studies will be richer if it *can* find a place for Pippin's work.

It is not the case, however, that Bessette is unsympathetic to Pippin's goals. On the contrary, he writes very warmly about Pippin's discussion of *The Searchers* in *Hollywood Westerns*, observing that "the philosophically incisive and cinematically novel chapter on *The Searchers* exemplifies a philosophical approach to film interpretation. There Pippin makes new close readings of the mise-en-scène and camerawork that support his political philosophical thesis" (Bessette 2013: 160). Bessette is, then, disappointed by Pippin's treatment of the more purely cinematic aspects of the films discussed. He seems to *require* any truly valuable reading to refer extensively to elements such as mise-en-scène and camerawork. This is a very important issue, one to which I will return in Chapter 6.

Photographing Mindedness: The Dardenne Brothers

I hope that at least something of what Pippin means by claiming that film noir is "an art form uniquely suited to the exploration of the uniquely temporal dimensions of action in such a critical situation (call it 'late modernity')" is now clear (2016a: 222). But this can hardly be the end of the story, given the pervasiveness of the implications of the account of agency that Pippin defends. Therefore it is not exactly surprising, though it is very interesting, that Pippin has also explored the same account of agency by means of a collection of films that might seem, on the surface, to contrast with film noir at almost every point: the work of the Belgian filmmaking brothers Jean-Pierre and Luc Dardenne. Coming from a background in political documentary cinema, after two features that they now largely disown, the Dardenne brothers have constructed a highly distinctive oeuvre of narrative cinema comprising nine films to date, from *The Promise* in 1996 to 2019's *Young Ahmed*. Almost all of them are set in Seraing, a deprived suburb of Liège, and focus on characters on the margins of society. Stylistically very consistent, they exhibit a distinctive form of realism involving some very unusual cinematographic strategies. Pippin highlights four in particular:

> (1) a striking lack of congruence between the cuts in the film and the normal beginnings and endings of actions or conversations; (2) the positioning of the handheld camera very close to the characters and from behind, as if the viewer is too close, following the action rather than seeing it; (3) the invocation of the cinematic conventions about close-ups, and then the frustration or refusal of these expectations; and (4) the display of the psychological lives of the characters in ways such that, very often, individual faces appear somewhat blank or empty, without detectable psychological inward motion, let us say, as if we might be at psychology degree zero in the sense in which Roland Barthes spoke of "writing degree zero."
> (Pippin 2020a: 238)

The final chapter in *Filmed Thought*, from which the above passage is taken, is dedicated to the films of the Dardenne brothers and entitled "Psychology Degree Zero? The Representation of Action in the Films of the Dardenne Brothers." Essentially the same chapter also appears in Ludwig Nagl and Waldemar Zacharasiewicz's collection *Ein Filmphilosophiesymposium mit Robert B. Pippin*, where it has a title that in some ways more clearly points to what lies at the heart of Pippin's interest in these films: "Photographing Mindedness: Cinematic Technique and Philosophy in the Films of the Dardenne Brothers" (see Pippin 2016c).

What would it mean to "photograph mindedness"? Surely, of all things, *mindedness* cannot be photographed? Pippin's counterintuitive claim is, however, precisely that mindedness *can* be photographed, and not merely in some metaphorical or symbolic sense. Pippin cites

Wittgenstein's famous remark that the human body is the best picture of the human soul (Pippin 2020a: 245; see Wittgenstein 2009: 187), and would, I think, entirely concur with Stanley Cavell's further remark, which he does not cite, that this is "not ... primarily because it represents the soul but because it expresses it" (1979a: 356). One way into this idea might be by means of what happens when we understand what somebody says. Sebastian Rödl notes that, according to John McDowell, "when we hear someone speaking and understand what she is saying ... we perceive her thinking" (2007: 179). The situation is, however, more challenging when we are not dealing with language, and many of the protagonists in the Dardennes' films are fairly inarticulate, or at least not given to speechifying at length about their actions. Much of the time, then, if we are to see their mindedness, we must do so without linguistic assistance.

Recall the first of the stylistic features that we saw Pippin identify above, namely the tendency of the editing in these films not to coincide with what we would consider the normal or natural beginnings and endings of the events we are shown; he argues that "this should be understood as a kind of cinematic interrogation of what really *is* a beginning and an end for action" (Pippin 2020a: 239; emphasis in original). We encountered earlier Pippin's insistence that it would be philosophically desirable "to break the hold altogether of the notion of 'a moment' of resolve or a moment of causal efficacy" (2008: 152), one that he shares with a number of other philosophers, such as—for example—Michael Thompson, who has announced his own aspiration of "break[ing] up" what he sees as "the tendency of students of practical philosophy to view individual human actions as discrete or atomic or pointlike or eye-blink-like units that might as well be instantaneous for all that it matters to the theory" (2008: 91). If we can start to understand actions as temporally extended in this way, it might begin to be plausible that, for example, what we see in *The Promise* is Igor (Jérémie Renier) *carrying out* the promise he makes to the dying Amidou (Rasmané

Ouédraogo) that he will look after his wife, rather than just the *consequences* of making the promise. There is an analogy here with the question of "imaginative seeing" that we discussed in Chapter 1. Just as, for Pippin, we do not see actors on screen and imagine or infer things about the characters they are portraying, but rather *imaginatively see* those very characters, so in human life and interaction in general we do not, in general, see physical movements and merely infer that they are the consequences of certain intentions. Rather, we *see* those intentions *in* action.[21] Understanding action in films is both a subcategory of this vast subject and—often—an allegory for or commentary on it, as Pippin argues about the editing in the Dardennes' films.

The situation is, however, much more complex than this because all of the Dardennes' films deal with situations where it is not merely difficult to say when an action begins and ends, but also *what action it is*. *The Son* (2002), which is the film to which Pippin devotes the most attention, is a perfect example of this. It tells the story of a man named Olivier (Olivier Gourmet), a carpenter who trains recently released young offenders and takes on Francis (Morgan Marinne), the boy who murdered Olivier's son five years previously. The film culminates in Olivier taking Francis on a lengthy drive to his brother's lumber yard, after which he extracts an account of the murder from Francis and finally tells him that he is the murdered boy's father, which prompts Francis to run away from him. Olivier gives chase and finds himself on the verge of strangling Francis, only to release him. The two of them then work together loading wood onto Olivier's trailer, at which point the film ends. Pippin remarks:

> What is quite credibly shown in the nonstandard representations of the mindedness of many of these characters, especially here with Olivier, is that there is nothing yet to be known, at least (and this is the crucial point) nothing *determinate*, even though he is certainly *acting*; things are not merely happening to him.
>
> (Pippin 2020a: 243; emphases in original)

Anybody who wanted to insist that, for an action to be an action (rather than, say, a reflex, or the expression of an unconscious drive) the agent of the action must be aware of a specific, determinate end would, argues Pippin, find themselves challenged by these films. At one point in the film Olivier's ex-wife Magali (Isabella Soupart), horrified that he has taken Francis on as an apprentice, asks him why, to which Olivier simply replies, "I don't know." This is not, Pippin argues, because of some emotional or intellectual inarticulacy: "There is no sense that this 'I don't know' is simply the best Olivier can do, as if someone more articulate or reflective could do better" (ibid.: 251). Pippin maintains that "the credibility" of his "I don't know" is "the insight on which most of the movie is based" (2015c). Note the repeated insistence, familiar from Pippin's discussions of film noir, of the importance of credibility. Without the cinematic experience of this credibility, there is no material to work on philosophically. A viewer who did not find it credible could not be *argued* by Pippin into finding it so, although his arguments might prompt them to reconsider their reaction, and to test Pippin's account against themselves during a subsequent viewing of the film.

So what *is* going on with Olivier and Francis? On one possible account, Olivier intends to harm or, probably, to kill Francis; the film traces the development and enactment of this intention until, finally, Olivier changes his mind. Alternatively, he had no such intention, and only begins to strangle Francis in the heat of the moment, something he quickly reconsiders. Lisa Trahair seems to believe something close to the second option, and thinks that Pippin must believe the first. This is because she finds Pippin's position to be directly analogous with Pasolini's notion of a cinematic free indirect discourse, writing that "for both Pasolini and Pippin the operation of free indirect point-of-view (or objective subjectivity) amount to an immersion of the entire film in the consciousness of one character or a conflation between inner states and external worlds," whereas Gilles Deleuze offers a more attractive account involving "correlation" rather than "immersion or confusion" (2016: 110). This is, however, a misreading of Pippin and what his notion of reflective form amounts to. Pippin argues for parallels between the viewers' situation and that of the characters, but never claims that "the entire film" is immersed "in the consciousness of one character." Trahair writes that "suggesting that in this sense the inner (psychological) and outer (external world) dimensions of the film are not clearly separable, Pippin concludes that the films are intelligible as a kind of 'objective subjectivity'" (ibid.: 109), whereas what he actually says is that the world of the Dardenne brothers' is one with "little room, if any, for such a possibility of such 'objective subjectivity'" (Pippin 2020a: 248). Pippin is referring to the notion, discussed in Chapter 1, that if we want to take on board the challenges to our self-understanding presented by thinkers such as Darwin, Marx, Nietzsche, and Freud, the really difficult question is what *difference* their work should make to the way we act, even when their arguments are at their most convincing. The central question is what it would mean

> *to be free* of the grip of ... illusory Cartesian or Christian or subjectivist pictures, what it would be like to live out a whole form of life, day to day, in complex interactions with others, *not* informed (and self-deceived) about itself in such ways, and credibly set in a world that determines what forms such interactions shall take (and may not take).
>
> (ibid.; emphases in original)

So his point is that *even though there is so little* "objective subjectivity," the Dardennes' films help show us what living out a non-Cartesian account of subjectivity might *look like*—and so, given what we have already encountered about witnessing mindedness, *be like*.[22] It's not, I think, possible to get Pippin much more wrong than this:

> Olivier's inscrutability, his "psychology degree zero," as Pippin calls it, which makes his thinking about his choices impenetrable to us,

is consistent with Kierkegaard's contention that movements of the spirit or soul are internal, not necessarily visible from the outside.
(Trahair 2016: 114)

Pippin's whole project—with regard to the Dardennes in particular, but also with regard to film and to the philosophy of action in general—is to challenge the notion of subjectivity as something "concealed" within people (which of course by no means entails that it is instead entirely transparent).[23]

All this being said, Trahair's account of the camera's mindedness in *The Son* is extremely interesting, and many of her observations are perfectly compatible with Pippin's analysis:

> Coupled with the contrast between her open and reflective countenance and his distant impassivity, the contrast between the framing of Magali and Olivier serves not just to block our access to his thought in order to arouse our curiosity about him, as commentators have noted, but to make us suspicious of him.
> (ibid.: 111)

This is quite true, but instead of claiming that this tension must either reflect Olivier's potential for violence (as Trahair maintains a "free indirect discourse" account is compelled to), *or* that it is a question of the camera being unfair to him, a cinematic device to trick the viewer into misevaluating what they are seeing (so that on a second viewing the camera "frees itself from its own suspicions and prejudicial disposition … a second viewing of the film greatly diminishes the plausibility of the claim that Olivier ever was in a state of temptation or bent on vengeance" [ibid.: 114]), Pippin concludes that the question is not determinate enough to be so neatly separated into two possibilities. Olivier *doesn't know* whether or not he will be violent toward Francis, but not because he is unusually lacking in self-insight, or indeed because he is self-deceived (like Michael O'Hara) or because, like Ethan Edwards, he "avow[s] principles that [are] partly confabulations and fantasy" (Pippin 2010: 131).[24] Instead, there simply *is no such* determinate knowledge either to accurately represent or to misrepresent. Olivier does not know what he intends, and this not because he has, say, an unconscious desire to injure Francis but because his intentions are in a continual process of formation and revision. It is perfectly plausible that he really does need to visit the lumberyard (this need not merely be a pretext), but he is also certainly capable of hurting Francis; see the moment when he brakes the car suddenly while Francis is sleeping. (Trahair's claim that Olivier was never accurately described as "bent on vengeance" is quite reasonable, but it seems very odd to claim that he was never even *tempted* towards revenge.) Nor does saying that fully determinate knowledge is lacking means that we can't say *anything* decisive. Clearly, for example, strangling Francis brings about, for Olivier, *some* kind of understanding of Francis's strangling of his son.[25] Seeing things this way is entailed by finding Olivier's "I don't know" truly credible and fully thinking through its implications.[26]

Pippin concludes that the Dardennes' famous technique of filming characters from behind (number two in the list of stylistic features cited at the beginning of this section) need not be taken as indicating that something is being hidden from us: "It may also mean that our expectation of some punctuated moment of insight is being deliberately frustrated because such an assumption is misleading, looking for the wrong thing, for some hidden content, rather than attentive to a still indeterminate and more temporally extended and socially embedded formation process" (2020a: 246).[27] Just as with the question of the nature of Olivier's intentions, our access to the characters we see on-screen need not be a binary, all-or-nothing affair. Pippin refers approvingly to Richard Rushton's work on the Dardennes, in which Rushton refers to something he calls "empathetic projection" as characterizing the viewer's relation to the characters, insisting that "this notion is not one of seeing things from a character's point of view or of 'feeling the same feelings' as a character; rather, it is one of being cut off from but nevertheless emotionally connected to a character at one and the same time" (2014: 313). There is much we don't know about these characters but also much we *do* know, and they are in a comparable—but by no means identical—situation in relation to themselves. At worst, Pippin believes that moving from the experience of difficulty or obscurity toward belief in something *essentially* hidden, fundamentally ineffable, risks conveying "the idea that the Dardennes' unusual technique shows us that their characters are mysteriously other," something he describes as a "mystification" (ibid.: 248):

> None of this, I hasten to add, should be taken to suggest that our moral lives are to be understood as consisting of nothing but epiphanic moments, expressive moments of great emotional power, intimating a rationally inarticulable but deeply real bond, unity or even identity with other persons. Perhaps the Dardenne brothers believe this. I am not sure. But I certainly don't.
> (Pippin 2016b)[28]

There is much in Pippin's discussion of the Dardenne brothers' work that I have had to omit or gloss over here, in particular his discussion of its political implications, its depiction of "a world where a ruthless form of competitiveness is forced on workers (American-style capitalism, as it is now rightly put), where one person's job is another person's unemployment, and where the two persons often know each other," undercutting clichés about the anonymity of modern capitalism (2020a: 232). But I hope to have at least begun to indicate some of the ways in which Pippin's explorations of fatalism in film noir and of the Dardennes' "very unusual attempt[s] to represent human mindedness in situations of great moral turmoil when a crucial decision has to be made" (2015c) have resulted in compelling readings of films that bring to the fore the challenging implications these films should have for the philosophy of action, if we find them credible and are prepared to take them seriously.

5

Unknowing One Another: Film as Practical Moral Psychology

Building on the account of agency sketched in the previous chapter, this chapter explores Pippin's defense of the importance of a psychology whose object is something other than what can be studied experimentally, specifically what he describes as a *moral psychology*. It demonstrates the grounding of this idea in an unusual reading of Nietzsche, the only one of the "masters of suspicion" mentioned in Chapter 1 to whom Pippin has devoted extensive attention (one book and numerous articles), and who he describes as "Hegel's most problematic opponent, the thinker who best raises the question of the whole possibility and even desirability" of the kind of "self-conscious justification" of agency and rationality to which Hegel dedicated himself (Pippin 1999: 14).[1] This chapter assesses Pippin's proposal that the study of film has a major contribution to make to such a moral psychology; whether his claims in this regard are borne out is explored via Pippin's third book on film, *The Philosophical Hitchcock*—a book-length study of Alfred Hitchcock's *Vertigo*—as well as his writing on Almodóvar's *Talk to Her*, Hitchcock's *Shadow of a Doubt*, and Nicholas Ray's *In a Lonely Place*.

"Confounding Morality": *Shadow of a Doubt* and *Talk to Her*

Before discussing precisely what Pippin means by "moral psychology," it will be useful to get something of a handle on his general approach to questions of morality in film. The second section of *Filmed Thought* is entitled "Moral Variations" and includes chapters on two films: Pedro Almodóvar's *Talk to Her* (2002) and Hitchcock's *Shadow of a Doubt* (1943). Both films, Pippin suggests, show that to complicate and render problematic the notion of moral judgment need by no means equate to justifying or excusing unethical behavior. (We shall see that, whereas the moral difficulties in Almodóvar's film are immediately apparent, in the case of the Hitchcock film part of what interests Pippin is just how easily its ethical complexities can be overlooked.) In both cases, Pippin acknowledges, he is engaging in questions of casuistry, taken not in its pejorative sense of special pleading, but in the more technical sense of the ways that moral principles can be brought to bear on difficult cases. His point is not merely "that abstract distinctions can be extremely difficult to apply in hard cases"—which is something that "every serious moral philosopher realizes" (Pippin 2020a: 13)—but is something that, stated abstractly, is also essentially rather simple; namely, that there is a "difference between morality and moral judgement, on the one hand, and moralism, on the other" (ibid.). If we think of moralism as the view that the moral judgments we make always require us to ascribe blame, and "that such judgements have a kind of absolute, all-trumping importance in assessing one another's deeds" (ibid.), it is easy to see that such a position could easily become unattractively absolute, a rigid and judgmental approach to ethics that we would prefer to avoid. But in attempting to avoid such an approach, how is it possible to avoid thereby confusing the *explanation* of blamable action with its *justification*, of sliding from a reluctance to condemn toward a reluctance to hold one another morally responsible at all? Or of, as Pippin puts it, "too easily 'excusing' or patronizingly pitying or treating another as less than a full agent" (ibid.)? The simplicity mentioned above evaporates as soon as we engage with situations complex enough to raise these questions with any urgency; Pippin's position is that any answers pitched at too high a level of abstraction or generality are likely to be unsatisfying, that we need to keep closer contact with concretely specific examples if we are to get any real purchase on them, and that (some) films can serve just this purpose. The difficulty of thinking through these questions with regard to films like *Talk to Her* or *Shadow of a Doubt* is precisely what makes it rewarding and illuminating to do so.

In *Filmed Thought*, the section discussing these more individual questions of morality precedes the section on "Social Pathologies," one of whose chapters, on Polanski's *Chinatown*, we have already discussed. The sequence followed in *Filmed Thought*—morality before society—might seem more natural than the sequence followed here. However, given the unfamiliar (and often counterintuitive) nature of Pippin's views on the social character of subjectivity, it seemed more helpful to get these on the table first, as I have tried to do in the preceding chapters. Indeed, Pippin's interest in questions of individual morality is precisely in the ways that situations of great moral complexity can put enormous pressure on some of our most automatic assumptions about the nature of our subjectivity and our relations to our feelings and actions. Pippin is concerned to highlight "the potential illusions of thinking of what are experienced as a character's 'ownmost feelings,' especially romantic feelings, as unproblematically and directly accessible as such" (ibid.: 14). But the solution cannot be, he thinks, to dismiss such feelings as *purely* illusory and work in terms of social critique instead because, "however paradoxical and strange it can seem" that a society could be said to have something like a psychology, we also need to pay attention to forms of *social* ignorance, "an ignorance that shows up particularly in attempts at the greatest and riskiest intimacy we seek: in romantic relationships" (Pippin 2020a: 15).

Prefiguring the Nietzschean ideas we will encounter later in this chapter, Pippin believes that not only can we be wrong individually about what we most strongly feel, but that our collective assumptions about what, Pippin notes, Henry James once called "what 'goes on' irreconcilably, subversively, beneath the vast, smug surface" (1977: 22) can *also* be wrong. We therefore need what Pippin calls a kind of "stereoscopic attentiveness" (2020a: 14). This is another version of a point that will be familiar by now: that in a great many ethical and aesthetic situations, we need to take account both of the complicated, often dialectical, relationships between what is "going on" in an objective sense, and of what the participants in these situations *take* to be "going on" (as Jonathan Lear puts it, "*what it is* to be a person is shaped by *what it is like* for that person to be" [1990: 4; emphases in original]). When human agents—whether real or fictional—are involved, to simply delete the latter as illusory will distort our understanding of the very phenomena we are grappling with. (Not to mention the fact that it seems likely that Pippin would also agree with James that "the agents in any drama, are interesting only in proportion as they feel their respective situations" [1977: 9].) To repurpose the terms derived from Daniel Yacavone that we discussed in Chapter 3, there are both moral *worlds-of* narrative films and moral *worlds-in* them and we need to come to terms with both.

Pippin's strategy of "stereoscopic attentiveness," then, means that he strives to avoid plumping either for "an individualist psychology" or, alternatively, "a potentially reductionist 'ideology critique'" (2020a: 14). But actually doing so is, he thinks, "much more difficult than it can initially appear"; his proposal with regard to film is that the "imaginative richness of these films is an invaluable means of access to the issues" (ibid.). Of course, the question of "what difference it makes that this form of reflection on issues posed with such generality is a form of *aesthetic* reflection in general, and cinematic reflection in particular" (ibid.: 15; emphasis in original) is itself a very challenging question, but it is one that, thinks Pippin, has to be answered *specifically*, because not to do so would beg the question.

We need to *find out* what difference it makes, not *stipulate* it. I do not have space here to go into the detail required really to make good on the preceding claims, but some indications of the ways that Pippin attempts to do so can be given. His discussion of *Talk to Her*, for example, centers on what is obviously the most problematic aspect both of the film's narrative and its aesthetic strategies or reflective form: the rape of the comatose Alicia (Leonor Watling) by her nurse Benigno (Javier Cámara), and his friend Marco's (Darío Grandinetti) continuing loyalty to Benigno thereafter (indeed, the marked increase in intensity of their relationship). Although the problems raised might easily seem vertiginous in their complexity, Pippin insists that many things are entirely clear. Benigno is, for example, "barely sane" and "largely delusional"; nevertheless, "Benigno and his act *are* partly treated sympathetically by Almodóvar," particularly in that the rape—somehow—seems to bring Alicia out of her coma: "Alicia clearly seems brought back to life by what Benigno does, even though what he does clearly calls for moral recoil" (ibid.: 55; emphasis in original).

Pippin brings a substantial range of material to bear in his investigation of how we might be supposed to take the complicated and troubling situation that the film presents us with, including noting the fairy tale resonances in the narrative and pursuing comparable patterns and devices that can be found in other films by Almodóvar. But essentially his strategy involves a close attention both to the film and to what we might call the texture of our response to it, of what the film *shows us* if we are prepared to engage with it on its own terms. He has no knockdown argument to present; as he notes, a philosopher such as "Kant, for example, would have no trouble condemning Benigno, full stop. There is no discursive case made in the film, no implied argument, that could 'refute' Kant, but we are *shown* something of the limitations of the moral point of view. In some sense, it is inhuman" (ibid.: 59, n. 11; emphasis in original). If we do hesitate simply to condemn Benigno, Pippin does not think that "our 'hesitation,' such as it is, is based on an appreciation of Benigno's psychopathology"; not, that is, simply on facts of the case that render Benigno not fully culpable (ibid.: 52). But if our moral response to him is somehow qualified then the difficult question is, precisely, "*what* sort of qualification is it?" (ibid.: 51; emphasis in original). Pippin doesn't pretend to be able give a neat answer, but instead works through the film and its implications. The purpose is less to classify this qualification than to characterize it.

Ultimately, Pippin thinks that the film credibly demonstrates that, from Benigno's point of view, for example, "he sees himself in some fantasy as sacrificing himself" for Alicia (ibid.: 62), and that it is possible to sympathize with—and perhaps even to endorse—aspects of this attitude, even while recognizing it as a fantasy and without at all justifying the actions it ultimately leads to: "Almodóvar is trying to render credible the idea of both condemnation of and solidarity with Benigno" (ibid.: 64). This difficult combination is what Pippin's "stereoscopic attentiveness" seems to ask of us. This will be, for many, a great deal to swallow, but Pippin asks what "anyone uncomfortable with what I have called our 'moral hesitation' about Benigno" would "really want? That Benigno be punished *more*? [He takes his own life while in prison for Alicia's rape.] That Alicia remain comatose? That Marco abandon his friend in disgust?" (ibid.: 65; emphasis in original). One response, of course, would be to point out that all of these responses remain on the level of the fictional narrative, and that one answer might be: "For films that use rape as a symbolic narrative device invoking a mythic register not to be made." Pippin is, of course, well aware that it is "by making use of rape" that the film "takes the greatest risks with viewer reaction, and an obvious question is whether this can be said to work" (ibid.: 59). But unless we are to ban the treatment of certain types of event in fiction, Pippin believes that what—uncomfortable as this is—I think we have to call the *aesthetic* dimensions of this question will remain pertinent. Even if we chose to condemn *this* film,

Almodóvar's film, as aestheticizing rape in an unacceptable fashion, it is not possible to rule out in advance that another film might complicate, in a serious and profound fashion, our attitude towards something as reprehensible as rape. Were this to happen, it would—in the first instance—be because that film had managed to succeed aesthetically, to have achieved sufficient credibility to warrant a serious and detailed response rather than a dismissal.

Something of this is figured by the film's treatment of Benigno's friend Marco. Pippin writes that "the movie works ... by concentrating a good deal of our attention on Marco's point of view and his reasons for neither abandoning Benigno nor, it is crucial to add yet again, excusing him at all, but for expressing some kind of solidarity with, even partly merging with, Benigno," all of this partly because Benigno's "care for Alicia and especially his desperate attempts to 'talk to her' were acts of faith that he [Marco] was not capable of, much to his detriment" (ibid.: 65). Pippin notes the way that the film visually expresses this partial merging between the two men in the way each replaces the other in the reflection in the glass when Marco visits Benigno in prison (ibid.: 58). It is, I think, unclear as to whether this is best seen as each *becoming* the other or as, somehow, *replacing* the other, of seeing only themselves where they should be seeing another, of turning a window into a mirror. The images seem—remarkably enough—ambiguous about whether they represent a kind of merging between two subjects or, instead, some kind of *failed* encounter (see Figure 7). If we are unsure how to read Marco's relationship with Benigno *within* the film, why should we be any more confident about exactly what is the appropriate stance for us as viewers to adopt? Further than this, there are some tricky ethical questions regarding Marco's behavior that interfere with any possibility of seeing him as straightforwardly put forward by the film as its ethical center or as a model for the viewer's reaction to Benigno. Although Pippin remarks that Marco manages to relate to Benigno without "excusing

Figure 7 *Talk to Her*: merger or failure?

him at all" (ibid.: 65), he does tell Benigno's landlady unambiguously that Benigno is innocent. Also, when speaking to him at his grave, Marco lies to Benigno. He says that he rushed over when he heard that Alicia had reawakened, whereas in fact Marco had acquiesced to his doctor's request *not* to tell Benigno and only rushed over when he got Benigno's message implying that he was going to kill himself (see ibid.: 65, n. 14). Marco keeps faith with Benigno's memory by adopting his strategy of talking to someone not in a position to hear and respond (Alicia because she is in a coma; Benigno because he is dead) at the same time as he betrays him by lying. The film ends by suggesting that Marco and the reawakened Alicia will embark on a relationship. If we feel, as we surely do, that there is something deeply morally problematic about this, actually spelling out why that is so proves very hard to do. These complications should not, I think, simply dissuade us from *any* kind of ethical identification with Marco, but, nevertheless, the film warns us against ending up like him, "naively convinced that it will all be ... 'simpler' than one imagines" (ibid.: 66).

With respect to *Shadow of a Doubt*, Pippin focuses his discussion on our confidence that we understand the difference between innocence and experience, or between a good person and a bad person; that we know, further, how we come to understand these things; and that we can reasonably successfully make such distinctions. He reads Hitchcock's film as destabilizing all these confidences—by dramatizing an instance of a loss of confidence—and argues that "it is enough of a philosophical achievement simply to say that many Hitchcock films compellingly, credibly, greatly complicate *any* such self-confidence" (ibid.: 71; emphasis in original). We should note once again how much weight Pippin's account places on the notion of credibility, a concept that has already appeared a number of times in this chapter, and that we saw in the previous chapter to be very important to Pippin's sense of the significance of film noir and the work of the Dardenne brothers. It could certainly be argued that Pippin puts too much weight on the notion of credibility, as if, in claiming that some films render credible the various philosophical notions he wants to explore, he is begging his own questions, using the credibility of a film as evidence for precisely what is in question (such as, e.g., that—in the case of the Dardennes—our understanding of the relationship between act and intention is in need of revision; or that—prompted by *Shadow of a Doubt*—we should doubt the security of the distinctions we make between goodness and evil). I think such a claim would misrepresent Pippin's enterprise, however. He is not attempting to *prove* credibility; one cannot be simply *argued into* finding an aspect of a film credible that one does not find to be so, any more than one can be argued into finding something beautiful. The experience of credibility is, rather, the starting point for Pippin's investigations. (Compare this remark about Nicholas Ray's *In a Lonely Place*, Pippin's reading of which will be discussed later in this chapter: "Something like the compellingness of the narrative will have *illuminated something* in a way ... much closer to having *understood someone*, than it is to having *proved something*" [2020a: 180; emphases in original].) If we already find credible the aspects he points to, his writings help us explore the consequences of this; if we do not, we may end up more prepared to entertain the possibility that some aspects of a film be regarded as credible, but whether we eventually come to revise our opinion must always take place by means of a renewed encounter with the film itself.[2]

Shadow of a Doubt tells the story of a serial murderer, Charles Oakley (Joseph Cotton) lying low with his sister and her family in small-town California, the ways that his niece Charlie Newton (Teresa Wright) comes to discover the truth about him, and what she chooses to do about it. As with the strange merger between Marco and Benigno figured by the prison visit scene in *Talk to Her*, much is made of the connection between Charles and Charlie, which seems almost to involve genuine telepathy (Charlie thinks of telegraphing Charles when he has already sent the family a telegram, and the "Merry Widow Waltz"—Charles is the Merry Widow Murderer— comes into her head from nowhere). Their relationship also, as Pippin and many other commentators have noted, has incestuous overtones. Something of this is humorously hinted at very early in the film, in the distinct tone of disgust at sexual deviance we hear in the post office mistress's response to Charlie's questioning her about telepathy, which she mishears as "telegraphy": "I only send telegrams the *normal* way."

It is, precisely, Charlie's bond with Charles that lets her know that something is wrong. This not only means that moral vision is not simply a question of accumulating evidence; it also suggests that Charlie herself is somehow intrinsically compromised. As Pippin observes, when Charlie is willing to risk the life of the widow Mrs. Potter in order to get her uncle out of town, "this indication that

Charlie can deal with Charles inside the amoral world he inhabits, can accept the terms of that world and prevail, is the most disturbing element of their 'bond' that we have yet seen" (ibid.: 91). Whereas *Talk to Her* causes problems for the audience's moral judgment, *Shadow of a Doubt* is much more of a dramatization of a character's experience of a profound quandary. It is, nevertheless, one that, according to Pippin, is powerful enough to suggest a genuine gap in the philosophical literature. When Charlie visits the library and finds the newspaper article that unambiguously indicates that her uncle is a murderer:

> This revelation ... confounds our security in moral distinctions, in our ability to ascribe motives to others, and so to be able to describe properly what they are doing. ... there is not a recognized philosophical literature on such a state of confusion and unknowingness, or on the virtues appropriate to such states.
> (ibid.: 86–8)

(We shall have more to say about unknowingness in the last section of this chapter.) And yet our sense that we are merely witnessing a character experience a confounding of morality covers over our own *lack* of moral consternation; we should be much more unsettled than we tend to be, given what Charlie later does and—credibly—threatens to do: "We, the viewers, tend to think of Charlie as such a good girl, that I would wager that for most viewers, the dense moral complications of Charlie's attitude, threatening to kill [Charles], not helping the FBI, goes, if not unnoticed, not judged. This is a remarkable effect" (ibid.: 88). The "confounding" in Pippin's section title, "Confounding Morality," then, works in two ways. Morality is often confounded in these films, but they also demonstrate that morality is itself confounding (it can confound us). Uncle Charles's nihilism, according to which "killing is no different than talking or eating; the universe is devoid of any moral structure" (ibid.: 74), is ultimately much *simpler* than the world that young Charlie is gradually introduced to during the film. In contrast to the nihilist's view that the moral perspective is a way of evading the nasty, messy truth, wrestling with the full complexities of moral psychology proves to be by no means the easy way out.

Nietzsche and Psychology

Candace Vogler has written a useful and extremely succinct summary of what moral psychology refers to; it indicates "those aspects of mental life that admit of ethical assessment, express ethical assessment, inform deliberation and conduct, and frame the larger practical orientations of individual agents" (2007: 6). Despite a number of divergences from Pippin's point of view, she provides a helpful summary of his attitude to the moral relevance of works of fiction: for Pippin, as for Stanley Cavell, "the philosophical importance of exemplary literary material is not that such material tells us what to do. Rather, it provides exquisite help in formulating the depth and character of an ethical challenge that we may be presumed to face … the challenge of producing a reflective, engaged, meaningful life with very little substantive guidance enshrined in established custom" (ibid.: 19).[3] True as this is, such a position is often conflated with one that Pippin does *not* share. He is extremely skeptical of the suggestion (expressed here in terms of literature, but equally applicable to film)

> that one of the best ways *to become* a better judge is *by* reading literature; that literature might sensitize us in the proper way, improve our discriminatory powers and sensitivity to morally salient features of situations, and so on. … it is not at all clear (and very likely untrue) that one even becomes a better reader in the sense that we are interested in simply (or only) *by* reading … This is as implausible (or at least as radically incomplete) as the claim that one becomes better morally by doing better moral philosophy.
> (Pippin 2005a: 269; emphases in original)

This is not at all to say that Pippin does not believe that the skills involved in "reading" books or films well—of being a sensitive, discriminating, and exacting reader—do not resemble the "skills" (if we can call them that) involved in being a perceptive moral agent. If he did not think this, little of what we examined in the previous section would have any foundation. But the argumentative step that Pippin believes is often presumed or glossed over—in texts such as, for example, Martha Nussbaum's *Poetic Justice* and Elaine Scarry's *On Beauty and Being Just*, the objects of his attention in the passage quoted above—is that, by virtue of this analogy, one can become a better moral agent simply by reading the right books or watching the right films. It is equally true that one cannot become excellent at cricket without playing a lot of it, but it in no way follows that if I play a lot of cricket I will necessarily get any better at it.

This thought has a Nietzschean flavor to it. Pippin is at pains to point out that the caricatured Nietzsche who believed that there were no truths but only interpretations is a complete fiction; Nietzsche's (in some ways even more radical) point concerns what *difference* it makes that there are truths, profoundly destabilizing the connection between the true and the good that has reigned at least since Plato and is very hard to avoid thinking in terms of.[4] Why should what is true be any more effective, any more *useful*, than what is false? As Pippin puts it, "there is no evidence that Nietzsche is committed to the extremely radical (and incoherent) view that 'there are no facts, only interpretations,' or that 'there is no truth'" (1983: 159); instead, "his main, overarching or master question is always the *value of truth*, or what we think 'the truth' will accomplish, and more generally always the question of the various ways in which attachments to various possible lives come to be and are sustained" (Pippin 1997: 326; emphasis in original). This latter question—"the various ways in which attachments to various possible lives come to be and are sustained"—resonates with the questions of political psychology that, as we saw in Chapter 2, Pippin finds so compellingly explored in some of the greatest Westerns. Nietzsche's interest in it also goes some way to explaining why he thought that psychology—which, as §23 of *Beyond Good and Evil* has it, had "hitherto remained anchored to moral prejudices and timidities"—could "again be recognized as the queen of the sciences" (1990: 53–4).

In many ways, Pippin finds the view of agency that Nietzsche expresses in his psychology to be—rather surprisingly—congruous with Hegel's.[5] In §13 of the first essay in *On the Genealogy of Morality*, Nietzsche writes that

> the common people separates lightning from its flash and takes the latter to be a *deed*, something performed by a subject, which is called lightning ... But there is no such substratum; there is no "being" behind the deed, its effect and what becomes of it; "the doer" is invented as an afterthought,—the deed is everything.
> (Nietzsche 1997: 26; emphasis in original)

Pippin does not subscribe to what is probably the most prevalent view as to how we should interpret this passage, namely that Nietzsche believes that the intentions we espouse and ascribe to others are merely so many illusions or epiphenomena; that all that is *really* going on are the workings of fundamental—essentially biological—"drives." For Pippin, "if the Nietzschean enterprise is deflationary, it is not reductionist" (2010c: 4); for Pippin's Nietzsche, if drives "are to explain behavior, they cannot determine the psychological from 'outside the psychological,' as extrapsychological phenomena" (ibid.: 88). We still need to think in terms of "stereoscopic attentiveness," looking at agency both from the outside and in terms of how it appears to the agent. Although, on Pippin's reading, Nietzsche—in common with a number of philosophers[6]—"does not think self-knowledge is ever directly observational or introspectable ... what makes his position so unusual is that he *also* does not, by contrast, consider it immediate, self-presenting, or incorrigible" (ibid.: 99; emphasis in original). One of the consequences Nietzsche draws from this is that—in keeping with the reluctance that he shares with Hegel to think of "individual human actions as discrete or atomic or pointlike or eye-blink-like units" (Thompson 2008: 91)—self-knowledge is best thought of as "the result of provisional and testable interpretation" (Pippin 2010c: 99).

In *Shadow of a Doubt*, Charlie does not merely discover some unpleasant truths about the world but has radically to reconsider, to reinterpret, her self-knowledge. Her previous "goodness" had not involved "an active struggle with evil" and hence was "innocence more than goodness" (Pippin 2020a: 82). As we saw above, Pippin's discussion focuses on the collapse of her previous confidence about the ways one might distinguish good from evil and its consequences for her understanding both of herself and those closest to her. For Pippin, there is something profoundly Nietzschean in this, particularly in the sense that the apparently drastically different "moral postures" of Charles and Charlie are in fact "not strict contrasts"; for example, her "dawning distaste for bourgeois domestic life"—for what she sees as its stultifying and deadening qualities ("We just sort of go along and nothing happens," she tells her parents)[7]—"*is* on a continuum with Charles's nihilistic rage at it" (2020a: 82–3; emphasis in original). The existence of this continuum is a profound challenge to moral certainty; in such a situation the most pressing issue—both for Charlie and for the viewer of *Shadow of a Doubt*—becomes coming to terms with

> the unique kind of difficulty one faces in attempting to know such things as why one (or anyone) did what one did, what it actually was that one did, what one (or some other) truly values, why one values what one does, and whether one could come to know what sort of a life one might truly affirm, and if so, how.
>
> (Pippin 2013c: 182)

Pippin names this particular theme "unknowingness," and we have already encountered it. For him, for example, the films of the Dardenne brothers "explore the issue of unknowingness with respect to oneself" (Pippin 2020a: 232, n. 2). But there is one film that explores this theme with such a degree of complexity that it merits a book-length discussion; this film is Hitchcock's 1958 film *Vertigo*, and the book is Pippin's third book on film, *The Philosophical Hitchcock: Vertigo and the Anxieties of Unknowingness*.

The Anxieties of Unknowingness: *Vertigo* and *In a Lonely Place*

The plot of *Vertigo* is famously convoluted; Pippin describes it as "immensely complicated, massively improbable and risky" (2017a: 12).[8] Put crudely, the film's narrative is as follows. The detective Scottie Ferguson (James Stewart), retired from the police force because of his acrophobia and vertigo, is asked by an old college friend, Gavin Elster (Tom Helmore), to follow his wife Madeleine (Kim Novak), because Elster believes she has become mentally unstable, obsessed— and possibly even possessed—by an ancestor called Carlotta Valdes (although in her lucid moments she knows nothing of this). Scottie comes to fall in love with Madeleine, but after taking her to an old Spanish mission south of San Francisco called San Juan Bautista in an attempt to rationalize and so cure her delusions, she ascends a tower and falls to her death, with Scottie unable to follow her due to his acrophobia. Scottie is cleared of wrongdoing but descends into a state of "acute melancholia," as his doctor calls it, and becomes almost catatonic for a year. Wandering listlessly after his release from hospital, he spots a young woman named Judy Barton (also Kim Novak) and is struck by her resemblance to Madeleine. At this point it is revealed to the audience that Judy *is* Madeleine, that the entire

Madeleine narrative in the first half of the film was an elaborate ruse concocted by Elster in order to enable him to kill his wife, with Judy, his now-abandoned mistress, pretending to be Madeleine. (When Judy ran up the tower, Elster threw his wife's identically dressed body from the roof.) Scottie, however, does not know this and becomes obsessed with remaking Judy into (he thinks) a copy of Madeleine. No sooner is this achieved, however, than a necklace that was supposed to belong to Carlotta gives Judy away. Scottie forces her to return to San Juan Bautista, and proves able, this time, to ascend the tower. Judy protests that she does indeed love him, that she could have run away when he discovered her, but after a final kiss she is startled by a nun ascending the stairs and really does, this time, fall to her death. The film concludes with a famously ambiguous image of Scottie standing on the ledge of the tower looking down at Judy's body. As Pippin puts it, "The strange position of his hands could bear scores of different meanings, and everything is left open" (ibid.: 121).[9]

Pippin begins his investigation of *Vertigo* by noting the—appropriately vertiginous—complexities of the number of "persons" involved "in any romantic relationship between two people" (ibid.: 12). If we count the two persons "they actually are," the further two persons that "they see themselves" as, the two "as they are each seen by the other," the distinct two persons *"they aspire to be seen as* by the other," and the two persons *"they take themselves to be seen as* by the other" (which are by no means identical with the persons each participant actually sees in the other) we get to ten different persons (ibid.; emphases in original). Not to mention that, "if we import a Freudian thesis, the opposite-sex parent of each participant would also be involved"; clearly the situation is "quite crowded, no matter the size of the drawing room or bedroom" (ibid.)! Despite this complexity—or rather, perhaps, because of it—Pippin structures his book very simply, working through the film's narrative from beginning to end. Although he clearly believes that it would confuse matters more than clarify them to attempt to track these ten "persons" all the way though the film, he also believes that we do need to entertain at least "something very like this complexity" in order "to understand the relation between Scottie and Madeleine" (ibid.). Although he does not put things in quite these terms, one could say that the elaborate deceptions, the sustained creations of fictional personas, that go on in *Vertigo* are literalizations of the procedures involved, as Pippin says at the outset, in "any romantic relationship." We all try to be (or to become) *somebody lovable* at the same time as wanting to be loved *for who we are*, and there is no way for this process (given that the other person involved is inevitably doing exactly the same thing) to be straightforward and not involve complexities that at times verge on the contradictory.

Pippin points out how repeated viewings of *Vertigo* gradually unfurl and deepen this complexity. When Madeleine hurls herself into San Francisco Bay and Scottie fishes her out and brings her back to his apartment, we will think, first time around, that we are witnessing the "accidental intimacy between them and what seems to be a budding love affair" (ibid.: 59). The second time around, in the full knowledge of the murder plot, it is not only obvious that "what Madeleine is doing is staged and manipulative"; knowing this puts us in a position to notice what may have evaded notice before, "that Scottie does not reveal to her who he is or why he is following her" (ibid.). But at the same time as we notice this duplicity in Scottie, our sense of the power relations between them shifts. The power relationship that seemed both "grotesque" and "uncomfortably completely one-sided" on first viewing (Scottie, after all, stripped naked an unconscious woman and put her to bed, something that he later very nearly admits to her that he "enjoyed") is reversed and "now seems completely one-sided in the *other* direction, as Scottie is the one manipulated" (ibid.: 60; emphasis in original). Madeleine (actually, of course, Judy playing Madeleine) knows that Scottie is being economical with the truth, but he does not have the same benefit. But having entered fully into this web of deceit, a third viewing—Pippin suggests—may well increase the complexity still further by suggesting that it is not *merely* a matter of interwoven deceptions, but that, indeed, "something *is* beginning between them, on her side as well" (ibid.; my emphasis).

It is a definite achievement of Pippin's that he brings out this and many other of the film's complexities without his prose or his argument becoming convoluted or bewildering, at the same time as demonstrating his desire to respect the film's complexities rather than to "solve" or "unravel" them. As the book's subtitle indicates, his chief aim is to explore the film's presentation of "unknowingness" and of the "anxieties" it provokes. He acknowledges that the word unknowingness is rather "clumsy," but he thinks the neologism is useful in helping him "to avoid suggesting that the problem is a kind of skepticism about interpreting others rightly, or skepticism about self-knowledge, or skepticism about the possible intimacies of romantic love" (ibid.: 16). It is not that we can know—nor, even, at least in the case of *Vertigo*, *think* we know—that such things are impossible or nonexistent; on the contrary, "there *are* occasions when we do get things right and we know that we do and have some sense of how we know, but not such that we could lay out evidence, or explain discursively how we know" (ibid.; emphasis in original).[10] Instead, in "Hitchcock's representation we simply often (but not always) fail to know in situations where we most need to know, but we have no option but to persist in such attempts. Not to persist would be not to lead a life at all" (ibid.: 16–17). Clear as I think these formulations are, there is something potentially confusing in Pippin's insistence on keeping unknowingness separate from skepticism, which is that (as he acknowledges and as we shall see in slightly more detail later) what Pippin means by unknowingness has a great deal of resonance with Stanley Cavell's studies of, precisely, skepticism. Pippin means to distinguish the problem he is investigating from skepticism as a kind of certainty about the impossibility of knowledge, but he is fully in sympathy with—and greatly influenced by—Cavell's explorations of skepticism as something that must, instead, be lived out, a renewable condition involving the ebb and flow of certainty and confusion in our lives and our dealings with one another, something that cannot be simply refuted (see, e.g., Cavell 1979a: 109).[11] So, to avoid confusion: Pippin's point is that "we don't know enough to be *globally* skeptical" (2017a: 16; my emphasis) about the possibilities of correctly interpreting one another, of self-knowledge, or whether romantic love involves genuine intimacies; what is needed instead is precisely what Cavell calls the study of skepticism, namely an "exploration of the unresolvable uncertainties involved in coming to understand and trust another" (ibid.: 17, n. 28).

Vertigo, then, both dramatizes and explores—compellingly, Pippin thinks—living under the condition of unknowingness. In this it has a great many resonances, a number of which Pippin brings out in the book, with the challenges that Nietzsche's writings pose. Particularly important, given the centrality of Hegel's work to Pippin's thinking, is the challenge that Nietzsche represents for Hegel:

> *Vertigo* does raise an issue that is a problem for Hegel. Said very crudely, Hegel thinks that, like everything else, the human practical world is in principle fully intelligible. We can in principle make some sense of the way we live. Even if there are all sorts of apparent irrationalities in such a life, they are ultimately only apparent. Films like *Vertigo* as well as the great Greek and Shakespearian and French classical tragedies in our tradition are a very deep challenge to this assumption, and I am not sure Hegel has a satisfactory response to the implicit challenge they raise.[12]
>
> (Pippin 2018b)

We saw above, for example, Pippin's observation that Nietzsche's attempt in *Beyond Good and Evil* to demonstrate "our ignorance about why we do what we do in significant choices, given how subject we are to deception, even eager to be deceived in some cases" is extremely relevant to an understanding of *Vertigo* (2017a). One could also pick out other pertinent themes in Pippin's work on Nietzsche that he does not highlight. For example, on Pippin's reading Nietzsche's interpretation of modern nihilism indicates "that the problem of nihilism does not consist in a failure of knowledge or in a failure of will, but in a *failure of desire*, the flickering out of some erotic flame," one that is figured in images such as "perhaps the most intuitive metonymy of failed desire, boredom" (2005b: 177; emphasis in original). And though Scottie may perhaps be depressed at the beginning of the film, I think he is also clearly *bored*. He is looking for something that might kindle an "erotic flame," something that his old friend (and one-time fiancée) Midge (Barbara Bel Geddes) clearly—and in some ways tragically—fails to do.

Pippin's insistence that Nietzsche's interest in the possibility of creating new values cannot mean that he is recommending wishful thinking is also helpful in approaching Hitchcock's film. In asking the question, "What is possible, possibly affirmed, loved, 'now'?" Nietzsche is, thinks Pippin, quite clear that although (1) answering this question must involve the production of a narrative about why the candidates that previously seemed to be potential answers are no longer acceptable,[13] and (2) "this narrative too will be an 'attempt,' a kind of story that itself might make possible some sort of life now," it is nevertheless clear that (3) "it cannot be wishful thinking, any more than one can make oneself believe anything about a loved one" (Pippin 1997: 370).[14] Nietzsche is quite clear about the "impossibility of living whatever lie seems most beautiful or pleasing" (Pippin 2003: 24). Scottie's actions in the second part of the film seem to me to demonstrate this impossibility. We can view them as an attempt to live out a kind of wishful thinking in the full knowledge that it *is* wishful thinking, an attempt to demonstrate that a beautiful and pleasing lie *can* be lived, even in the knowledge that it is a lie. Scottie thinks that remaking Judy as Madeleine—while fully aware that this can only result in a copy—will, somehow, produce a life that is in contrast to the life of melancholic blankness, a life that he can once again really *lead*, one that is not merely the "we just sort of go along and nothing happens" kind of life that Charlie rejects in *Shadow of a Doubt*. This is the case even though Scottie is not able to articulate this fully, being able to answer Judy's question as to what good the whole rigmarole will achieve only by saying, in a direct expression of unknowingness, "I don't know. No good, I guess." But, of course, the attempt fails anyway, with the ironic twist being that the reason that it fails is that Scottie is *actually doing* what he thinks he is only, we might say, "wishfully thinking that he is doing"—that is, bringing Madeleine back—because Judy-playing-Madeleine is all that his Madeleine ever was. (Although, as always with this film, there are further complexities to be reckoned with because, as Wendy Doniger puts it, "Judy Barton from Kansas is surely not the same after she has played Madeleine and fallen in love with Scottie," and hence *this* Judy-playing-Madeleine cannot be the same as *that*, earlier, Judy-playing-Madeleine [2005: 165].)

One central question in *Vertigo*, then, both for its characters—chiefly Scottie—and its viewers is what it is that we are attempting to interpret. Scottie thinks he is attempting to understand Madeleine but discovers that he could never have been doing that because he never even met the real Madeleine, Elster's wife, but only Judy-playing-Madeleine. *Vertigo* raises what we could see as Fregean questions of the difference between sense and reference with a quite peculiar urgency and intensity. Is it possible, that is, to love somebody under one description and not under another? Is it the *referent* of the description that is loved, or do the different *senses* of each possible description affect whether or not they pertain to the person loved? If love is to be genuine, "we want to be able to say that the 'spark' between [Scottie and Judy] is independent of the various descriptions available as we get to know someone" (Pippin 2017a: 62). After all, as Pippin notes:

> It would seem strangely restrictive to say that Scottie can love "the haunted wife of Elster," but would not be able to fall in love with "Judy who is pretending to be haunted," that he does not love the woman under that description. That *is* "whom" he falls in love with!
> (ibid.: 62, n. 76; emphasis in original)

Yet it is clear that love cannot survive just *any* redescription, but this is something that we cannot find out in advance; Pippin suggests that "a woman who loves her husband qua faithful may avow that she would not love her husband qua betrayer, but then find that the situation is much more complicated, and that she still does love him" when his betrayal comes to light (ibid.: 63, n. 76). These issues involve us in questions of surface versus depth that are central to the interpretation of film. The importance of surfaces in any erotic attachment—"something as mysterious and disturbing as a mere 'look,' or dress, or hairstyle (or scent, or profile, or gait, or, indeed someone's back, at some moment, in some context)" (ibid.: 63)—can make any plea, such as Judy's, to be loved purely for oneself "sound naïve" (ibid.: 64). Pippin cites a passage from Henry James's *A Portrait of a Lady* in which Isabel Archer's claim that her clothes have nothing to do with her true self, that they express nothing genuine about her—"it's not my own choice that I wear them; they're imposed upon me by society"—is met by Madame Merle's dry rejoinder: "Should you prefer to go without them?" (ibid.: 101).

Pippin also points out how important faces (which, for all that they are, as T. J. Clark puts it, "machine[s] for exteriorizing—exchanging, universalizing—subjectivity" [2014] are also *surfaces*, and particularly so in film) are in this attempt to understand, both for Scottie and for us as viewers: "So often our only means of determining what is real and what is theatrical is what we see, what we think we see, in what a person does, and *in a person's face*" (2017a: 24; emphasis in original). He explores the ways that this is figured in the film's use of profiles, in particular two prominent profiles of Madeleine/Judy. The right-profile shot of Madeleine at Ernie's is recalled by the much later left-profile silhouette of Judy in her apartment, both reminding us of Scottie's "first, deep infatuation with her profile" and, by being a silhouette, suggesting that "from his point of view," she is "a blank slate on which he can reinscribe Madeleine" (ibid.: 106). There are in fact a rather large number of profile shots of Kim Novak in *Vertigo* (see Figure 8 for a selection), and there is a distinct emphasis on right-profile shots. Given this emphasis, the fact that the silhouette is a left-profile might be seen to raise—perhaps at the same time as it satirizes—the notion of a person having a "true" and a "false" side. Are we finally to get to see the "real" woman who has hitherto been hidden from us? The film's figuration here literalizes the metaphor of someone "having two sides to their personality," at the same time as, just as with its use of color (see ibid.: 27–8, 59), it undercuts any simplistic symbolism. There is no question of Judy simply having a "good side" and "bad side," and the starkness of the profile shots seems to poke fun at any viewer tempted to think there was.

The film's treatment of these profiles can be seen as a single instance of a much broader complex of questions tackled by Pippin involving relationships between authenticity and inauthenticity and the ways coming to understand this film's narrative, characters, and form involves complex interplay between, or mutual impingement among, these various relationships. The artificiality of an image in profile is not simply a symbol for something about a character or characters, but—in another variant on Pippin's "stereoscopic attentiveness"—resonates with those characters' own relationships with artificiality, within the film's diegesis. Similar processes are at work with regard to questions of, for example, film genre. *Vertigo*, Pippin argues, asks us "to consider the relationship between romantic love and neurotic

Figure 8 A series of profiles in *Vertigo*.

obsession," and at least to entertain "the suggestion that there is little difference between them," and it does so partly by "invoking elements of the film noir genre [specifically, the overwhelming power of the appearance of the femme fatale] both to make this point and, in effect, to quote the cinematic convention" (ibid.: 51). This helps to demonstrate that thinking in terms of a film's reflective form and its relation to the moral psychology of its characters by no means need involve any simplistic choice between "realistic characters" *or* "directorial pawns."[15] A version of this point comes out in the possibility of the simultaneous truth of two claims made, one page apart, by William Rothman: that "Hitchcock's signatures are expressions of his unwillingness or inability ever to forsake his mark, ever to absorb himself unconditionally in the destinies of his characters, ever to leave his own story untold" (2004: 239) and that "Hitchcock's films are also demonstrations that human beings *can* be known" (ibid.: 240; emphasis in original).

If *Vertigo* can be said to invoke film noir, this is something it shares with Nicholas Ray's *In a Lonely Place*, Pippin's investigation of which has many affinities with his study of *Vertigo*. In Ray's film, Humphrey Bogart plays Dix Steele, a Hollywood screenwriter with a bit of a temper, who becomes suspected of murdering a hatcheck girl he brings home with him to tell him the plot of a novel he is being invited to adapt. His neighbor Laurel Grey (Gloria Grahame) gives him an alibi, and the two fall in love. But after witnessing his violent temper she comes increasingly to believe that he is capable of murder. At the same time, he becomes more and more jealous and suspicious, forcing her to accept his proposal of marriage. The final revelation of Dix's innocence of the murder comes too late, after he has attempted to strangle Laurel in a jealous rage, ruining any possible future for their relationship. The question of what sense it makes for somebody to have a "true self" beneath all their surfaces is raised by this film, just as it is by *Vertigo*, but with a very different texture. Pippin frames the question in terms of Cavell's distinction between "active" and "passive" skepticism about other people, about the relationship between the fear that one cannot ever really *know* anyone else and the fear that one cannot, oneself, *be known* (which is of course also very closely related to the fear *of being known*, of being "found out").

One could say, then, that *In a Lonely Place* explores what it means for the questions of "mutual interpretability" (Pippin 2017a: 54) to involve *being* true (as in "I'll be true to you") rather than it being primarily a matter of *finding out* "the truth." The process of investigation changes the object under investigation. As Jonathan Lear remarks about psychoanalysis (*contra* much of what Freud claimed but in keeping with what, Lear thinks, his practice implies), given that "the reality that mind is trying to capture is mind itself ... in its attempt to understand itself, mind does not leave itself unaltered" (1990: 11). Laurel is "in an intimate relationship of trust with Dix," but

> once she allows the question of whether this trust and faith are justified to arise, the possibility of answering it immediately changes, as her relationship to Dix has just changed; he notes the change, is wounded, *he changes*, and then, and only then, does he begin to evince what could be, and are taken to be, indications that he really *is* "capable of murder."
>
> (Pippin 2020a: 174; emphases in original)

The film puts a good deal of pressure, Pippin argues, on what it means to think of someone as being the "type" who would commit murder. (Scottie, at the end of *Vertigo*, appears ready to kill Judy; does the fact that her death is an accident prove that he is not the type of person who could be a killer?) Pippin argues that, although Dix has shown plenty of evidence of his hair-trigger temper, it does not make sense to call the Dix we see later on in the film "the true Dix coming out" (ibid.: 192).

We could also ask comparable questions about the appropriateness of Dix's description of Laurel, early in the film, as a "quitter," which he immediately glosses as the "get out before you get hurt type."

Emotionally, the events of the film don't prove her to be that "type," but she does indeed "get out" before suffering serious physical harm. Her behavior at the end of the film is clearly not best described as "quitting," but the film still leaves open the possibility that she might have been wiser not to get involved at all. I think Pippin rather underplays the importance of Dix's previous girlfriend Frances Randolph (Alix Talton), toward whom he was very violent, something she seems to have been willing to accept. "Alleges nose broken by running into a door" is the very dark comment contained in the relevant police file.[16] Frances shows herself at the beginning of the film to be willing to take Dix back, and the film only gradually unfolds the story of what happened between them previously. I find it hard to see the film as suggesting that Frances and Laurel represent two equally possible options; Laurel's choice seems clearly the more dignified and justifiable. Be that as it may, in her life before meeting Dix, Laurel—it seems—did tend to "get out before she got hurt." But of course by "getting out," one will never know whether one would have been hurt, which is in a way what the phrase really means; it means, that is, "not taking the risk of getting hurt," and Laurel is only hurt—emotionally—because she *does* take that risk. Of the film's famous concluding line, "I lived a few weeks while you loved me," Pippin points out the ironies involved in the fact that it was of course Dix who wrote those lines, which we hear earlier as part of his screenplay. But when he concludes that "astonishingly, in her mind *Dix left her*" (ibid.: 199; emphasis in original), Pippin can only say so by including the unspoken line "I died when you left me." (The lines are: "I was born when she kissed me. I died when she left me. I lived a few weeks while she loved me.") Clearly, we are meant to *remember* the other lines, but I think it is equally significant that Laurel does *not* say them. She doesn't know when (or whether) she (or they) was (or were) "born" and "died"; but she does affirm that the entire relationship wasn't an illusion; she did "live a few weeks."[17] Ultimately the film does not makes it at all easy to articulate either what Dix and Laurel could have done differently, or whether, and in what senses, the moments of happiness Dix and Laurel clearly *do* experience could be said to have made it all "worth it." This, I think, is why Pippin believes that Nicholas Ray "would agree" with Cavell that "skepticism about other minds … is not properly skepticism in the philosophical sense but tragedy, and that there is no human alternative to tragedy" (ibid.: 199).[18]

Pippin aims to demonstrate of all the films mentioned in this chapter both that they are not fully comprehensible unless we think in terms of moral psychology, but also that doing so raises questions about which consequences of so doing are "worth it." One reason why moral psychology is distinct from moralism is that attending to the former can result in a kind of "suspension" of moral questions, "as if the judgements are available, but not somehow appropriate in this context" (Pippin 2017a: 124). Pippin remarks on the very "unusual moral tone" of *Vertigo*, by which he means "the absence of any grip of moral categories on the characters" and the way that "such notions never seem to arise, despite adultery and murder" (ibid.: 15, n. 24). This is the case partly because "our awareness of the fragile and uncertain self- and other-knowledge apparent all seem to reduce our confidence that we really understand … what is actually happening," with the result that "moral judgement comes to feel hubristic" (ibid.: 125–6). Much of what I think is distinctive in Pippin's approach to these questions is precisely the "suspension" that his readings also achieve, a suspension that is not an evasion. Pippin neither, as we have seen, takes it that the right conclusion to draw from this lack of confidence is that we should attempt a global skepticism about morality, nor that we ought to dismiss the compelling and credible ways in which films like *Vertigo* dramatize problems of unknowingness and of moral psychology as merely trickery, as aesthetic sleight-of-hand that only pretends to have relevance to our actual moral lives. On the contrary, his conclusion is that the exploration of these problems within aesthetic contexts—such as the interpretation of films—can usefully bring the *appropriate application* of morality (something which it must always be possible to challenge or to reconsider if morality is not to become a kind of tyranny) into question.

Pippin points out that it "is not infrequent in Hitchcock's films that the voice of morality is ... a posing, strutting fraud," as is the case with the judge or coroner in *Vertigo* (ibid.: 67). But what comes to take place in that film is "a general suspension of the conditions for moral assessment" which, Pippin insists, is "not at all of course the same thing as the suspension of moral distinctions" (ibid.: 124). Ultimately, Pippin aims to demonstrate that the "psychological complications of *Vertigo*"—as well as, in their different ways, the other films mentioned in this chapter—raise what could be regarded as very Nietzschean question, namely "*the point* of attempts at moral blame, and especially the question of, whatever blame can be assigned, what the point of holding someone forever accountable would be" (ibid.: 128; emphasis in original). If it is unclear both, as Nietzsche insists, that the truth can be equated with what "works best," and that—as we saw in the previous chapter—we can always and immediately say what we ourselves (to say nothing of other people) are doing and why, why bother insisting that moral evaluation is always possible, let alone "worth it"? But are there possible ways of resisting such an insistence that do not resort to moral skepticism? Pippin thinks the study of film can give us as vivid a purchase as any on the consequences of the inescapability of unknowingness, as well as on the richness of romantic love as a site for the exploration of these consequences. Toward the very end of his study of *Vertigo*, Pippin makes some remarks that will serve well to draw this chapter to a close:

> We seem to be invited by all of this to ponder the significance of Nietzsche's famous aphorism from *Beyond Good and Evil*:

"Whatever is done out of love takes place beyond good and evil." The aphorism seems to be saying that people in love are indifferent to moral assessment, don't care about rightness or wrongness in what they do. But that would be to misinterpret Nietzsche as well as the film. In *Beyond Good and Evil*, Nietzsche is out to show something quite relevant to Hitchcock's movie. He wants to point out first the frequent opacity in human self-knowledge, our ignorance about why we do what we do in significant choices, given how subject we are to deception, even eager to be deceived in some cases, and given the almost inevitable self-deceit in many of our ascriptions of motives and in the act descriptions we give. He means that this is true *especially* in cases like love, where what we interpretively see is so intertwined with our own powerful passions and with our own evaluation of how others see us, that the moral psychology required by the moral point of view can no longer be said to apply.

(Pippin 2017a: 127–8; emphasis in original)

6

Pippin and Film Studies

This chapter will situate Pippin's work on film among other contemporary works in Film Studies more explicitly than has been my practice in other chapters. It will also address some possible limitations of his work, singling out two concerns as particularly worthy of attention: (1) the almost exclusive focus of Pippin's writings to date on the traditional canon of films made by white male filmmakers and (2) the suggestion that Pippin's work on film pays insufficient or inadequate attention to the specifically cinematic aspects of the films under discussion. I will explore the latter question chiefly via an examination of Pippin's treatment of cinematic irony (irony being a subject whose relation to visual art forms is notoriously thorny) in two contemporaneous films: Douglas Sirk's *All That Heaven Allows* (1955) and Nicholas Ray's *Johnny Guitar* (1954). The chapter will close with an examination, in the light of Pippin's work, of some of the ways different philosophical approaches intersect within the philosophical study of film and consider whether his work suggests ways these relationships might be reconceived.

Pippin and the Canon

Pippin's reliance on the notion that the films he studies are examples of "great art" might appear to be one of the weakest aspects of his approach. He gives no general defense of this position, and if the claim is that some films are valuable to study *because* they are great artistic achievements, the claim might appear to be circular. (Each of his readings aims to establish that its subject is a work of art; but this subject was only selected for discussion on that very basis.) But this is not really the case. Whatever the actual reasons for his choices of film—which, as with most scholars, are presumably rooted in the fact that he simply happened to find himself particularly interested in these films, for a complex range of reasons not all of which will be accessible to Pippin himself—we need only be broadly convinced by his interpretation in order to agree that the film discussed is indeed a work of art; nothing in what he says relies on our acceptance *at the outset* that the films he discusses are art. The situation has parallels with aspects of Stanley Cavell's discussion of skepticism. A critic could certainly try to show that a single film was *not* art, just as a particular goldfinch might turn out not, in fact, to be a goldfinch (the example of the goldfinch derives from J. L. Austin; see Cavell 1979a: 49–64). Persuasively showing that an individual film is not a work of art, however, could never prove that *no* film can be art, just as showing that what we took to be a goldfinch was actually a painted piece of wood does not demonstrate that we are *never* sure, in any circumstances, that we are looking at a goldfinch. But Pippin would have no response to any feeling of disappointment that we can't prove a priori that films can be art, nor indeed provide a general definition of what it means for a film to be a work of art, because there is, he believes, nowhere else to look in the pursuit of such questions than to (or, rather, at!) films themselves.[1] What else could the claim to the artistic status of films be based on, other than interpretations of specific films?

One answer to this question could, of course, be: on an account of the material and discursive conditions under which films are *received* as artworks. The result would be a broadly sociological account of art. As valuable as such an account would be, however, it is difficult to see how it could entirely *replace* an aesthetic account without thereby dismissing the aesthetic realm as ultimately illusory, as—for example—nothing but a device for clandestinely reinforcing social hierarchies. Pippin would certainly accept that art *can* serve this— and many other—social functions (both positive and negative), but he does not think that this in any way exhausts the meaning and function of artworks. Neither, however—even though most of the films he has written about were originally produced in Hollywood as mass entertainment—does Pippin wish to defend mass entertainment as art *in general*:

> When someone hears that you have written books about Hollywood movies, they almost always assume that you are an opponent of the distinction between "high" and "low" or popular or mass art; that if you write about John Ford, you might just as well write about one of the *Hunger Games* or *Star Wars* movies, or *The Simpsons* TV show. (Not infrequently such interlocutors also tell you what a masterpiece *Groundhog Day* is, or what a genius the dreadful Woody Allen is.) But the point is to claim—and this is a bit easier a point to make now than thirty years ago—that many Hollywood movies categorized as commercial vehicles destined to entertain and sell popcorn were not at all such mere vehicles.
>
> (Pippin 2016a: 225)

Such a position might sound unfashionably mandarin, as if the claim is that some mainstream films have the good fortune to "escape" or "transcend" their mainstream status. But unless one wishes to remove evaluative concerns from criticism entirely—an attempt which Pippin agrees with V. F. Perkins would be an impossibility because, for example, "even description depends upon forms of evaluation which are no less 'subjective' than judgement" (1972: 191)—then it is surely entirely reasonable to conclude that many films are more interesting commercially than aesthetically and to choose not to concentrate one's aesthetic attention on such films. It is, however, important to remember that for Pippin "art" works, as a category, in a similar way to "subjectivity": neither term refers to a metaphysical nor an empirical property but to a normatively—hence ultimately *collectively*—achieved status. In order to *be* art, artworks have to be held to be art by a community. Pippin does not, however, believe that this means that such a status is simply in the eye of the beholder and has nothing to do with the properties of the artwork. Instead—fittingly for a Hegelian such as Pippin—there is a complex historical and dialectical relationship between a work, its reception, and its status as art (see Pippin 2014).

The sense in which Hollywood films can, for Pippin, achieve the status of art is very different from David Bordwell's formalist claim (originally proposed in 1979), that "art cinema" represents a specific mode of film practice made at a specific time and with specific formal characteristics. It might be helpful here to distinguish "art cinema" from "cinematic art." Bordwell's category enables the demonstration of a film's status as an example of "art cinema" with minimum interpretation. (Can we tick off the requisite features? If so, we're dealing with art cinema, and the normative issue of whether the film in question is a particularly *good* or *interesting* example of it is a subsidiary question.) For Pippin, however, the argument that a specific film is an instance of film achieving the status of art—of being an instance of cinematic art—stands or falls on the convincingness of the interpretation offered, and whether or not it successfully demonstrates that the film exhibits a sufficiently "reflective form."[2] Such an argument will certainly point out specific features of the film but it will do so in order to articulate their function within the film as a whole (rather than simply indicate their presence) because, as noted above, a more dialectical mode is required. As Andrew Klevan argues, the "meaning or effect" of, say, "an image, a gesture, a cut, or a camera movement within a film" is something that "shifts depending on the context" and cannot be assumed to be "equivalent to images, gestures, cuts, and camera movements in other films" (2018: 77).

It is, however, true that, despite the fact that Pippin spends very little time discussing the canon as such, one could say that he leaves himself open to attack—or denies himself some ammunition for the defense of his position—by choosing only to focus on films that have already come to be seen as canonical. As he himself acknowledges, the battles as to whether Westerns and film noirs can be art were to all intents and purposes won years ago; claiming that the study of Hollywood film in and of itself challenges notions of canonicity (which he does not in fact choose to do) no longer seems a terribly plausible move.[3] Pippin would, no doubt, argue that the films he writes about are canonical largely *because* of their aesthetic value, rather than the other way round, but it would be interesting to see him test this with a discussion of some less securely canonized films. That a film has already been much studied can, in and of itself, no more be an argument for ceasing to write about it than it could be to say that we've heard quite enough about *King Lear* and *Emma* by now, thank you very much. Nevertheless, given the increasing awareness in many quarters of the ways that artistic canons perpetuate entrenched privilege, it can only be regretted that Pippin has nowhere published an extended study of a film directed by somebody who wasn't a white man.

He is also certainly capable, at least in passing, of giving the impression of being a little tone-deaf to such concerns, as when he offers a list of novelists and dramatists who are philosophically sensitive to the issues of agency that interest him—"Fontane, Tolstoy (above all Tolstoy), Hardy, James, Musil, Döblin, Dreyser [sic], Kafka, Ibsen, Beckett" (Pippin 2010b)—or a list of contemporary film scholars in whose company he would be "happy enough to find a home"—"Stanley Cavell, Victor Perkins, Tom Gunning, Robin Wood, William Rothman, Murray Pomerance, George Wilson, Gilberto Perez, George Toles, and their like" (Pippin 2017a: 11, n. 17). Both lists are overwhelmingly white and entirely male. Pippin, however, does not quite do himself justice with such lists. With regard to issues of gender, for example, his oeuvre contains sustained philosophical engagement with Hannah Arendt (Pippin 2005a: 146–67) and Christine Korsgaard (Pippin 2008: 75–85), and *The Philosophical Hitchcock* alone—in which the list of contemporary film scholars quoted above appears—makes reference to the writings of Tania Modleski, Frances Ferguson, Susan S. Levine, Elsie B. Michie, Katie Trumpener, Katalin Makkai, and Wendy Doniger. In the first chapter of *Filmed Thought* Pippin declares explicitly his belief that in most of the films he discusses "the social worlds depicted in the movie worlds are deeply poisoned by patriarchy, and the films would be far less credible if that were not acknowledged," even though this fact is not his chief focus; he claims that "the aspiration here is to suggest a philosophical framework for such a deeper interrogation," but it is not clear whether or not he thinks himself suited to be the one to conduct it (Pippin 2020a: 14).

Pippin gives a good indication of the logic of his general position on issues of representation, inclusion, and institutionalized prejudice in his response to an article on his work on Hegel by Purushottama Bilimoria. Pippin insists that he "would never dream of defending the racist and orientalist remarks Hegel made about East and South Asia and about Africa" and that this cannot be excused simply by Hegel's historical positioning; Pippin names Herder and Montesquieu as examples of "scholars and philosophers in his own and even prior ages who tried much harder than he obviously did to understand these cultures with depth and sensitivity" (2018c: 450). But he does not think that this, in and of itself, necessarily compromises any of Hegel's arguments. Therefore,

> when Bilimoria quotes [Amartya] Sen writing that "The West is seen, in effect, as having exclusive access to the values that lie at the foundation of rationality and reasoning, science and evidence,

liberty and tolerance, and of course rights and justice," then we simply need to note Hegel's error in claiming such *exclusive* access and then note that the values and practices Sen mentions are universal, wherever they appear, in whatever form. The important question concerns the content of these norms, and whether Hegel was right about that content, or whether anyone else is, from wherever in the world, at whatever time.

(ibid.: 451; emphasis in original)

Similarly—to put things excessively crudely—Pippin does not think that the fact that a director was a white man can be, in and of itself, a reason not to write about their work. It is hard to disagree with such a position. But one further potential consequence of his failure, to date, to write about any other kinds of director is that it might give the impression that his interest in the cinematic canon is more orthodoxly humanist than it is. As we have seen (particularly in Chapters 1 and 4), Pippin's interest in subjectivity does not result from a desire to dismiss the challenges presented by the likes of Nietzsche, Marx, and Freud, but rather to properly think them through. His position can nevertheless mislead even a sympathetic and perceptive commentator such as Richard Rushton, whose comment that "Pippin … cannot seem to fathom quite why thinkers have given up on the notion of subjectivity" (2013: 11) underestimates the extent to which Pippin is in sympathy with many of the reasons why they have done so, even if he thinks that such approaches are ultimately untenable. It would be a shame if Pippin's focus on canonical cinema led his readers to assume that he subscribes, for example, to a conventional view of the therapeutic and educative values of great (cinematic) art. On the contrary, one of the things he finds in one example of such art, Hitchcock's *Vertigo*, is—precisely—a satirical *attack* "on the view that one thing art can 'do' is make us better, healthier, etc." (Pippin 2017a: 95, n. 113).[4]

Cinematic Irony and Visual Style: Nicholas Ray and Douglas Sirk

In Chapter 4 we encountered Eliot Bessette's view that *Fatalism in American Film Noir* was a disappointment because, in contrast to *Hollywood Westerns and American Myth*, it did not involve enough "new close readings of the mise-en-scène and camerawork that support his political philosophical thesis" for it to manage successfully to be both "philosophically incisive and cinematically novel" (2013: 160). In that chapter I defended the view that Pippin's work on noir has a great deal to offer a philosophically inflected Film Studies, not merely a philosophy that treats films as conveniently potted examples. But the central assumption behind Bessette's evaluation was left largely undiscussed: that there are such things as "cinematically novel" close readings and that they are impossible without detailed and explicit discussion of the uniquely cinematic aspects of the films under discussion. According to such a view, a close reading of a film that made extensive reference to, say, characterization and narration but did not provide any fresh insights into at least some specific aspects of the cinematic medium such as mise-en-scène, camerawork, editing, and so forth, could never achieve the status of a truly *cinematic* criticism.

It is certainly the case that cinematic techniques, per se, are not at the heart of Pippin's philosophical readings of films. If one is looking for studies that focus primarily on such evidently cinematic phenomena as editing and camera movement, or on more borderline cases such as color or visual composition, one should look elsewhere. But is it the case that this means that Pippin's writings on film are best thought of as philosophical *rather than* cinematic? Pippin is explicit that he thinks that the specifics of cinematic style are central to the meaning of films, as are the equivalent dimensions of other visual artworks. He thinks, for example, that Thomas Elsaesser is entirely "right that the meaning of what we see in family film melodramas and especially in [Douglas] Sirk is to a great degree a matter of décor, lighting, music, camera movement, composition of frame, color and gesture" (Pippin 2020a: 125, n. 22). Similarly, he is clear that "painterly intelligibility" could very well be "interrogated" in terms of "shape, pictorial organization, color, relations among colors, solidity and weight, paint itself, brushwork, thickness, different representational regimes thematized as such, expressive tonality, elements of line and boundary, and so on" (Pippin 2015b: 324). It is true, as Pippin would I think be the first to admit, both that his discussions of films and paintings do not revolve primarily around such aspects, and that we very much need studies that *do* so revolve. But is Pippin's contrasting approach the result of simply ignoring, or at least, downplaying, such "cinematic," "painterly," medium-specific aspects?

Pippin would deny that it is. Throughout this book I have discussed instances of his attention to specifically cinematic phenomena (see, e.g., the discussion in Chapter 4 of the Dardenne brothers' positioning of the camera and the relation between editing and narration in their films), as well as noting his insistence on the importance of considering, for example, "why the camera moves and frames events one way rather than another" or "to what end a musical score signals something sad or ominous" (Pippin 2020a: 11). But simply counting references to specific cinematic phenomena is not, perhaps, the most productive path to follow; Bessette's remark, ultimately unfair as I believe it to be, does identify something important about Pippin's priorities and what kind of criticism he considers himself to be writing.

It may be that Pippin's views on this subject are somewhat obscured for some readers by the fact that he does not often aim in his writings to evoke the sensation of watching a film (a goal that has led others to some extraordinary writing but that can equally well lead to inflated purple prose that muddles rather than clarifies). What might seem the dryness of his writings is not, I want to claim, aimed at *diminishing* the sensual dimension of art but is rather an attempt to *leave space* for it, to encourage the reader to return to the film in question and really test Pippin's account against their own experience of it.[5] (This remark is not in itself a response to Bessette, merely a preliminary clarification.) Writing philosophically about film does not—or at least *should* not—aim to *replace* film in any way. This is a pitfall that attempting to conjure, in prose, the experience of watching a film is at least as open to as the kind of philosophical writing that sees films simply as examples to be chewed up and, eventually, excreted. Pippin aims for a kind of middle way, in which his writing will sharpen and refresh our attentiveness without getting in the way of the film in question.

Pippin's tendency, then, is to attend to visual meaning in a particular mode, one that follows naturally from his overarching interest in reflective form. His visual interests tend to focus, we could say, on what something *looks like* (in the sense of how it *comes across* visually, rather than what it resembles).[6] Pippin insists both that "we should never assume that one has to choose between attention to aesthetic form or attention to thematic content" and—recalling the discussion in the preceding section—that the extent to which this form and content are inseparable can be a measure of the extent to which we are dealing with "a great work of art" (2016a: 222). In narrative film, one avenue of enquiry that Pippin's work demonstrates can be very fruitful is to think in terms of what in literary studies is called free indirect discourse, or free indirect style, and thereby to see the visual qualities of a film as having a relation to the way that the film's characters see their own worlds.[7] Sirk's melodramas are a perfect case in point. As many commentators have noted, they involve an "excess emotionality [which] is expressed by an unusually intense, bright color palette in sets and clothes (again anti-illusionistic), sometimes almost garish lighting, hyper-sharp, deep focus, frequent close-ups of such expressivity [which is to say a form of expression "that is hyperbolic, excessive, overwrought"], a lush, romantic, and quite unsubtle sound track, and transparently phony, and even ominous (because phony), happy endings" (Pippin 2020a: 122) but it is also the case, thinks Pippin, that the "garishness of Sirk's presentation of such worlds always appears to suggest that this world, a clearly artificial world ... is some sort of projection of *the characters' own sense of themselves*, how *they* see themselves" (ibid.: 124–5; emphases in original).

Entertaining the possibility that visual style and our understanding of character can be connected in such a manner involves more than just enriching our sense of the ways that character is expressed in narrative films (though this is certainly interesting enough to be worth pursuing). Pippin follows the remark about Elsaesser's view of Sirk quoted above with the claim that thinking in these terms can clarify our understanding of the way intention relates to aesthetic meaning because it "helps destabilize the dualism" (2020a: 125, n. 22) between "the author's intentions expressed in what is said and done, and meaning carried more visually and ideologically" (ibid.: 123, n. 18). This "false duality" has important philosophical consequences, because it is "itself based on the assumption of a Cartesian ideology of the private, self-ownership view of individual mindedness, versus some 'outside' determination" (ibid.).[8] Too strict a distinction between the "visual" or "cinematic" aspects of a film and its "narrative," "literary," or "dramatic" aspects can, then, perpetuate the notions—all of which Pippin wants to resist—that other distinctions are also mutually exclusive. These distinctions include those between the private self and the surrounding world (so that we *either* get to determine our own actions *or* have them determined by external forces but not both; I hope Chapter 4 has begun to make it clear why Pippin thinks any such account is inadequate) or between "formalist or socio-historical" accounts of aesthetic meaning (Pippin 2018a: 377).

Examining some of Pippin's treatments of cinematic irony will help make these ideas a little more concrete. Early in his chapter in *Filmed Thought* on Douglas Sirk's *All That Heaven Allows* Pippin offers "Nicholas Ray's *Johnny Guitar*, Josef von Sternberg's *The Scarlet Empress*, and Stanley Kubrick's *Barry Lyndon*" as three further examples of "*how* a cinematic style can suggest irony," and the subsequent chapter is in fact devoted to *Johnny Guitar* (2020a: 118; emphasis in original). In Sirk's melodramas, Pippin notes, we find both visual ironies and ironies that revolve around character:

> Aside from the purely visual dimensions of irony—that dimension of artificial color, lighting, and close-up, overheated expressions of emotion—there is a more subtle dimension of such estranging irony. We see characters who sincerely avow what they believe, but who have no substantive idea about what in fact they are actually avowing, what the implications would be … or characters whose expressed self-understanding is clearly a manifestation of a self-ignorance; again, even if also sincere and well-meaning.
>
> (ibid.: 120–1)

A number of important points emerge from this. First, although Pippin fully subscribes to the view that Sirk's melodramas are deeply ironic, he does not think that to say so equates to saying that they take place, as it were, at the expense of the characters that populate them: "Unknowingness posing as knowingness can be a rich subject for irony, especially if the irony is not patronizing or mocking, as it rarely is in Sirk's films" (ibid.: 121). Once more, we need to avoid assuming the existence of an exclusive disjunction, this time between an engaged form of viewing that takes characters seriously and a distanced position that sees them as targets for irony. The behavior of Sirk's characters can serve as a vehicle for, or expression of, all sorts of ironies, without it being a naive misunderstanding of the film to *care* about those characters, as much as one might care about the characters in any narrative film.

Irony is both a particularly fascinating subject, in and of itself, and a very useful one for Pippin's purposes, then, because it demonstrates the dangers of insisting too rigidly on separating the "visual" or "cinematic" aspects of a film from its other dimensions.[9] We will not understand the way irony operates in a film like *All That Heaven Allows*—whose very title, Pippin notes, contains an ironic ambiguity (ibid.: 117)—unless we attend to the relationships between all these different forms of irony. Some of these will be particularly cinematic, while others will have more obvious continuities with the way irony operates in other art forms and, indeed, in our own daily lives. James MacDowell, whose work on irony in film Pippin cites approvingly (ibid.: 118, n. 4), very helpfully notes that "the fact that a given element may not be *exclusively* filmic need make it no less specifically so" (2016: 45; emphasis in original). MacDowell presents a nuanced and persuasive case for the importance of cinematic irony, one that dissents from Gregory Currie's distinction between images, or films, that merely *show* an ironic situation and those that actually *are* ironic forms of communication (something which for him necessarily involves a form of pretense), a distinction that leads Currie to conclude that films have a "limited palette" with which to generate irony (2010: 169). On MacDowell's view, to say so is to stipulate the nature of irony in advance rather than allow films to reveal their ironic possibilities to us; he remarks that "we will give ourselves a better chance of elucidating the nature of irony, in any medium, not by demanding that a medium satisfy our theory of ironic expression, but rather by moulding our theorising better to fit the ways a medium seems able to express itself ironically" (2016: 24–5). With, rather appropriately, a certain degree of irony, it is precisely the fact that the possibilities of cinema overlap with those of so many other forms of artistic expression—literature, visual art, drama—that enables the medium to generate its own distinct forms of irony: "film's particular ironic capacities are bound to lie precisely in this medium's ability to draw simultaneously upon the properties of many other art forms" (ibid.: 21).

Having said this, and despite his recommendation "that the pretence theory should perhaps not be our sole framework for approaching all ironic expression, regardless of medium" (ibid.: 24), MacDowell is willing to endorse Currie's notion of irony as pretense a little more extensively than I am. Pippin's studies of cinematic irony help bring out other aspects. MacDowell writes, for example, that "communicative irony usually requires some real or imagined other figure associated with the point of view that one is pretending to express," and so—for example—if someone was to look out of a window at the pouring rain and declare to their friend "What lovely weather!" this "other figure" would be "a hypothetical person who might truly misinterpret pouring rain in this fashion" (ibid.: 63). Such a figure, however, seems to me to be superfluous. The ironic effect of such remarks comes from the fact that the speaker knows, and is confident that their friend agrees, that the downpour outside is *not* an example of lovely weather. How does the friend know that the source of the remark is being ironic? Possibly, certainly, partly through tone of voice and other such features of the delivery, but chiefly because of this agreement; there is a disjunction between what is said and what is the case (it is *not*, in fact, lovely weather).[10] As Wittgenstein famously puts it in the *Philosophical Investigations* §242: "It is not only agreement in definitions, but also (odd as it may sound) agreement in judgements that is required for communication by means of language" (2009: 94). Saying "lovely weather" during a thunderstorm with a truly convincing pretense of belief would be liable to provoke puzzlement, at the very least ("What are you on about? Oh, I see, you're being ironic!").[11] It would also be just as ironic—albeit in very different ways—if someone were to say "What lovely weather!" during a thunderstorm with ironic intent, and if someone were to say "What lovely weather!" with full sincerity, a thunderstorm having erupted without their knowledge since they last looked out the window. One can certainly take up an ironic attitude towards the world or anything in it, but it is not simply a matter of picking an attitude; irony involves not only what we think about the world, but what is *actually true* about it.[12] It is, therefore, important that we recognize that, as Pippin puts it, "there are two senses of 'not meaning what one says,' the traditional understanding of irony"; there is "a knowing form" but there is also "an unknowing form" (Pippin 2020a: 162).[13] (Saying "lovely weather!" with an ironic intention is an example of the former; saying the same thing when I think the sun is shining but it is actually tipping it down could, in certain circumstances, be an instance of the latter.) Although artistically "unknowing," creatively unintended ironies—such as the fact that irony is largely absent from the lyrics of Alanis Morissette's song "Ironic," or almost everything about Tommy Wiseau's film *The Room*—are not the object of Pippin's attention, he is very interested in the fact that dramatizations of both the "knowing" and "unknowing" forms of irony are crucial to films such as *All That Heaven Allows*. Within the diegesis, characters frequently *betray* themselves ironically as well as deliberately *expressing* themselves ironically.

We may seem at this point to have moved some distance from the question of Pippin's treatment of visual and cinematic meaning, so let us try to find our way back. I will conclude this section with a discussion of some of the ironies of the conclusion of Sirk's film, but before getting there I want to briefly mention some aspects of Pippin's discussion of *Johnny Guitar*, of which irony is the main focus; the chapter in question is called "Cinematic Irony: The Strange Case of Nicholas Ray's *Johnny Guitar*." Ray's film involves, it is claimed, a knowingly ironic play with the conventions of the Western, deployed in such a manner that, as V. F. Perkins (in a piece that Pippin confesses to being "much indebted to" [2020a: 152, n. 10]) puts it, "intensification is calculated to arrive at, but not to pass, the edge of absurdity. The daring in this process constructs an aesthetic suspense that defines the film's special thrill" (2020: 360). Pippin points out a detail that is more subtle than the film's more extravagant gestures (such as the moment when the posse arrives to confront Vienna [Joan Crawford]—all dressed in funeral black—and "the arrangement starts to tip the film dangerously in the direction of dance musical" [Clayton 2015: 212]), but whose ironic functioning is comparable:

> In this film, the theme [of the "end of the West," or at least its coming transformation] is pictorially invoked, or ... rather more "cited" imagistically as a theme than straight-forwardly assumed. The presence of the images seems too "self-conscious" to be natural. For instance, over the back of the bar there is a large replica of a railroad engine—the future, it would seem. Over the entryway to the kitchen, on the other hand, there is a replica of a stagecoach.
>
> (Pippin 2020a: 148)

What Pippin points to here are examples of precisely the kind of visual ironies that MacDowell wants to claim, contra Currie, can be properly described as instances of the film *being* ironic, rather than simply depictions of situational irony (see 2016: 22–36). As Pippin repeatedly insists, we cannot understand a film without thinking not only about what it presents to its audience but *how* it presents itself. Criticism is frequently a matter of puzzling over precisely this question. Are the models of modes of transport—one representing the past, the other the future—instances of crude symbolism? Given the richness and complexity of the film as a whole—not to mention the rest of Ray's oeuvre—this seems unlikely, offering up for exploration the possibility of an ironic reading, that symbolism is being cited or referred to as much as simply being deployed. None of the above refers very specifically to cinematic devices (neither I nor Pippin have made reference to the specific angle from which the models of the train and the stagecoach are filmed, though Pippin does refer to their placement in the mise-en-scène), but it does, surely, represent a way of attending to a film *visually*—and indeed *cinematically*, because what is at issue is how *the film* shows us these model vehicles and what we are to make of it—albeit also as part of the wider network of patterns and implications that go to make up the film and its meanings.[14]

As a final example of this mode of attention, I want to look at Pippin's account of the ending of *All That Heaven Allows*, comparing and contrasting it with Andrew Klevan's account of the same (which itself draws on James MacDowell's work on the film). Sirk's film tells the story of the romance between a wealthy middle-aged widow, Cary Scott (Jane Wyman), from the town of Stoningham, and her younger, somewhat more bohemian lover Ron Kirby (Rock Hudson), who grows trees out of town. The film traces the evolution of their relationship from burgeoning love affair, via a hiatus when Cary is taken aback to be proposed to by Ron, to their engagement. But society gossip, and in particular the "cruelty and insensitivity" (Pippin 2020a: 128) with which Cary's children react to the news, prompts Cary to suggest that they live in her house, rather than the barn that Ron has been renovating with a view to them moving into it together. Ron responds that "it wouldn't work" because he "couldn't live that way," and Cary breaks off their relationship. Eventually—when Cary's children demonstrate that they don't in fact care about the reasons that they had previously offered as impossible barriers to the marriage and Cary discovers that Ron is not in fact dating the younger woman she thought he was—she returns to Ron's home, but cannot quite bring herself to knock on his door. Ron, waving to her from a hillside, falls and is seriously injured. The film ends with Ron on his sickbed, having just returned to consciousness, with Cary prepared to nurse him back to health and declaring to him that she's finally "come home." Prominent in this conclusion, and much discussed by commentators, is a deer that is visible through the large picture window that Ron has installed in the barn.

As outlined by Barbara Klinger in her book *Melodrama and Meaning* (which Pippin describes as "indispensable on the various receptions of Sirk and on the significance of that variation" [ibid.: 118,

Figure 9 *All That Heaven Allows*: an ironic conclusion?

n. 3]), responses to Sirk's melodramas varied sharply. Particularly relevant here is that for some reviewers they represented "'soap operas,' typical not only of the crass commercialism of the film industry, but also of the frightening mediocrity of a mass culture with fascist tendencies" (1996: xv), whereas for some academics—beginning in the 1970s—they were best seen as epitomizing the potential for melodrama to dramatize a "subversive relationship to the dominant ideology" (ibid.: xii). With regard to the ending of *All That Heaven Allows*, Klevan wants to reject both alternatives: "The implication of both a sentimental thesis and an oppositional rupture thesis is that the 'happy ending' is one-dimensional. The development of the window within the narrative and the characters' involvement with it within individual scenes enables the ending to be multi-dimensional" (2018: 154). Klevan notes that the deer is quite specifically delineated, being "an antlered young buck, and not a fawn or a doe. In this sense, the deer is associated with Ron who, among other things, represents sexual potency" (ibid.: 151). Pippin makes the same point about the deer's association with Ron, and—while not going as far as Pippin, who declares the film's ending "bizarre" (2020a: 125)—Klevan certainly agrees that "like a life with Ron, with whom the animal is associated, [the deer] is strange and unsettling" (2018: 150). (For Pippin, the deer seems "confused and stunned a bit, as if to remind us that Ron has no idea what he is in for, will be in the same state for some time" [2020a: 137].) But Klevan is quite clear that neither the deer nor the ending as a whole are ironic. He quotes a rhetorical question from James MacDowell, whose account of the ending aligns closely with his own: "Why, MacDowell asks, would the film want to 'ironise the putative triumph of a mode of living and set of values [i.e., Ron's] which [it] has in general ... affirmed?'" (Klevan 2018: 147).[15] For Klevan, the oddities of the ending—and in particular the deer—are not intended "to ironise, undermine, or even compromise the happiness, but rather to enrich a comprehension of what is at stake in it, or its fulfilment" (ibid.: 150). Pippin, however, although he is fully in agreement with Klevan and MacDowell that the film's ironies should not be read as simply inverting the film's surface meanings, is clear that the ending is "quite complexly ambiguous" (2020a: 129) and that "the effect of the deer" represents "a near-perfect embodiment of Sirk's unique version of cinematic irony" (ibid.: 138).

What are we to make of this divergence in readings that are otherwise united in agreement about the limitations of seeing Sirk's irony as based in what Klevan calls an "oppositional rupture thesis"? The divergence hinges on MacDowell's view, endorsed by Klevan, that Ron's way of life is itself broadly endorsed by the film; Klevan is willing to admit that "if the film has a potential problem it is that its drama is too patently diametrical, setting the good Ron against the bad Stoningham, and that neither is sufficiently complicated" (2018: 147). Just as with the deer's confusion, however, Pippin notes at various points in the film a smugness in Ron's demeanor and manner of expressing himself; his "sometimes smug and self-satisfied air' are 'the first signs of trouble with this character" (2020a: 127).[16] Indeed, although Pippin does not mention it, there is at least one hint that

Cary may be aware that Ron doesn't simply live a Thoreauvian life, but that "he preaches it, and rather self-righteously too" (ibid.: 127, n. 24). Cary is rather surprised when she first visits Ron's abode to find that he "lives in his greenhouse" (ibid.: 127). When Ron says that "it does very well for me," Cary replies: "If one likes to live in a glass house." This might indicate that his life is all too unguarded for her bourgeois sensibilities (anyone passing could look in!), but it also alludes to the proverb that those who live in glass houses shouldn't throw stones, and thereby—just possibly—suggests a knowing irony on Cary's part (which, in a further irony, Ron fails to notice). Ron isn't the kind of person to live in a glass house precisely because of his tendency to throw stones.[17]

Though I do not have space to go into the full details of Pippin's argument, the crucial point is that—although the limitations of Stoningham are too obvious for any viewer to miss, and the limitations of Ron and his world are much more subtly presented—Pippin does not agree with Klevan and MacDowell that the film endorses Ron's perspective in an unqualified manner. Instead, what Ron "never realizes is that authenticity is a cooperative or a social virtue" (ibid.: 142); he thinks that he can be authentic simply "by himself." Further, "the naïveté of Ron's sense of what authenticity requires is linked to his constant avoidance of the dialectic of dependence and independence that is often raised by the film's point of view" (ibid.: 141).[18] The richness and subtlety with which the film demonstrates this is, for Pippin, an instance of Sirk's achievement—one that he shares with "Nicholas Ray, Max Ophüls, Alfred Hitchcock, and a few others"—in producing what we might call "a politics of American emotional life" (ibid.: 144). Or, to put it another way: "The full claim would be that Sirk treats America's deepest understanding of itself, its self-narration, as a kind of melodrama" (ibid.: 130).[19] None of this means that Pippin reads the film as entirely dismissing Ron's way of life—clearly it is preferable to Stoningham in many ways—but the blinkered aspects of Ron's worldview makes possible the various ironies with which the film concludes. These ironies concern Ron's affinities with the deer at the end of the film and what the film hints about the future of his relationship with Cary, a relationship which only begins to be repaired when he is rendered entirely the passive partner.

In arguing this, Pippin never attempts to attend to the film's visuality in separation from all the other aspects of its construction, but neither does he ignore the cinematic specificity of the film's meanings. Pippin may not be the critic to turn to for an exhaustive analysis of, say, editing patterns, but his claims are thoroughly grounded in cinematic detail; Michael Wood is quite right to say that very few philosophers writing on film have "written with so long and so close an attention to individual films" (Pippin 2020a: back cover).[20] The details of *All That Heaven Allows* on which Pippin builds his interpretation are variously conveyed: Cary's (possibly) ironic reference to glass houses is expressed verbally; Ron's smugness comes across both through verbal content, tone of voice, and facial expression; the deer's lostness and its connection to Ron are indicated entirely visually. Recalling once more MacDowell's point that "the fact that a given element may not be *exclusively* filmic need make it no less specifically so" (2016: 45; emphasis in original), it is ultimately via the relationships between these and many other details that what I, like Pippin, would insist on calling the film's cinematic ironies are generated.

"Continental" and "Analytic" Film-Philosophy

Distinctions that do not overlap neatly within philosophy more generally are sometimes taken, within film-philosophy, to be—at least roughly—equivalent. For example, the label of "analytic" film-philosophy is applied chiefly to forms of cognitivism (note the existence of the Cognitive/Analytic Scholarly Interest Group within the Society for Cinema and Media Studies), while "continental" work is taken to refer largely to post-structuralist or, increasingly, phenomenological approaches.[21] Or, to take another example, analytic work is seen as having a focus on clarity, rigor, and evidence while continental approaches are associated with abstract, quasi-literary prose. Pippin is a philosopher whose chief interest is in that most continental of philosophers, namely Hegel; and after all, "one can make a good case that this supposedly divergent tradition began with Hegel and his influence on later European philosophy" (Pippin 2011: 3). But Pippin's work is equally distant from either cognitivism or post-structuralism, and his prose is both extremely clear and argumentatively rigorous. Jensen Suther has argued that *Hegel's Realm of Shadows*, Pippin's recent book on Hegel's *Logic*, as well as making "evident contributions to Hegel scholarship, engaging as it does with a host of analytical idealists, from McDowell to Brandom to Houlgate to Longuenesse," can also be considered "a crucial philosophical intervention in critical theory with radical implications for our understanding of social critique" (2020: 97). The impossibility of fitting Pippin's work neatly into one camp or another is as true of his work in film-philosophy as it is of his more purely philosophical work. As one of the reviewers of the initial proposal for this book put it, "Pippin is a unique figure in the realm of film philosophy, somebody who does not fit neatly into any of the established academic camps."[22] As we have seen, he is as happy to draw on the work of George Wilson as of Theodor W. Adorno. The last section of this chapter aims to demonstrate some ways in which trying to situate Pippin's work might productively muddy the waters of film-philosophical classification, thereby offering some suggestions of ways that future philosophical work on film might avoid being straightjacketed by categories.

As is evident in phenomena such as the increasing levels of interest in Hegel among analytic philosophers, there are as many reasons for wanting to break down the distinction between analytic and continental philosophy as there are for recognizing that it points to some genuinely important divergences. (The two sets of reasons come together rather entertainingly in the fact that Michael Thompson draws extensively on Hegel's philosophy, while still feeling the need to declare that Hegel employs "a completely indefensible form of expression in writing" [2008: 12].) Maintaining a rigid distinction is, therefore, unhelpful; the terms "analytic" and "continental" are best thought of as having heuristic value rather than as marking fundamental differences. Some, like Robert Sinnerbrink, have argued that we might try to do without them entirely, replacing them with the terms *rationalist* and *romanticist*:

> Rationalist approaches to theory seek to provide explanatory models of various aspects of film experience. They elaborate empirically grounded models of our experience of moving images, of film ontology, of how we understand film narrative, and so on. Romanticist approaches, for their part, seek to reflect upon, interpret, or extend the kind of aesthetic experience that film evokes. They seek not only to explain and comprehend but to question and understand the significance of film experience; they search for apt ways of expressing this aesthetic experience in a philosophical discourse that aims to elucidate and thus deepen our understanding of film.
>
> (Sinnerbrink 2011: 7–8)

The proposal is attractive, and certainly Pippin's work is much closer to Sinnerbrink's "romanticist" category, but I have reservations. There is at the very least a problem of terminology, given that Pippin—like Hegel before him—is a card-carrying rationalist and certainly not—once again, just like Hegel—any kind of romanticist. Pippin is, though, indubitably signed up to Sinnerbrink's advocacy of an approach (I think Pippin might be reluctant to call it a "thesis"; see, e.g., ibid.: 123–32) whose "validity ... rests less on general theoretical arguments than on robust and detailed philosophical film criticism" (ibid.: 10).

Nevertheless, for all their limitations, the sheer regularity with which the "analytic" and "continental" labels are used can be helpful. How might they help us see where Pippin's work fits among other contemporary approaches to the philosophical study of film? What avenues for future study does that work suggest? One simple suggestion is that it might remind us that cognitivist philosophy is not the only sort of analytic philosophy that could be productively brought to bear on the study of film. It would be fascinating to see more works on film that engage with the likes of Anscombe, McDowell, Brandom, and so on, and Pippin's work might provide some inspiration in this regard. That work might also serve as a valuable point of contact with the various ways that the distinction between the analytic and the continental is coming under pressure in philosophy more generally. Pippin's anti-Cartesian account of subjectivity—which we have seen him put to work throughout his writings on film, albeit most prominently in *Fatalism in American Film Noir*—stands at least a chance of putting him in good stead with both camps. After all, Heidegger's *Being and Time* and Gilbert Ryle's *The Concept of Mind* are equally hostile to Cartesianism. But Pippin's Hegelianism could potentially have the opposite effect; if there is one thing that links a great many—perhaps even the majority—of analytic and continental philosophers, it is their hostility to Hegel! Despite the fact that resistance to his work can be seen as having given rise to the analytic/continental division in the first place, a list of those philosophers who "considered Hegel their chief opponent" (namely "Marx, Adorno, Derrida, Lyotard, and Levinas," as well as Schelling, Kierkegaard, Heidegger, Deleuze, Bataille, and Foucault; see Pippin [2019c: 350]) contains a great many of the figures most influential in Continental film-philosophy,[23] while for the analytic branch, of course, Hegel has often seemed to be the epitome of impenetrable armchair-based system building. Admittedly, this hostility to Hegel now appears in many philosophical quarters to be diminishing; more attention to Hegel in all the various branches of film-philosophy would contribute to this welcome development, as well as interestingly recontextualizing some of the field's orienting assumptions.

John Mullarkey (now John Ó Maoilearca) advocates a deliberate catholicity of approach in the face of the whirl of competing approaches to film-philosophy. He notes that "what frequently claim to be 'open' readings of film as philosophy still remain prefigured philosophical interpretations" (Mullarkey 2009: 4) and recommends "that film-philosophy should be catholic rather than puritan, a messy mix of methodologies and eclectic, random examples, rather than exemplars that illustrate one's point perfectly" (ibid.: 6). Though he would use different language, Pippin would be quite in sympathy with the claim that "film doesn't reflect (illustrate, illuminate or represent) our philosophy—it refracts it, it distorts it with its own thinking" (ibid.: 11). But the very interesting and lucid book in which these remarks appear does not include any extended, detailed close readings of films. Cavell and Pippin both insist that for film truly to have the chance to "refract" and "distort" philosophy in productive ways one needs to get as close as possible, for a sustained period, to the film or films in question, and to their details.[24] In many ways Cavell—whose work also has a very complex relationship to the analytic and continental traditions—is, indeed, Pippin's closest film-philosophical precursor. Fundamentally, *theory* links both analytic and continental approaches; the lion's share of work in film-philosophy, of whatever tradition, has assumed that it is the job of philosophical work on film to provide a theory of film. Ó Maoilearca does not consider that film might have a relationship to philosophy that is not based on theory but, as we saw in Chapter 1, Pippin believes that this *is* possible. But this need not imply that his work is incompatible with theory. It might well be very fruitful to explore the compatibilities and incompatibilities between Pippin's *readings* and a variety of film-philosophical *theories*. What kinds of frictions and resonances might we find between Pippin's work and, say, Deleuze's taxonomy of "movement-images," "time-images," and so forth (2005a and 2005b)? Does Pippin simply concentrate on the movement-image or does his work challenge the way Deleuze draws the distinction? Such questions are very interesting, and if I have not chosen to address them in this book, that is because Pippin's nontheoretical practice of film-philosophy is sufficiently unusual to merit sustained exposition and interrogation on its own terms.[25]

It is, then, this orientation away from theory-building toward giving sustained, detailed, and accurate accounts of individual films and the way they work through philosophical questions that ultimately distinguishes Pippin's film-philosophical work as much from Deleuze's writings as from, say, Gregory Currie's, and marks his affinity with Cavell who, as Charles Bernstein has put it, "was not interested in theory but in thought" (epigram to LaRocca 2020). There is, admittedly, a large dose of the polemical in this remark (with its implication that theory need not, or often does not, involve thought), and Pippin tends in general to avoid the polemical sparring that has marred much discussion of the relationships between different forms of philosophy, or film-philosophy. That being said, we are not dealing with bland platitudes of the "can't we all just get along" variety. As Pippin clearly articulates, philosophical approaches to film that *do* focus on the construction of theories "need not be considered a competitor" to his preferred approach of "concentration on a cinematic treatment of a complicated philosophical problem," but, instead, "something simply different," even if "there will inevitably be some disagreement" (2019a: 540).

Where do we find examples of "something simply different," and where more emphatic "disagreement"? Despite Pippin's dissatisfaction with philosophical naturalism—because it does not, for him, adequately account for the normativity of the reasons a subject takes to be motivating—I see, for example, little (or at least less than one might have expected) that Pippin would disagree within a piece such as Murray Smith's "'The Pit of Naturalism': Neuroscience and the Naturalized Aesthetics of Film" (2014).[26] But the divergence of priorities can be seen in the final section of the article. One of the subjects of the chapter is the role of the startle response in our viewing of films. Smith asks what we can learn from neuroscience that we couldn't learn from "reflection on our experience, [or] exploration of the practices and discussions of filmmakers" (ibid.: 41). He wonders how, for example, "learning and cultural context ... bear upon the role of the startle response in our experience of films?" (ibid.). But the succeeding final eight hundred words of the article make no more reference to films; everything they say applies to the general value of the neurosciences, not to their specific relationship to our understanding of films and their operation.

Another chapter in the same volume in which Smith's piece appears sets out explicitly to demonstrate the value of cognitivist film theory "with respect to the illumination of individual movies," taking as its test case the very same film Pippin's reading of which we examined in the introduction, namely Hitchcock's *Rear Window* (Seeley and Carroll 2014: 236). William Seeley and Noël Carroll make use of terms (familiar from Carroll's work elsewhere) such as "indexing," "scaling," and "bracketing" that are potentially very helpful in articulating the ways that Hitchcock's film engages and directs the attention of its viewers. The chapter proposes that "one may construe *Rear Window* as a self-conscious model for an entire class of movie making and thus a perfect opportunity to display the explanatory power of cognitivism" (ibid.: 237). In doing so it neglects the question of what Pippin calls reflective form, presumably because its argument is aimed at generalizability. The chapter's method encourages takings things at face value, which is conducive to clarity but also risks banality: "narrative expectations about what we currently cannot see outside the bracket of the camera give life and pressing significance to particular narrative possibilities, increasing the level of suspense in the scene" (ibid.: 244). The chapter does not, therefore, consider Pippin's idea that the film might be taken as a *negative* model for spectatorship, for the *wrong* way of watching a film. Still, much of what is in the chapter could simply be supplemented by attention to the way we are shown things, their tonal or ironic aspects; we could say that Seeley and Carrol give a helpful account of the film's surface form, putting us is in a better position to explore its reflective dimensions. Sometimes, though, "disagreement" is broached: compare the claim that at the end of the film "Lisa and Jeff are closer than ever before" and that "the narrative comes to an end, or achieves *closure*" (these two possibilities being treated as equivalent) with the discussion of the end of *Rear Window* that closes the introduction to this book (ibid.: 242; emphasis in original).

Having very briefly considered Pippin's relationship to two "analytic" examples, do we find more congruence with "continental" circles? The answer, in some ways, is no. Pippin has had an interesting and ongoing exchange with the thinker who is probably the most famous continental film-philosopher working today, namely Slavoj Žižek. The meat of this exchange, however, revolves not around films but around the interpretation of Hegel, concerning which Pippin finds much to approve, as well as some areas of profound disagreement: "there is nothing more un-Hegelian than the idea of the 'emergence of the pure drive beyond fantasy'" (2015a: 113). But despite the fact that he has some spiky criticisms to make of Pippin's philosophical views, there is something almost suspiciously enthusiastic in the way that Žižek responds to Pippin's writings on film. In his book *Absolute Recoil*, Žižek refers to *Fatalism in American Film Noir* in entirely positive terms. He refers to Pippin's "perspicuous readings" and appears to endorse them without reservation; there is not a single detail he wishes to challenge or reinterpret (Žižek 2014: 318). One wonders whether Žižek has really let the films themselves, as we earlier saw Ó Maoilearca recommend, "refract" and "distort" his thinking.[27]

There are, however, certainly debates within continental philosophy which Pippin's work on film bears on directly; I will offer a single example. J. M. Bernstein has attacked Pippin's *After the Beautiful* because "in place of all the detailed structural analyses of reification, alienation, rationalization, illusory identification, bureaucratization, and so on that tie subjective mortification to the social forms producing it (operating through individuals but behind their backs), Pippin suggests the 'starkness' or 'nakedness' of relations of independence or dependence as the deep issue"; Bernstein sees this as a "dismissal of the sociology of modernity" that is "hard to fathom" (2017: 203). In his discussion of *Vertigo*, however, Pippin talks in terms of a past in which, as Pop Leibel (Konstantin Shayne) says, "a man could do that in those days," by which he means throw away a mistress and keep a child. (The issue is made more complicated—is, one might say, mythologized—because this account of "those days" is both in some ways accurate and also matches a fantasy of Elster's, a fantasy of a time when he wouldn't have needed to bother with the pretense that generates the film's plot.) In the modern world of the film, however, "the same kind of hierarchy still exists, only in a *more disguised, less openly brutal*, but now quite manipulative way" (Pippin 2017a: 54; my emphasis). It is, I think, only apparently contradictory that Pippin can claim this while also insisting that modernity involves the "emergence of a logic of social subjectivity in which the starkness or nakedness of relations of independence and dependence is ever more visible" (2014: 60). Modernity involves both new forms of laying bare and new modes of concealment, and films can help us investigate how on earth this can be the case.[28] I think Pippin would want his claims about, for example, social pathology and political psychology to be read in relation to precisely the kind of "sociology of modernity" that Bernstein refers to. Perhaps the Dardenne brothers' films show some of the ways the "logic of social subjectivity" has become visible, while Hitchcock concentrates on how it still gets concealed or repressed.

Ultimately, however, rather than any explicitly philosophical work on film—with the possible exception of Cavell, whose prose is much more consistently dense and sustainedly self-referential than Pippin's—the writing that Pippin aspires to come closest to in texture and intent is, I suggest, that of V. F. Perkins, to whose memory *The Philosophical Hitchcock* is dedicated. Pippin's writings bring out the ways that the kind of patient, attentive, and reflective criticism that Perkins dedicated himself to *is* philosophical, despite the lack of explicit claims to such a status—and, indeed, some explicit claims that could be read as tending towards the contrary. One of these touches on the issues of obviousness and concealment that were touched on in the previous paragraph, but in terms of the function of film criticism rather than the philosophical analysis of modernity. In a passage that I also quoted from in my introduction, Perkins writes that in discussing some aspects of Max Ophüls's *Caught*, he was writing "about things that I believe to be in the film for all to see, and to see the sense of" (2020: 248). We might, however, be fully willing to grant that interpretation "is not an attempt to clarify what the picture has obscured" (ibid.) and yet still wonder: if both the "things" and their "sense" are truly there for *all* to see, why is it worth taking the trouble to point them out in prose? Pippin suggests an answer. He observes that "cinematic conviction can be at least temporarily created for any sort of content," but that we cannot simply rest there; we need to examine this "conviction" and its grounds (Pippin 2016b). As a consequence, "it cannot be the film alone that should be said to be the bearer of some sort of philosophical intelligibility, but the film and the 'reading' it is given, a reading which, because articulate, can both be disputed as a reading and as a claim on our moral attention"(ibid.).[29] It is largely because we can *disagree*—in good faith—with what another might see as present in a film "for all to see, and to see the sense of" that philosophical readings of films need attempt neither to "translate" films directly into words, nor to co-opt films into alien realms of thought. They should, instead, provoke their readers both to return to the films themselves and to carry on the conversation about them; Pippin's position is that both activities can be richly philosophical.

Afterword: On the Nonexistence of Pippinian Film-Philosophy

In Chapter 2, we encountered Pippin's view that Howard Hawks deliberately risks a kind of bathos at the end of *Red River*. I also want to end this book with a claim that might initially appear to partake of the bathetic, even though I think it is one of the reasons Pippin's work is so stimulating: that there is no such thing as "Pippinian film-philosophy."

***

One chapter of novelist and critic David Lodge's book *Consciousness and the Novel* has a title that neatly fits the span of Pippin's writing on the arts: "Henry James and the Movies." Pippin's first book not explicitly covering philosophical texts was his book on Henry James (2000a) and, as we have seen, he has also written five books on film, making cinema the art form to which he has, to date, dedicated the most published material.[1] Lodge claims to see the relationship between James's achievement and that of the movies very differently from Pippin. He writes that the kind of consciousness that James excels in delineating, "which is self-consciousness, is precisely what film as a medium finds most difficult to represent, because it is not visible" (2002: 202–3). We have seen throughout this book that Pippin does not believe this to be the case, and that films can represent self-consciousness with enormous degrees of subtlety and can also be said to be themselves self-conscious, in the sense that the most philosophically interesting films have a reflective form. This simply means that these films require viewers to consider both *what* they present and *how* they present it, *what* they do and *why* they do it in the ways they do. It is, therefore, reasonable to think of some films as examples of, as the title of one of Pippin's books has it, *Filmed Thought*.

It is not clear that either Lodge's criteria or his judgments are entirely consistent. He declares ambiguity to be a failing in one screen adaptation of James—"It is not at all clear whether ... " (ibid.: 207)—even though he seems to value James's novels in part precisely for their "obscurity" and "ambiguity" (ibid.: 202). But toward the end of his piece, it comes to seem that Lodge's problem of adaptations of James to the screen has nothing to do with the properties of the two forms—novel and film—but are more to do with the fact that he thinks that some of the adaptations are simply not very good. When Lodge encounters the Merchant-Ivory version of *The Golden Bowl* he is very impressed, claiming that "the Master would not be displeased by this thoughtful and carefully crafted film" (ibid.: 233). But it is not at all clear how the film avoids what earlier seemed to be the crippling limitations of film. As arguably the apex of James's deeply psychological late style, the novel is certainly no less psychological than the others discussed. We read that *The Golden Bowl* is "extremely well cast, and James Ivory has drawn from his performers ensemble acting of a very high order" (ibid.: 229).[2] In fact, "all are adept at acting with their eyes, implying layers of unspoken thoughts" (ibid.: 230), which seems almost entirely to undercut a claim that Lodge makes at the beginning of his piece, namely that "facial expression, body language, visual imagery, and music can all be powerfully expressive, but they lack precision and discrimination. They deal in broad basic emotions: fear, desire, joy. James's fiction, by contrast, is full of the finest, subtlest psychological discriminations" (ibid.: 203).

It seems to me that Lodge is misled by trying to find exact equivalence between scenes in the novels and scenes in the films; he considers anything lacking in the film, compared with the corresponding scene in the novel, as demonstrating a failing or a limitation of the medium. But it is also the case that he finds himself persuaded out of his original argument—though he does not acknowledge that this is what has happened—not by reconsidering his argument, per se, but by really *attending to*, and finding himself *convinced by*, a particular film. Pippin's response would, I suspect, be that novels and films are capable of equal richness, even if the virtues of one *specific* example can't be translated directly into another art form. That the film of *Portrait of a Lady* fails to achieve everything that the novel achieves—in terms of psychology—does not mean that another film could not achieve a comparable *level* of psychological achievement, one that itself could not be "translated" into, say, a novel without loss and alteration. As we earlier saw James MacDowell rightly claim, "the fact that a given element may not be *exclusively* filmic need make it no less specifically so" (2016: 45; emphasis in original). The same is true of the *achievements* of either medium. Gilberto Perez writes that he "takes film to be a medium poised between drama and narrative, between enactment and mediation," and makes a powerful case for such a view, one that resonates with Pippin's views on film narration, outlined in Chapter 1 (1998: 16). We might take this to be a unique, or at least a distinctive, value of film as a medium. But James, in his preface to *The Wings of the Dove*, discovers a suggestively similar relationship in his novels between what he calls "picture" and "drama." He discusses this relationship in terms that, to me, cry out for an exploration of their relevance to film, as ways of stimulating deeper exploration of the way that, as Perez puts it, film is "poised." James writes of "the odd inveteracy with which picture, at almost any turn, is jealous of drama, and drama (though on the whole with a greater patience, I think) suspicious of picture" (1986: 43). Therefore, having claimed in Chapter 6 that Pippin's film philosophy is emphatically *film-philosophy* (as well as film-*philosophy*), I want to now risk at least the appearance of contradiction. If it is true that Pippin practices *film*-philosophy in the sense that his work is attentive to film as films (as V. F. Perkins recommended), it is not the case that he thinks this entails hermetically sealing film off from other aspects of our lives, whether aesthetic, romantic, political, or otherwise. Indeed, we are not truly responding to narrative films *as films* if we try to do so. This means that much of what we find in films—such as dynamic tensions between "drama and narrative," or between "picture ... and drama"—we might also find (in different ways) in novels, or indeed in our everyday lives. I want to therefore say that while in one sense Pippin's film-philosophy very much deserves that name, in another sense it is simply part of his broader practice of philosophy, period.[3]

I also want to claim that it is not best thought of as "Pippinian," as launching a brave new subgenre of philosophical possibility complete with its own jargon and hot topics. Much of the philosophical excitement of Pippin's work on film lies in the fresh ways in which it reconnects films to some of the central texts in modern European philosophy; his reinterpretations of films go hand in hand with his reinterpretations of Hegel, Nietzsche, and others. If there is a sense that much (though by no means all!) of Pippin's writings on film boil down to an exploration of the account of agency and normativity set forward in *Hegel's Practical Philosophy* (albeit with its relevance to the sociality and moral psychology of modernity always to the fore), this is not a failing. Fleshing out a philosophical account is a different kind of project than simply illustrating a set of theses, let alone applying or—worse—forcing a set of theoretical propositions onto a group of films. Pippin finds films so valuable in fleshing out his Hegelian account of agency precisely because of how much there is for us to learn *from* (and not only *about*) films—hence the repeated references in this book to the centrality, for Pippin, of the ways in which we are *convinced* by a film, or find what it shows us to be *credible*.[4] Given that it is so often assumed in film studies—as in literary studies—that attending to character and narrative in ways that relate to how we attend to other people in our real lives (politically, ethically, psychologically) must involve being naïve, ignorant, uninformative, or misleading, or entail ignoring the truly "cinematic" aspects of films, only an extensive demonstration that this need not be true is likely to have any success. Such a demonstration is precisely what Pippin's writing on film offers its readers.

***

Despite the centrality of Hegel's thought to Pippin's work, which I hope this book has articulated, I have mainly chosen not to quote from him directly, in large part because of his famously challenging prose. But it is appropriate to close with Hegel, however fleetingly. It is, it seems to me, still the case, as the epigraph to this book claims, that the attempt to employ "fixed and determinate thoughts" in the service of "actualizing and spiritually animating the universal" seems much more promising—and pressing—than any project of "purifying the individual of the sensuously immediate" (Hegel 2018: 21).[5] Cinematic cognitivists and phenomenologists, for all their differences, are in agreement that getting rid of the "sensuously immediate" would be quite the wrong path to follow; one could make the case that the Althusserian and Lacanian studies of film that are regularly lumped together as "1970s film theory" too often fell into the trap of doing so. But this does not mean that, despite the persistence of claims to the contrary, "the sensuously immediate"—either purely *qua* "sensuously immediate" or as the generator of cognitive activity in the viewer—is the only proper object of the contemporary philosophical study of film.[6] The position that this book has defended is that as far as the detailed philosophical study of agency and self-consciousness as manifest in individual films is concerned (an activity which is a form of "animating the universal" in Hegel's sense), nobody has achieved such an "actualization" with greater precision, elegance, or suggestiveness than Robert B. Pippin.

Notes

Introduction: "I'm Just Trying to Understand the Goddamn Film"

1 The last of these was published as this book was being completed, and thus it receives less thorough coverage here than Pippin's other works on film. A version of its chapter on *All That Heaven Allows* is, however, also included in Pippin (2020a) and is discussed here in Chapter 6.
2 This is not to say that Pippin would by any means dispute the helpfulness of the philosophy Klevan examines here, only that his practice demonstrates that non-theoretical philosophy is not the *only* kind of philosophy that can be of use to a non-theoretical film-philosophy. Indeed, Pippin has explicitly expressed his interest in the kind of ordinary language philosophy to which Klevan is referring. See Pippin (2018d), where he argues that the point is not to avoid all claims of any generality, but rather to challenge "'the rage for generality' at work in theory" (2018d: n.p.). James Zborowski elegantly expresses the heart of the issue when he writes that he is not convinced that the "best route" by which Film Studies might achieve "precision in its accounts of its objects of study" is to pursue "the generation of a set of categories which offer a means of framing (one might go so far as to say 'pre-empting') our encounter with any conceivable instance of narrative fiction film" (2016: 111). Better, instead, to think of theoretical categories as "places to begin, rather than places to end" (ibid.: 113).
3 To say this is, of course, by no means to accuse Pippin of philosophical prejudice! Indeed, despite its focus on European thought, the work of, e.g., English and American philosophers including Elizabeth Anscombe, Robert Brandom, John McDowell, and Bernard Williams has had a profound impact on Pippin's work.
4 The recent shift in attitude is in no small measure due to Pippin's influence; Paul Redding writes that "Pippin's work can surely be counted as among the most successful and influential attempts to challenge the implicit picture of Hegel" that led to his "generalised dismissal from the analytic perspective" (2018: 356).

5 For some, this is best thought of as a *rediscovery*. The theologian Nicholas Lash argues that the idea that "human nature is as much a project as it is a given fact" is originally a *pre*modern notion that has been obscured by the legacy of Descartes and modern science (2008: 67). While fully acknowledging the influence of Aristotle on Hegel, Pippin would deny that Hegel identified "what happened with what must be so" (ibid.: 63), and argue that Hegel's modernity lies in the way he connects subjectivity with the development of autonomy, with the "historical novelty" of the idea of the "struggle to actualize a free life for all" (Pippin 2008: 281). See Chapter 1 for more on autonomy.

6 Pippin notes that "Bordwell is, in general, skeptical" about precisely the sense of interpretation that he wishes to defend (2012: 107, n. 3).

7 It seems to me that a similar point lies behind some of the resistance to Stanley Cavell's ideas about the ontology of film. What Cavell means by ontology can only be pursued by thinking about concrete instances of film viewing, whereas what some of his opponents understand as ontology can be investigated by exploring the nature of the cinematic medium itself, in the absence of much—if any—reflection on (the experience of) specific films. On this point see Shuster (2017: 33).

8 A concise and helpful discussion of similar ideas with relation to art in general, rather than film in particular, can be found in Pippin (2021b: 69–73).

9 Pippin believes a certain agnosticism regarding the specifics of such a position is possible: "I don't mean to be taking a position on auteur theory as such; only to be indulging the useful fiction of an imputed governing intelligence behind the aesthetic decisions. If elements in the film cannot be made to fit an interpretation controlled by such an imputation, then we have to look elsewhere for explanation—to the studio's interference, for example. But we should exhaust the first possibility before we do so" (2012: 107, n. 1). In fact, I see no reason why "the studio" might not be part of what gives rise to the sense of a film's "governing intelligence." The logic of Pippin's position—which seems to me sound—is that the aesthetic, interpretational question of the extent to which a film can be judged in terms of what Pippin calls its "reflective form" are distinct from the empirical facts of its production and authorship. This is not to say that the latter may not usefully

impinge on or inform our view of the former but only that they do not *necessarily* do so in every case.

10 One possibility would be to repurpose some terminology of Robert Brandom and distinguish between directorial intentions *de dicto* (what the director, we might say, *intended their film to intend*) and filmic intentions *de re* (whatever self-conception we can actually discover in the finished film); see Brandom (2002: 94–107). For Pippin, the former are mostly of interest insofar as they help to establish the latter, whereas for historically or empirically minded scholars of a different stripe, the latter are often primarily useful to the extent that they can serve as evidence for the former. Cf. this remark by Brandom: "So long as one is explicit about what sort of methodology one is pursuing ... assessments of the *legitimacy* of one approach or another should give way to assessments of their hermeneutic *fruitfulness*: the sort of understanding they yield" (ibid.: 117; emphases in original).

11 This example neatly indicates the limitations of Bordwell's distinction, cited earlier, between comprehension and interpretation. What Pippin call's Jeff's "maladroit" interpretations are not the result of engaging in unwarranted interpretations of some solid facts; it comes about because his interpretive habits cause him *not to comprehend* those facts. It is his treatment of "apparent, manifest, or direct meanings"—not "hidden, nonobvious meanings"—that is at fault (Bordwell 1989: 2).

12 After spotting the flash, I found a few mentions of it on the internet but no discussions in the critical literature. See, e.g., http://chrissturhann.blogspot.com/2017/07/flash-in-upstairs-rear-window-apartment.html (last accessed July 17, 2020).

13 Although I referred earlier to a "lingering auteurism" in Pippin's thinking, if auteurism is taken to mean prioritizing the patterns of a director's body of work over the interpretation of any individual film, then Pippin is certainly not an auteurist critic; he would, I am sure, concur with V. F. Perkins's claims that "it is necessary to observe a distinction between auteurism and other practices of director-centered criticism" and that auteurisms tend to display an "exaggerated concern with the continuities and coherence across the body of a director's work" (2020: 220).

14 See Chapter 6 for more on Pippin and cinematic irony.

1 Modernism, Self-Consciousness, and Film

1 A helpful, if very brief, survey of Pippin's view of the historical details can be found in Pippin (1999: 16–22). On the notion of the "break," it might also be useful to say that it is crucial for Pippin that modernity is *both* a form of self-understanding (the way some participants in a historical period understood, or understand, that period) *and* an—at least partially—accurate account. On the latter point, see Pippin's rhetorical rejoinder to Stephen Toulmin's doubts: "Can so much in the success of the projects of [Descartes and Hobbes] be accounted for by reference to a kind of hysterical quest for certainty generated by social, economic and military crises?" (ibid.: 185, n. 7). The form of this view has many resonances with Pippin's notion of narrative film as a reflective form, as a medium that both presents and reflects on—takes up an attitude towards—what it presents. This will become clearer during the course of this book.

2 Alternatively, one could say that the distinction concerns "a 'logical' or categorical issue about the natural and the normative, or as [American philosopher Wilfrid] Sellars first formulated it, the space of causes and the space of reasons" (Pippin 2008: 236). This said, in the often complex and sometimes fractious philosophical debates about the relationship between causes and reasons, Pippin does not seem to belong to the camp that wants to draw an *absolute* distinction between them. He is quite happy to accept that things such as "a desire, or respect for the moral law" can be said to cause an action (Pippin 1997: 428), and—although he might want to argue about some of the details—he would not, I think, fundamentally dispute the claim by Jonathan Lear (with whose account of individuality as something best seen "as a social and psychological achievement" [cf. 1990, chapter 6; and Pippin 2005b: 184, n. 24] he is fully in sympathy) that "a hermeneutic account of human motivation and action may also be causal" (Lear 1990: 49, n. 36).

3 For Pippin, it is Hegel who most thoroughly and radically thinks through the implications of this claim. In this regard Hegel "can sound so extravagant, I want to claim, because he is not, as it were, hedging any bets, because his enterprise stands as one of the most rigorous attempts to avoid completely any form of 'dogmatism' or what

would later be called (in the Critical Theory tradition) 'positivism.' The Hegelian experiment, we might call it, involves entertaining and thinking through the view that, in accounting for the fundamental elements of a conceptual or evaluative scheme, there is and can be no decisive or certifying appeal to any basic 'facts of the matter,' foundational experiences, logical forms, constitutive 'interests,' 'prejudices,' or guiding 'intuitions' to begin or end any such account. We can appeal only to what we have come to regard as a basic fact or secure method or initial, orienting intuition" (Pippin 1997: 163).

4 This passage should not, incidentally, be taken as suggesting that Pippin would dispute the "twofoldness" of aesthetic experience as proposed in the work of Richard Wollheim on the perception of visual art. According to Wollheim, 'I can simultaneously be visually aware of the y that I see in x and the sustaining features of this perception' (2015: 142). See the following paragraph. (This kind of "twofoldness" should, incidentally, be strictly distinguished from the idea of perception as a "two-stage" or "two-step" process, which—as we shall see in the next section of this chapter—Pippin does strongly dispute.)

5 A comment on Pippin's relationship to Arthur Danto is in order, given that Danto is, as Dan Yacavone has reminded me, "by far the most influential Anglo-American philosopher of art to make Hegel central to his reflections on modernism, post-modernism, self-consciousness" (personal communication). In Pippin's view, Danto's story of art becoming ever more abstract and self-referential (as in conceptual art)—culminating in the disappearance of the very distinction between art and non-art—is not Hegel's story: "Hegel's claim about the *end of art mattering in the way it always had* is not a claim about the 'end of art' in Danto's sense (about the end of the purchase *of the category of art*, of the art/nonart distinction)" (2005a: 282, n. 1; emphases in original). Whatever the strengths and weaknesses of Danto's account on its own terms, Pippin believes that "a great number of issues are confused by Danto's invoking Hegel" with regard to the distinction between art and non-art (ibid.; see also Pippin 2014: 70–2).

6 Compare some of Wittgenstein's remarks about faces in the *Philosophical Investigations* in, e.g., §285 ("the description of facial expressions ... does not consist in giving the measurements of the

face!") and §537 ("one might say, courage *fits* this face. But *what* fits *what* here?") (2009: 105, 153; emphases in original).
7 Compare Murray Smith's discussion of Wollheim's "twofoldness," in which he emphasizes its 'normative aspect' and observes that "judging a depiction to be *realistic* is not at all like mistaking it for a *real scene*, because our awareness of the differentiated surface runs alongside—is a part of the same experience as—our awareness of what is depicted" (2011: 291; emphases in original).
8 The famous paragraph of the B text (1787) of Kant's *Critique of Pure Reason* is B131–3.
9 As Pippin is very fond of quoting, in the *Science of Logic* Hegel writes that "it is one of the profoundest and truest insights to be found in the Critique of Reason that the *unity* which constitutes the *essence of the concept* is recognized as the *original synthetic* unity *of apperception*, the unity of the '*I think*,' or of self-consciousness" (2010: 515; emphases in original). In fact, despite the novelty of Kant's insight, this idea has ancient roots. Aristotle was clear that although "when we perceive we are aware that we perceive" and "when we contemplate we are aware that we are contemplating," in neither case do we "require a separate mental faculty which has mind actively thinking as its object" (Lear 1988: 131–2).
10 Wittgenstein explores similar issues in the *Investigations*: "But how is it possible to *see* an object according to an *interpretation*?" (2009: 211; emphases in original). And cf. Richard Wollheim's gloss on Wittgenstein, according to which "the fundamental point in Wittgenstein's argument … is that, when I see x as f, f permeates or mixes into the perception: the concept does not stand outside the perception, expressing an opinion or conjecture on my part about x, and which the perception may be said to support to this or that degree" (2015: 147).
11 Arthur Danto speculates that "perhaps films are like consciousness is as described by Sartre with two distinct, but inseparable, dimensions, consciousness of something as its intentional object, and a kind of non-thetic consciousness of the consciousness itself: and it is with reference to the latter that the intermittent reminders of the cinematic processes as such are to be appreciated," but does not pursue the Kantian/Hegelian point about apperception: "We are aware of the world and seldom aware, if at all, of the *special way* in which we are aware of the

world" (2006: 111; emphasis in original). I think Pippin would find the first of these passages suggestive and the second mistaken. Contrast Richard Wollheim's famous distinction between *seeing-in* and *seeing-as*; Wollheim notes that "in those cases where there are sustaining features of my seeing y in x, then seeing-in contrasts with seeing-as in that I can simultaneously be visually aware of the y that I see in x and the sustaining features of this perception" (2015: 142). It would be very interesting to pursue the relationship between Wollheim's distinction and the arguments by Pippin with which I am concerned here (Pippin refers enthusiastically to Wollheim 2015 in Pippin 2014: 103, n. 15), but doing so would be complex and beyond the scope of the present discussion.

12 The equation of the **literal** (which is a mode of *statements*) with the real and the **imaginary** (which is a mode of *objects*) with the nonexistent seems to be a source of confusion, both in Carroll's account here and—in a different way—with regard to Wilson's assumption (which we will encounter below) that all seeing must be either literal or imagined. It is not, to me, at all obvious that it is necessarily any more helpful to say that we "literally see images of Buster Keaton" (or, more precisely, that the *statement* "we see images of Buster Keaton when we watch *The General*" is literal) than that we "literally see images that we understand to be intended to represent Johnnie Gray." Both statements are equally true.

13 There is a certain irony in this, given that "Williams seems to have had an absolutely toxic reaction to all things remotely Kantian" (Pippin 2010b, response to Karl Ameriks).

14 Austin also proposes a third kind of speech-act, the *perlocutionary* act, which is something achieved *by means of* a speech-act, such as when somebody persuades or frightens another person by what they say (see, e.g., Austin 1975: 101–2). One could say that a great deal of both cognitivist and phenomenological Film Studies that focuses on the experience of the film viewer (whether emotional, haptic, or otherwise) concentrates on the "perlocutionary" aspects of film.

15 Although Pippin does not cite it, his claims here intersect in interesting ways with works on the relationship between film *narration* and *enunciation* by the likes of (the later) Christian Metz; Francesco Casetti;

Dominique Chateau; François Jost, and others. See Buckland (1995) for a useful anthology of English translations of some of this work.
16 In an effort to avoid what he feels are the sometimes unhelpfully literary connotations of the term "narrative," Douglas Pye has suggested a very interesting alternative metaphor to refer to this phenomenon, namely the idea of *inhabiting* a film: "Films, like buildings, are the product of human agency and are informed by more or less complex intentions; they imply—though not always straightforwardly—how they are, as it were, to be inhabited" (2013: 136).
17 In the afterword I briefly address the fact that Pippin finds similar critical-philosophical approaches equally productive with regard both to films and to novels.
18 See Michael Wood's claim—offered not as evidence for moral skepticism but rather of the moral complexity of literature—that there is "no way of describing the morality of what is happening" in James's *The Wings of the Dove* "without getting it wrong" (2005: 32). In Chapter 5 we will see Pippin argue something very similar with respect to Hitchcock's *Vertigo* and *Shadow of a Doubt*.

2 The Political Psychology of the Wild West

1 Lévi-Strauss wrote, e.g., that "all mythemes of whatever kind, must, generally speaking, lend themselves to binary oppositions, since such operations are an inherent feature of the means invented by nature to make possible the functioning of language and thought" (1981: 559). These oppositions tend to reflect fundamental contradictions, because "the purpose of myth is to provide a logical model capable of overcoming a contradiction"; something which is, however, "an impossible achievement if, as it happens, the contradiction is real" (Lévi-Strauss 1963: 229).
2 Particularly given that Pippin discusses *Stagecoach* in relation to Alexis de Tocqueville in Pippin (2010: 6–7) (and more extensively in Pippin 2013b), it might be worth noting Doc Boone's drunken play-acting at the start of the film. Doc pretends—for the benefit of the women of the Law and Order League—that his walk with Dallas towards the

stagecoach is actually that of two aristocrats heading to their deaths during the French Revolution: "Take my arm, Madame la Comtesse! The tumbrel awaits, to the guillotine!" Fully unpacking the various ironies of class and culture at play here would take some doing.

3   A similar reading of Liberty Valance's obliviousness to the hand is certainly possible. Even though no other characters seem to recognize the "dead man's hand," one could still say that his failure to understand its symbolism informs us about his character's overconfidence and lack of perceptiveness. It is worth noting, however, that the desire to avoid anachronism might have informed Ford's different stagings: Hickok was killed in 1876, well after the period in which the majority of the events in *The Man Who Shot Liberty Valance* are set, but *Stagecoach* is set in 1880. (Historically, however, it does not seem that the dead man's hand was associated with Hickok until substantially later than this.)

4   Either reading is possible but the former seems to me to be richer, given that it does not simply represent Ranse withholding the truth from her. Although if it is the latter, perhaps it was being told the truth that caused Hallie to persuade Ranse that they needed to return for Tom's funeral, as a form of atonement for her and penance for him, which might explain their leaving before it happens ("Ford, without any comment or highlight of the fact in the movie world of the film, shows us that Ranse and Hallie leave *before*, and so do not attend, Tom's funeral." [Pippin 2010a: 86; emphasis in original]), given that Ranse's confession (authorized by those slight nods) and the tribute of the cactus rose have been achieved.

5   I do not quite understand why Pye thinks that "Tom Doniphon can remain central to Shinbone only while Liberty Valance lives" (1996: 121); as Pippin indicates, Tom could perfectly well have killed Valance in a fair fight, and the old West would have carried on. Valance's death would have been "just one more episode in a cycle of violence, revenge, and intimidation" (Pippin 2010a: 81), and a new Valance—a new man "like Trampas"—would have come along sooner or later.

6   The truth could not be widely known without extensive consequences for the political psychology of Stoddard's admirers: "It is impossible to say to oneself: I know these legendary accounts are false, but we need to treat them as facts, so I will. You can't make yourself believe something because you think it is good that you so believe" (Pippin 2010a: 85).

7 We might, therefore, need to at least qualify Pippin's account of Tom as driven neither by "desire and appetite" nor "reason" but only by "the will to achieve distinction and status, to be and to be known to be the doer of great deeds" (2010a: 48).
8 Pippin thinks that the will scene "could have been a powerful scene," but that it "is undermined" by Jeffrey Hunter's performance (2010a: 174–5, n. 15). Disappointment with Hunter in *The Searchers* is not uncommon, but by no means universal; Edward Buscombe writes of his "unselfish and sympathetic performance" (2000: 50).

3 Worlds Apart: Polanski and Malick

1 The popular view of Fukuyama's ideas does not quite do them justice, but this does not change the fact that many of his remarks might serve as examples of precisely the kind of readings of Hegel that Pippin is determined to counter, such as the idea that he believed that "the material world is itself only an aspect of mind" (1989: 6, n. 5).
2 This does not mean that we have no emotional reaction to the massacre. Cf. Deborah Thomas's interesting claim that the film both distances its viewers from the family's "class-bound frame" and catches them "within the very same frame," with the result that "the family's destruction comes as a welcome relief … from the ideological tension of experiencing ironic distance and acute embarrassment at the same time" (2005: 177–8). (I wonder, incidentally, if some of the limitations, which Thomas points out, of the notion that viewers identify with characters might be addressed by conceiving of identification more as a *process* than as a state that either does or does not pertain. Aspects of my discussion of Pippin's reading of Almodóvar's *Talk to Her* in Chapter 5 are, I think, relevant here.)
3 Pippin's work enables us, I think, to see how investigations whose political relevance may not be obvious, such as those of Douglas Pye into the ways that "tone alerts us … to the pervasive evaluative and affective orientations implied by the film," can actually be extremely helpful in clarifying a film's political resonances (Pye 2007: 76).

4 The third section of *Filmed Thought* is entitled "Social Pathologies." It covers *Chinatown* (1974) and Douglas Sirk's *All That Heaven Allows* (1955); I am reserving discussion of the latter until Chapter 6.

5 Pippin is intrigued by this claim despite being skeptical about a number of aspects of Adorno's thought. He argues, e.g., that "from Hegel's point of view, Adorno's approach is regressive. It holds out hope for some isolation of the experience of sensuous immediacy that escapes the soul-deadening 'identity thinking' necessary for capitalist society and its technological apparatus to function effectively," something that for Hegel could only be an undialectical and escapist fantasy (Pippin 2015b: 327; see also Pippin's discussion of Adorno on aesthetic negativity in Pippin 2021b: 143–58). Miriam Bratu Hansen—Pippin's former colleague at the University of Chicago and the dedicatee of his book on film noir—offers a more sympathetic account of this aspect of Adorno's thinking in Hansen (2012: 230–3); e.g.: "natural beauty provides a *model* for art in its elusive appearance and indeterminateness" (ibid.: 232; emphasis in original).

6 A philosophically adequate account of a challenging film not infrequently, for Pippin, involves an adequate interpretation of the relationship between its various "plots." Cf. the discussion, in the introduction, of Pippin's reading of what he sees as *Rear Window*'s *triple* plot.

7 Pippin notes that Cross's remark about people being "capable of *anything*" is "not the film's finest moment," because "such nihilism is simplistic"; also, "although we are three years from the sexual assault on a minor charge that led to Polanski's exile, the assertion sounds creepily like his own all-purpose excuse for his behavior" (2020a: 112).

8 It is worth noting that, in keeping with his measured view of bourgeois modernism, Pippin finds Shetley's claim that "private property itself ... becomes identified with the horror of incest" (1999: 1100), to be "a rare overstatement," because "nothing in the film that I can see ... justifies this as a claim about 'private property itself.' Although it is true that one might say that Cross's debased understanding of the entitlement that comes with property is a possible pathological implication of the institution, one that becomes hard to resist if great wealth is concentrated in a few hands" (Pippin 2020a: 111, n. 18).

9 This is not to say that there can exist no limits to cinematic narration; in one of his relatively rare negative comments about a film (Pippin tends to operate, it seems, on the principle of not saying anything at all if you haven't got anything nice to say), he remarks that "my own candidate for the limit-case would be the recent, endlessly irritating film, *Inception*" (2013a: 335).
10 Another gesture toward some kind of universal humanity (one that verges on sentimentality) is the way Pvt. Dale (Arie Verveen) throws away the bag of gold teeth he's gathered from the corpses of Japanese soldiers; in the source novel Dale ends up, instead, with "one whole quart mason jar full of gold teeth as the beginning of his collection" (Jones 1998: 510). Pippin mentions this scene, but not this aspect of it. I don't personally find Dale to be "very difficult to identify" at this point; my greatest difficulties in character identification come elsewhere (Pippin 2020a: 211).
11 Pippin's recognition that the film's final words are not Witt's "afterlife voice," as Tom Whalen, along with many other commentators, assumes, clearly complicates things, but not sufficiently so for me to be able to dissent entirely from Whalen's discovery in the film of "questionable aesthetic decisions" and, ultimately, a "descent into the sentimental" (1999: 164, 162).

4 Film Noir and Agency: Do We Know What We're Doing?

1 Notes 30 and 31 in Pippin (2008) give the correct page numbers for this article but mistakenly attribute the passages cited to Korsgaard's (1997) book *The Sources of Normativity* instead. Note 32 also does this, but references p. 246, where it should be p. 247.
2 Pippin's citation inaccurately adds another "at least" to the quotation.
3 Pippin would also subscribe to a comparable account of the spatial, as well as temporal, extension of action, as in this summary of Elizabeth Anscombe's views by Frederick Stoutland: "To act is not to have one's bodily movements caused by one's beliefs and desires; it is to exercise the power to move one's body directly and intentionally. Further,

to exercise that power is not primarily to *cause* events outside one's body; it is to perform actions that extend beyond one's body and its movements. Walking, running, eating, drinking, pounding, skiing, greeting, writing—ordinary bodily activities all—do not consist of bodily movements plus events they cause; they *are* our moving our bodies in ways that extend beyond them" (2011: 19; emphases in original).

4 Unusually for Pippin, he slightly misquotes; Brando actually says "I could have been a contender. I could have been *somebody*." Pippin goes on to point out both that by actually *saying* such things such a "Hegelian brother" would lead one to "suspect that he is using existentialist rhetoric to excuse his own role, to appeal to his own good intentions as exculpatory," and that in actual fact "the Rod Steiger character *is* very much like this" (2008: 162; emphasis in original).

5 Perhaps rather surprisingly, Pippin does not take this opportunity to refer to Simone de Beauvoir's famous remark that "one is not born, but rather becomes, a woman" (1953: 273). On some accounts, entirely compatible with Pippin's views, the difference between being female and being a woman hinges on just this point.

6 Text silently amended; the passage actually reads "a model for the how."

7 Pippin also indicates that he believes that any rigid division "between treating characters as persons *or* treating fictional entities as properties of or instantiations of structure, words, images, social or libidinal forces, and so forth" seems to him "a false duality" (2012: 108, n. 3; emphasis in original).

8 Pippin finds this resistance to definition by means of a list of required features relevant not only to the normative concepts that film noir treats so interestingly, but also to noir itself as a grouping, or genre: "I am just going to assume that Stanley Cavell's suggestions about how to think about this issue in his book *Pursuits of Happiness* are correct. He notes that we should not think of a genre as an object with features in common" but think more in terms of "Wittgenstein's idea of a family resemblance" (2012: 5). (Stephen Mulhall also points out some disanalogies between Wittgenstein's families and Cavell's genres in Mulhall [2020: 91–8].)

9 Amia Srinivasan has compellingly argued that there is no such thing an unequivocally "lucid" norm, which is to say a norm concerning which

"a competent agent who knows the norm is in a position to know of every basic action available to her whether it would be in conformity with the norm" (2015: 277). The result is that we inhabit a world very reminiscent of that of Pippin's noirs, in which "there are no norms that can invariably guide our actions, and no norms that are immune from blameless violation" (ibid.: 273). Srinivasan makes the connection with Greek tragedy that Pippin also makes; compare Pippin's reference to "such retrospective situations as Sophocles' *Oedipus at Colonnus*, where Oedipus utters what I would half-seriously nominate as an early noir line, 'I suffered those deeds more than I acted them'" (2012: 40) with these remarks by Srinivasan: "The natural moral laws prohibit parricide, incest and cannibalism. But these laws are non-lucid. One cannot always be guided by them, and one can violate them through bad performance luck. The tragedy of Oedipus, then, is not of a great man brought down by moral weakness. It is rather of a great man brought down (to put it with thundering banality) by normative non-lucidity" (2015: 287). (If, incidentally, the applicability of these ideas both to Greek tragedy and postwar Hollywood cinema seems to undermine Pippin's arguments about the distinctiveness of modernity, we might do well to recall Bernard Williams's remark that "in important ways, we are, in our ethical situation, more like human beings in antiquity than any Western people have been in the meantime" [1993: 166].)

10 It is important to be very clear that Pippin does not intend this kind of question to suggest that humans are metaphysically anything other than material beings; it is not that a neurochemical description is *false*, it is that it cannot be relevant to an agent, *qua agent*. This is the Kantian point "that knowledge of such processes cannot be *practically relevant* to a deed unless it can be made to serve as a practical reason" (Pippin 2005a: 115; emphasis in original). Agency, for Pippin, is a normative status—a matter of holding one another to account—rather than a metaphysical property. Cf. Brandom's claim that one can use "practical attitudes" such as "taking or treating a performance as correct, attributing or acknowledging a commitment" in order to explain "our relations in perception and action to the causal order of nonnormative facts that we inhabit cognitively and practically" (1994: 626).

11   There is an Aristotelian dimension to this phenomenon. Cf. Jonathan Lear's discussion of Aristotle on the puzzle of incontinence: "The **incontinent** ... must confront the inescapable fact that what he says, however sincerely, is not like-natured with what he does. He is brought up short by his own action" (1988: 184).
12   Peter Dews objects that if Pippin's reading of Hegel is accurate, and "if freedom and rationality are as closely intertwined as Pippin rightly assumes, then were we not to *act* like free beings, we would not in fact *be* free beings, and there would be nothing beyond our existing practices to generate the demand that we *should* become free" (2010: 247; emphases in original). This seems to me an excellent summary of what Pippin does in fact believe.
13   Pippin thanks the philosopher Jim Conant for encouraging him to think along these lines; see Pippin (2012: 117, n. 10).
14   Whereas the film gives us, according to Pippin, more than enough rope with which to hang Michael. He therefore disputes Britton's claim that the way Elsa is treated at the film's conclusion makes it "indisputably, one of the cinema's most disgraceful endings" (1992: 219). Pippin writes interestingly about the complex ways that the film suggests we view Elsa Bannister and Rita Hayworth in the film "in terms of either the vast commercial and patriarchal system that has produced the Bannisters, the 'bad' against which she later says it is futile to fight, or the vast Hollywood entertainment-celebrity machine that swallowed up little Margarita Carmen Cansino at a very early age and produced the 'product', Rita Hayworth" (2012: 65).
15   Pippin sees the story as further evidence of Michael's unreliability as a narrator: "Michael's speech about sharks devouring themselves is so obviously lifted from chapter 66 of *Moby-Dick* that the point of such a 'borrowing' becomes a question. It may have something to do with increasing our sense of Michael's untrustworthiness" (2012: 117, n. 13).
16   We might suppose that these stories must be true in order for them to have the power they do, but the film's narrative of murders and framings shows that this need not be the case. Grisby and Elsa intended to "have something" on Michael for killing Bannister; as events play out, Bannister and Elsa end up "having something" on him for killing Grisby. Michael was not responsible either for the planned murder or

the one that actually takes place, but this diminishes the "hold" of the story—the "edge" it gives the others—not one bit.
17 Pippin thinks there are various ways in which Westerns and noirs comprise two usefully opposing categories: "If Westerns were mythic accounts of life before the rule of law could be established, many noirs give us a picture of life in a nearly postlegal order" (2012: 109, n. 11).
18 See Pippin's remarks about the conflicting signifiers of gender associated with Chris in Pippin (2012: 85–6).
19 Leo Braudy sees Renoir and Lang as emblematic of two fundamentally different ways "in which films present the visible world"; Renoir's approach he calls "open" and Lang's "closed" (Braudy 2002: 44; see 44–51 for the full discussion).
20 Cf. Anscombe's remark that "it is the agent's knowledge of what he is doing that gives the descriptions under which what is going on is the execution of intention" (Anscombe 2000: 87).
21 Cf. Rödl's remark that "there is a sense in which 'observation,' i.e., immediate apprehension, of actions and beliefs of another subject is an act not of receptive, but of spontaneous knowledge" (2007: 15).
22 I think Pippin would probably be very skeptical of the desirability of generating what Trahair claims Deleuze discovers in post-Second World War cinema and the self-consciousness of the camera, namely "nothing less than a cinematic cogito" (Trahair 2016: 110). Pippin's whole concept of reflective form might be seen as an attempt to articulate a non-Cartesian account of cinematic self-consciousness.
23 Pippin is as opposed as was Gilbert Ryle to what Ryle called "the official doctrine," according to which "the workings of one mind are not witnessable by other observers; its career is private. Only I can take direct cognisance of the states and processes of my own mind" (1949: 13).
24 Compare the discussion here with that, in Chapter 2, of Hubert I. Cohen's claims about John Wayne's characters changing their minds in *Red River* and *The Searchers*.
25 Pippin writes very interestingly about the film's exploration of what he calls "mimetic intelligibility" or "mimetic understanding," often expressed by means of different kinds of doubling; see, e.g., Pippin (2020a: 241–2, n. 26; 253).

26 Although perhaps something of an overstatement, Jonathan Rosenbaum's remark that "the Dardennes never seem to know more about their characters than they show" puts its finger on something important (2009: 8). A tiny example of this is the way, at the end of *The Son*, that the camera shows us Francis as soon as Olivier notices him. (The fact that, in contrast to this, Bruno [Jérémie Renier]—at the end of *The Child*—knows that his visitor is Sonia [Déborah François] some time before the camera reveals this to the audience seems a little jarring to me in the context of the Dardennes' wider practice.)

27 In some remarks on the Biblical story of Abraham and Isaac—a narrative which clearly influenced the development of *The Son*—Luc Dardenne comments on the way that Isaac "walks behind" Abraham and "sees his back," holding out the intriguing possibility—which I cannot pursue here—that the Dardennes may see some parallels between Isaac's situation and that of the film viewer (2019: 17).

28 Pippin does not share the enthusiasm of many commentators on the Dardennes' films for the philosophy of Emmanuel Levinas, remarking at one point that it is a point in favor of Adorno—another philosopher with whom he has many disagreements—that he "does not at all mystify 'the other' as some singular, ineffable 'Beyond,' or *Jenseits*, before which we must all pay the appropriate mute, respectful homage, à la Levinas" (2005a: 106). Slightly oddly, perhaps, Pippin also plays down the films'—to me undeniable—religious resonances (see the previous note); see Pippin (2020a: 242, n. 26).

5 Unknowing One Another: Film as Practical Moral Psychology

1 Pippin's reading of Nietzsche departs from many aspects of the "standard" reading, not to mention the version of Nietzsche one most frequently encounters in film-philosophy, which is heavily influenced by Gilles Deleuze. Pippin finds Deleuze's account of Nietzsche to be a "misreading"—not to mention that his views on Hegel are "tendentious and hopelessly misinformed" (Pippin 1999: 201). For more on Pippin's view of the shortcomings of Deleuze's reading of Nietzsche, see Pippin

(1983: 177, n. 28). Note that this view does not result from any general hostility towards Deleuze; Pippin is quite ready to argue, e.g., that "Deleuze's interpretation of the relation between 'la penseé' and 'la vie' is an excellent and much more defensible position" than Habermas's claim that Nietzsche's understanding of human interest is "positivist and naturalistic" (ibid.: 179, n. 58).

2 Although Pippin does not dedicate himself to this kind of task, his kind of writing about film could very well operate the other way, as an exploration of the reasons why what seems initially compelling should ultimately be rejected as *not* credible: "A film after all can be both powerfully compelling ... and, if the director is technically talented, can carry us along with this point of view, only for us on reflection to realize that the point of view we had been initially accepting is in fact infantile, cartoonish, pandering to the adolescent fantasies of its mostly male fans. I think of the undeniably powerful films of Quentin Tarantino as an example of this" (2016b).

3 Briefly on Vogler's divergences from Pippin: she writes that "fictional figures do not have ethical insight. If they have physical bodies, these are dispersed across multiple copies and editions of specific works of fiction. Whereas real people can't be in London and Paris and Boston at the same time, Merton Densher faces no such limitations" (2007: 8). As understandable and apparently commonsensical as such a stance is, all three of the claims made here seem to me to be false, and I think would so appear to Pippin as well. Whatever it is that can be in London, Paris, and Boston simultaneously (that thing that exists wherever there is a copy of *The Wings of the Dove*, or at least wherever one of these copies is being read), it is not Merton Densher, the man who is engaged to Kate Croy. If it is true that "fictional figures do not have ethical insight," it must surely also be true that Elizabeth Bennett doesn't have any ears. Later Vogler claims that "imaginary people exist in no one place. They sense nothing, feel nothing, and think nothing. If you prick them, they do not bleed" (ibid.: 9). If pricked, however, fictional characters certainly do bleed; the problem is that we (the readers or viewers) can't prick them. Elsewhere, I have found the term metalepsis—which refers to situations in which worlds which "should not" be able to meet nonetheless do intersect, such as when Buster Keaton enters the

screen in *Sherlock Jr.*—to be helpful in discussing these issues (see Lash 2020: 27–37). In finding real ethical significance in fictional events shown on-screen, some kind of moral metalepsis seems to be going on, which can certainly be disconcerting, and can prompt the kind of resistance we see in Vogler. But that we need to be cautious in what kind of moral insights we might try to draw from works of fiction—and that we can, certainly, be led to absurd conclusions if we are not careful—by no means suggests that the best approach is to avoid the attempt in the first place.

4 The "no truths, only interpretations" view of Nietzsche is completely misleading even though he did in fact make that claim. In context, it was a denial of positivism; Michael Wood points out that "against a philosophy which insisted that there are only interpretations, Nietzsche would no doubt have had something to say in favour of the facts" (2005: 160).

5 It is also true that Pippin's Nietzsche—who thinks "that views of the soul and its capacities vary with beliefs about and commitments to norms; normative commitments are subject to radical historical change; and so what counts as soul or psyche or mind and thus psychology also changes" (2010c: 3)—sometimes sounds positively Hegelian; see Pippin's remarks in Pippin (2013c: 192).

6 Pippin names Wittgenstein, Elizabeth Anscombe, Sartre, Richard Moran, and David Finkelstein (2010c: 99).

7 Note that "being able to will, in the general sense of affirm, direct a life in a way that evinces a sustainable, 'living' commitment, amounts to the realization of the will to power in the sense in which Nietzsche most uses it" (Pippin 2010c: 12). This is exactly what Charlie feels to be impossible before her Uncle Charles arrives.

8 Further on credibility: regarding the film's many implausibilities (of which he provides an extensive list in Pippin [2017a: 77, n. 94]), Pippin claims that "we pass over them effortlessly," or that "at least most viewers captured by the film would"; he does, however, also "concede that there may be many who find the murder plan a barrier to being so captured" (ibid.: 84, n. 101).

9 Pippin's own view, which I find convincing, is that the "most poignant" and "most likely" interpretation is that, rather than—say—being about

to jump to his own death, what we see "is the pose of a man whose outstretched arms have failed to catch something falling, pulled back, and who looks on in shock at the results" (2017a: 121).

10 Cf. Sebastian Rödl's point that "from the fact that, when I am fooled, I do not know that I am, it does not follow that, when I am not fooled, I do not know that I am not" (2007: 158).

11 It is of great relevance to the discussion of Nietzsche, in the following paragraphs, that Cavell points out in this passage that Nietzsche ridiculed both the philosophical tendency to view life as a puzzle or riddle, as a "problem of knowledge," *and* the notion that any philosophical position—including, of course, the one just mentioned— "can simply be 'refuted'" (1979a: 109).

12 "has" in the final sentence silently corrected from "as."

13 Note that Pippin is clear, in keeping with his general interest in modernity and modernism, that the world Hitchcock represents in *Vertigo* "is a historical world, a complex modern world of profound social dependence and corresponding uncertainty" (2017a: 17).

14 "any more" silently corrected from "anymore."

15 Very interesting, and extremely complicated, related questions are raised in the film by Kim Novak's acting. Hitchcock appears to direct her to play Madeleine (and Judy the first time we and Scottie meet her) almost entirely "straight." Is Kim Novak playing Judy-playing-Madeleine, or does she just *play Madeleine* (even though Madeleine "herself" is obviously being played by Judy)? Similar questions arise on Judy's first appearance in the film: "She opens the door, sees him, *and does not bat an eyelash, skip a beat*" (Pippin 2017a: 97; emphasis in original). Having said this, on repeated viewings there certainly are points where we can ask questions such as the one raised by Neill Potts about the first scene at Ernie's as to whether the "nervousness" we can see is "the Madeleine mask itself, or a sign that the mask is slipping" (2005: 95). Potts plausibly asserts that "there is no answer to the conundrum of Novak's characters, no definite place to draw the line" (ibid.: 87).

16 Pippin, I think, misreads V. F. Perkins (and the film) on the contents of the police files. Pippin claims that Perkins points out that the file is clearly composed of "press clippings, not … police records"

(2017a: 173). This is not the case—the files read out include "February 1946. Beer parlor brawl on Santa Monica Boulevard. Brought to station for questioning. Discharged with warning" and "June 22, 11:00 PM. Frances Randolph screams for help. Charges Steele beat her up. Then denies having made the charge. Alleges nose broken by running into a door"—but nor does Perkins make that claim. His claim is that the film contains here a kind of allegory of the methods Hollywood studios used to keep their employees in line; the file "*looks like* a cuttings file and it consists largely of the scandal queens' gossip and commissary tittle-tattle that studios compiled to control the employability of the talent," but diegetically it certainly is a police file (Perkins 2020: 336; my emphasis). The studio's practice of keeping such files was certainly not limited to acting stars but also extended to writers like Dixon Steele; as MGM and RKO story editor William Fadiman put it: "The story department in every studio has a cross-filed card index on writers that would make Linnaeus' *Systema Naturae* seem the jottings of an amateur" (quoted in Ceplair and Englund 1983: 5).

17 She also, of course, changes the third person from the screenplay to the second person; compare Pippin's comments about the pivotal beach scene when Dix discovers that Laurel has been speaking to the police behind his back, and "the extent to which he is enraged at finding himself treated in such a third- and not second-person way, let us say" (2020a.: 189).

18 Pedantically, I am not sure it is entirely correct to say that, for Cavell, skepticism about other minds *is* tragedy; but it is certainly extremely close to it, or very easily turns into it. In *Vertigo* the role of Midge, whose "'project' in all of this is as tragically impossible" as Scottie's, is a particularly interesting site for the further exploration of this idea (Pippin 2017a: 110). The question of the precise relationship between Pippin's "unknowingness" and Cavell's "skepticism" is worthy of an independent study. My sense is that there is very little in Cavell's work on this subject that Pippin would want to reject. In particular, Pippin's Hegelian insistence that "unknowingness" is not, as one reviewer helpfully (but I think incorrectly) suggested to me, a kind of existential condition *rather than* a kind of activity—and this chiefly because "our understanding of others is not observational, and punctual, but

interpretive and extended in time" (2017a: 123)—has many resonances with Cavell's work. To give just a single example: toward the end of *The Claim of Reason*, Cavell explores the relationship to tragedy of a question he explicitly declares to be inspired by Hegel's *Philosophy of Right* and *Phenomenology of Spirit*: "What happens to individuals if they tire of history, can take no further mediation, become lost or captivated on the path of self-realization and intersubjectivity—if they become 'reified' rather than 'concretized' "? (1979a: 471). What is Scottie if not "lost or captivated on the path of self-realization and intersubjectivity"?

6 Pippin and Film Studies

1 We might see this as an indication of Pippin's Aristotelianism (he frequently points out Hegel's debts to Aristotle); compare this remark by Jonathan Lear: "It is absurd, [Aristotle] says, to state an absolutely general definition of what soul is. We must look instead to the workings of the different types of living organisms—plants, animals, and man" (1988: 99–100).
2 Compare Robert Sinnerbrink's similar claim, to which Pippin would also fully subsribe, that "the only way to justify that a film has philosophized, or illustrated a philosophical idea, or exists in the condition of philosophy, is by way of a contestable philosophical interpretation of that film" (2011: 134).
3 John Ford, Howard Hawks, Alfred Hitchcock, and Nicholas Ray were among the favorite directors of what is usually seen as the original move to canonize Hollywood directors, the work of the critics of *Cahiers du cinéma* in the 1950s (see Bickerton 2009), and Pippin has written about all of them; indeed, he has written on more than one film by all of them, with the exception of Hawks. Also, the rethinking of Douglas Sirk's reputation was central to the establishment of academic Film Studies in the 1970s (see Klinger 1994). (Pedro Almodóvar, Roman Polanski, Terrence Malick, and the Dardenne brothers have more connection to what Bordwell would call art cinema, and all have been extensively

discussed in the academic literature and thus also have a canonical status, albeit of a slightly different kind.)

4 See the beginning of the section entitled "Nietzsche and 'Psychology'" in Chapter 5 for more discussion of this point.

5 Something comparable could be said about the lack of obvious autobiographical reference in Pippin's writing. Something that William Rothman has written about V. F. Perkins—that "his assertions seem made with certainty—disinterestedly, dispassionately, from the security of an aesthetic distance" but that, nevertheless, "expressing himself in this impersonally rational voice was his *way* of being personal" (2020: 123; emphasis in original)—also resonates with Pippin's practice.

6 Similarly, his interest in the aural dimensions of film is oriented toward what they "sound like," taken in a parallel sense, as in the way that a remark or a car might "sound right" or "sound wrong." Wittgenstein's discussion of aspect perception or "seeing-as" should, of course, come to mind here.

7 See the discussion in Chapter 3 of the inflection Pippin gives to Daniel Yacavone's distinction between the *world-in* and *world-of* a film.

8 See Zborowski (2016) (and in particular chapter 1 therein) for another recent defense of the value, for film criticism, of attempting not to get trapped by this dualism.

9 Investigating irony also requires Pippin to move beyond his tendency to take Hegel as the chief point of orientation for his thought because, as he notes, Hegel is simply "not particularly good on the issue of irony. He thinks it must erode the wholeheartedness and reconciliation that is the goal of modern societies in his account" (2020a: 120, n. 8).

10 The contrast I am pointing to here is between *what is said* and *what is the case*; I agree with Currie that invoking a distinction between semantic meaning and the speaker's meaning is useless, because there is no such distinction (see 2006: 113). I do not deny that irony *can* involve pretense (Currie [2006] gives some interesting examples) but some kind of distance or contrast still seems to me a more fundamental basis of irony than pretense. In the next sentence in the main text I go on to cite Wittgenstein; if speaking ironically is a language game (or a family of language games) there may be no need to invoke pretense because—as in the "lovely weather!" example—I need not pretend to be playing

any other language game. (Here is a personal anecdote to illustrate the point. I once spent Easter in Italy with my parents as a child, and during the trip our hotel room was robbed. My father reported that while giving his statement to the police a particularly dour-looking policeman stood looking out of the window at the rain that was bucketing down and exclaimed, in the gloomiest of deadpans, "Bella Pasqua!", or "Beautiful Easter!" It does not seem to me that he was pretending to think that the weather was beautiful.)

11 Stanley Cavell frequently points out something similar in comparable cases; see the discussion of Cavell's views on Wittgensteinian criteria in Affeldt (1998).

12 This is one reason why irony can also serve as "a kind of ethical stance," a strategy for dealing with the "contingency and frustration" we may experience in our dealings with the world and one another (Pippin 2020a: 120).

13 Clearly the interpretive activity of the audience is crucial in instances of "unknowing" irony, but I am not wholly persuaded by MacDowell's claim that in this kind of case "it is certainly true to say that it will not be the intentions of artists or works but rather those of interpreters which make irony 'happen'" (2016: 166). It is also crucial that the artists involved *did not* intend any irony. Deliberately writing a song called "Ironic" that contains no irony would be just as ironic as doing so inadvertently, but these two cases represent two extremely different forms of irony: precisely what Pippin calls its "knowing" and "unknowing" varieties.

14 It is not easy to see how a novel, e.g., could include the model vehicles without seeming to "mention" them, as the film manages to do, although a stage play could perhaps do so. Pippin notes that the interior scenes of *Johnny Guitar* can indeed generate "the feeling that we are watching a filmed version of a stage play" (2020a: 155). This seems to me true, but this feeling is also—particularly at the beginning of the film—subtly dislocated. There is often a jarring or apparently unmotivated quality to the editing that is hard to put one's finger on, but which contributes an off-kilter aspect to the mood which would be impossible to replicate on stage.

15 The work referred to is MacDowell (2014), and the passage quoted appears on p. 165.
16 In Pippin (2021a) Sirk's presentation of a character as smug—which, Pippin notes, is a frequent occurrence—is always interpreted as particularly damning.
17 Compare this "diegetic" use of proverb or cliché with the moment in Sirk's *Written on the Wind* when Kyle (Robert Hadley) enters Lucy's (Lauren Bacall) hotel room only to discover that she has left: "Lucy, you decent? … Guess she was!" The whole film (whose screenplay was by George Zuckerman) is full of this kind of ironic play with language. (While he does not mention this particular remark, Pippin suggests many further ironic twists on its content in his chapter on the film; see Pippin [2021a: 71–100].)
18 In Pippin (2021a) it is noted that the sheer eagerness to see Cary that Ron exhibits before his fall complicates this aspect of the film a little: "His desperate attempt to reach her and then his fall and injury suggest, very briefly, a dimension of Ron we had not seen before … his bravado seems now more a protective device than genuine" (2021a: 57).
19 The original title of Pippin (2021a) was in fact *The Politics of Emotional Life: Douglas Sirk and Subversive Melodrama* (2020b). Recalling the language of "social pathology" we have encountered earlier, Pippin's fuller socio-historical claim is that Sirk's melodramas can contribute to demonstrating that "the intricacies of social dependence in modern mass-consumer societies, the near-feudal power of managers in corporate empires, and a heightened awareness of the difference between public and private attitudes make any settled sense of just 'being' oneself immediately naive" (2020a: 141; see also 2021a: 64).
20 Wood actually writes "none" rather than "very few," but I take this to be legitimate promotional hyperbole!
21 This being said, many scholars do carefully distinguish between the notions of "analytic" and "cognitivist" film-philosophy; see, e.g., Slugan (2019), in particular Chapter 4.
22 This has not stopped others from placing him in one category or another. In *The Palgrave Handbook of the Philosophy of Film and Motion Pictures* one author tells us that Pippin is "working from a

Hegelian background" while another refers to him as "an Analytic film philosopher" (Carroll et al. 2019: 253, 278).

23 Pippin adds the second group of names in Pippin (2018e).

24 Ó Maoilearca's account of Cavell's work is sympathetic, but I am puzzled by his claim that "Cavell himself says" that "an ontology—a science of the being of the medium itself... must precede any study of actual films a posteriori," because this strikes me as exactly what Cavell does *not* believe (Mularkey 2009: 121). Where exactly does Cavell say this? It is true that *The World Viewed* refers to "the *a priori* condition that its [i.e., film's] medium is photographic and its subject reality" (Cavell 1979b: 74), but if this were the same thing as its ontology there would be no need for most of the rest of the book. What Cavell says about painting he surely also believes about cinema: "What modernist painting proves is that we do not know *a priori* what painting has to do or be faithful to in order to remain painting" (ibid.: 106).

25 J. M. Bernstein has written an article critiquing Deleuze's *Cinema* books that suggests useful starting points for such an inquiry, given its reference to two notions—normativity and moral psychology—that, as we have seen, are central to Pippin's approach to film. Bernstein suggests both that Deleuze's notion of cinematic space "under-prescribes how stringent and complex the fit must be between the normative or ideal ends of human action and the causal structures of the world housing them in classical cinema" and that betrayal "is the pivot" of Alain Resnais's film *Hiroshima mon amour*, an understanding of which must involve "moral psychology" rather than the "speculative ontology" that Deleuze offers (2012: 80, 85).

26 Although I suspect that Pippin would certainly want to phrase some claims—particularly those about evolution and sociality—a little differently, and would be suspicious that a category mistake might be at work in the claim that "evidence of a mirror system [of neurons] provides a new form of evidence" (Smith 2014: 40) for the existence of empathy, because understanding empathy, for Pippin, necessarily involves the kinds of self-consciousness we have explored in this book.

27 Thus, what might seem like rather pedantic corrections of Žižek by Pippin are really indices of a much more substantive issue. E.g.: "The newspaper editor at the end of *The Man Who Shot Liberty Valance* did

not say, 'When reality doesn't fit the legend, print the legend' (420). He said something much more relevant to Žižek's concerns: 'This is the West, sir. When the legend becomes fact, print the legend.'" (Pippin 2015a: 95, n. 6; the page reference in the text is to Žižek 2012).

28 Compare the passage just cited with the remarks from Pippin 2021a cited above in n. 19 to this chapter and below in n. 4 to the afterword.

29 "that should be said" silently corrected from "than should be said."

Afterword: On the Nonexistence of Pippinian Film-Philosophy

1 He has also published on painting, photography, and the novels of Marcel Proust and J. M. Coetzee; see in particular Pippin (2014, 2021b, and 2021c).

2 A rather more technically sophisticated exploration of Henry James on print and on screen (one that sees James Ivory's *Golden Bowl* very differently) argues for a "homology ... between film's oblique angle in shot/reverse shot continuity editing and print fiction's free indirect discourse" (Butte 2017: 100); see ibid.: 73–119.

3 It is also worth saying that the fact that Pippin explicitly conceives of his work on film philosophically in no way diminishes its relevance to a host of important topics in Film Studies—particularly those centering around film characters and film worlds, but also including questions of, e.g., genre (What is a Western? What is a melodrama?)—that need not always be framed in explicitly philosophical terms. I hope the discussions of the individual films in the preceding chapters have brought this out at least to some extent.

4 The "Concluding Remarks" of Pippin's book on Douglas Sirk focus on the "powerful credibility" of narrative cinema, linking it to the shared sense we find in both Deleuze and Cavell that film can be seen as responding to "a historical crisis ... in any confidence we might have in various aspects of the intelligibility of the experienced external and social world" (2021a: 138). Pippin claims that Sirk's late melodramas give these ideas a very complex twist; the final sentence of the book (which, we might note, contains the word "credible" twice), reads: "The

need for a protective blindness and for projecting fantasies are as powerfully credible in his films as is the equally credible display of the destructiveness of such a need" (ibid.: 143).

5 For a discussion of the passage by Pippin, see Pippin (2021b: 42–8).

6 Art historian Todd Cronan nicely connects the two fundamentally different forms of enquiry with which we are concerned here with the idea of convincingness, close cousin to the credibility discussed in the previous paragraph: "disagreements about cause and effect, what actually happens to the beholder, differ entirely from what a work means, or how we interpret what happens. Effects are evaluated through verification (Did the effect happen?); interpretations of a work's meaning are evaluated in terms of the persuasiveness of one's claims (Is the account convincing?)" (2013: 3).

Bibliography

Works by Robert B. Pippin

(1982) *Kant's Theory of Form: An Essay on the* Critique of Pure Reason (New Haven, CT: Yale University Press).
(1983) "Nietzsche and the Origin of the Idea of Modernism," *Inquiry*, 26:2, pp. 151–80.
(1988) "Irony and Affirmation in Nietzsche's *Thus Spoke Zarathustra*," in Michael Allen Gillespie and Tracy B. Strong, eds., *Nietzsche's New Seas: Explorations in Philosophy, Aesthetics, and Politics* (Chicago, IL: University of Chicago Press), pp. 45–71.
(1989) *Hegel's Idealism: The Satisfactions of Self-Consciousness* (Cambridge: Cambridge University Press).
(1997) *Idealism as Modernism: Hegelian Variations* (Cambridge: Cambridge University Press).
(1999) *Modernism as a Philosophical Problem: On the Dissatisfactions of European High Culture* (2nd ed.) (Oxford: Blackwell).
(2000a) *Henry James and Modern Moral Life* (Cambridge: Cambridge University Press).
(2000b) "What Is the Question for which Hegel's Theory of Recognition Is the Answer?," *European Journal of Philosophy*, 8:2, pp. 155–72.
(2003) "Love and Death in Nietzsche," in Mark Wrathall, ed., *Religion after Metaphysics* (Cambridge: Cambridge University Press), pp. 7–28.
(2005a) *The Persistence of Subjectivity: On the Kantian Aftermath* (Cambridge: Cambridge University Press).
(2005b) "The Erotic Nietzsche: Philosophers without Philosophy," in Shadi Bartsch and Thomas Bartscherer, eds., *Erotikon: Essays on Eros, Ancient and Modern* (Chicago, IL: University of Chicago Press), pp. 172–91.
(2006) "Philosophy Is Its Own Time Comprehended in Thought," *Topoi*, no. 25, pp. 85–90.
(2008) *Hegel's Practical Philosophy: Rational Agency as Ethical Life* (Cambridge: Cambridge University Press).

(2009) "Natural and Normative," *Daedelus*, 138:3 (Summer), pp. 35–43.
(2010a) *Hollywood Westerns and American Myth: The Importance of Howard Hawks and John Ford for Political Philosophy* (New Haven, CT: Yale University Press).
(2010b) "Participants and Spectators," https://nationalhumanitiescenter.org/on-the-human/2010/04/participants_and_spectators (last accessed July 21, 2020).
(2010c) *Nietzsche, Psychology, & First Philosophy* (Chicago, IL: University of Chicago Press).
(2011) *Hegel on Self-Consciousness: Desire and Death in the Phenomenology of Spirit* (Princeton, NJ: Princeton University Press).
(2012) *Fatalism in American Film Noir: Some Cinematic Philosophy* (Charlottesville, VA: University of Virginia Press).
(2013a) "Le Grand Imagier of George Wilson," *European Journal of Philosophy*, 21:2, pp. 334–41.
(2013b) "Tocqueville, the Problem of Equality, and John Ford's *Stagecoach*," in Ewa Atanassow and Richard Boyd, eds., *Tocqueville and the Frontiers of Democracy* (Cambridge: Cambridge University Press), pp. 291–306.
(2013c) "Doer and Deed: Responses to Acampora and Anderson," *Journal of Nietzsche Studies*, 44:2, pp. 181–95.
(2014) *After the Beautiful* (Chicago, IL: University of Chicago Press).
(2015a) *Interanimations: Receiving Modern German Philosophy* (Chicago, IL: University of Chicago Press).
(2015b) "Response to Fred Rush and Adrian Daub," *Journal of Aesthetics and Art Criticism*, 73:3 (Summer), pp. 323–9.
(2015c) "Robert Pippin Discusses the Dardenne Brothers," *Criticalinquiry.uchicago.edu*, https://criticalinquiry.uchicago.edu/robert_pippin_discusses_the_dardenne_brothers/ (last accessed September 18, 2020).
(2016a) "Responses," in Ludwig Nagl and Waldemar Zacharasiewicz, eds., *Ein Film Philosophie-Symposium mit Robert B. Pippin* (Berlin: Walter de Gruyter), pp. 219–37.
(2016b) "Minds in the Dark: Cinematic Experience in the Dardenne Brothers' *Dans l'Obscurité*," *Nonsite.org*, https://nonsite.org/article/minds-in-the-dark-2 (last accessed August 7, 2020).

(2016c) "Photographing Mindedness: Cinematic Technique and Philosophy in the Films of the Dardenne Brothers," in Ludwig Nagl and Waldemar Zacharasiewicz, eds., *Ein Film Philosophie-Symposium mit Robert B. Pippin* (Berlin: Walter de Gruyter), pp. 18–42.

(2017a) *The Philosophical Hitchcock: Vertigo and the Anxieties of Unknowingness* (Chicago, IL: University of Chicago Press).

(2017b) "CCT MFS Film & Philosophy, University of Chicago, 'The Philosophical Hitchcock,'" https://www.youtube.com/watch?v=LIpg7WHe7AY (last accessed July 10, 2020).

(2018a) "Reading Hegel," *Australasian Philosophical Review*, 2:4, pp. 365–82.

(2018b) "Hegelian Themes" (Robert Pippin interviewed by Richard Marshall, 3:16, October 2018) https://www.3-16am.co.uk/articles/hegelian-themes (last accessed October 10, 2020).

(2018c) "On Idealism: Responses to Markus Gabriel, James Kreines, Christopher Yeomans, Purushottama Bilimoria, Gene Flenady, Lorenzo Sala, and Jonathan Shaheen," *Australasian Philosophical Review*, 2:4, pp. 440–57.

(2018d) "Review of Toril Moi, '*Revolution of the Ordinary: Literary Studies after Wittgenstein, Austin, and Cavell*,'" *Critical Inquiry*, January 17, 2018, https://criticalinquiry.uchicago.edu/robert_pippin_reviews_revolution_of_the_ordinary/ (last accessed November 9, 2020).

(2018e) "'Radical Finitude in the Anti-Idealist Modern European Philosophical Tradition,' Yale University, Franke Lectures in the Humanities, November 13, 2018," https://www.youtube.com/watch?v=ta44R593qks&t=656s (last accessed November 13, 2020).

(2019a) "The Bearing of Film on Philosophy," in Kelly Becker and Iain D. Thomson, eds., *Cambridge History of Philosophy, 1945–2015* (Cambridge: Cambridge University Press), pp. 529–41.

(2019b) *Hegel's Realm of Shadows* (Chicago, IL: University of Chicago Press).

(2019c) "Idealism and Anti-idealism in Modern European Thought," *Journal of Speculative Philosophy*, 33:3, pp. 349–67.

(2020a) *Filmed Thought: Cinema as Reflective Form* (Chicago, IL: University of Chicago Press).

(2020b) "Robert Pippin interviewed by Bill Schaffer," *New Books in Philosophy* podcast (June 11, 2020).

(2021a) *Douglas Sirk: Filmmaker and Philosopher* (New York, NY: Bloomsbury).

(2021b) *Philosophy by Other Means: The Arts in Philosophy and Philosophy in the Arts* (Chicago, IL: University of Chicago Press).

(2021c) *Metaphysical Exile: On J. M. Coetzee's Jesus Fictions* (Oxford: Oxford University Press).

Other sources

Abrams, Nathan. (2017) "review of *The Philosophical Hitchcock*," THES, November 30, https://www.timeshighereducation.com/cn/books/review-the-philosophical-hitchcock-robert-b-pippin-university-of-chicago-press (last accessed July 14, 2020).

Adorno, Theodor. (2005) *Minima Moralia: Reflections on a Damaged Life*, trans. E. F. N. Jephcott (London: Verso).

Affeldt, Steven G. (1998) "The Ground of Mutuality: Criteria, Judgment and Intelligibility in Stephen Mulhall and Stanley Cavell," *European Journal of Philosophy*, 6:1, pp. 1–31.

Anscombe, G. E. M. ([1957] 2000) *Intention* (Cambridge, MA: Harvard University Press).

Austin, J. L. ([1962] 1975) *How to Do Things with Words* (Oxford: Oxford University Press).

Bernstein, J. M. (2012) "Movement! Action! Belief? Notes for a Critique of Deleuze's Cinema Philosophy," *Angelaki*, 17:4, pp. 77–93.

Bernstein, J. M. (2017) "'Our Amphibian Problem': Nature in History in Adorno's Hegelian Critique of Hegel," in *Zuckert and Kreines*, pp. 193–212.

Bessette, Eliot. (2013) "Book Review: *Fatalism in American Film Noir: Some Cinematic Philosophy* by Robert B. Pippin," *Film Criticism*, 37/38:3/1 (Spring/Fall), pp. 157–60.

Bickerton, Emilie. (2009) *A Short History of Cahiers du cinéma* (London: Verso, 2009).

Bordwell, David. (1979) "The Art Cinema as a Mode of Film Practice," *Film Criticism*, 4:1 (Fall), pp. 56–64.

Bordwell, David. (1989) *Making Meaning: Inference and Rhetoric in the Interpretation of Cinema* (Cambridge, MA: Harvard University Press).

Brandom, Robert B. (1994) *Making It Explicit: Reasoning, Representing, and Discursive Commitment* (Cambridge, MA: Harvard University Press).

Brandom, Robert B. (2002) *Tales of the Mighty Dead: Historical Essays in the Metaphysics of Intentionality* (Cambridge, MA: Harvard University Press).

Brandom, Robert B. (2013) "Norms, Selves & Concepts (Animating Ideas of Idealism – Kant and Hegel 1)," https://www.youtube.com/watch?v=fUczOHn2n-c (last accessed July 21, 2020).

Braudy, Leo. ([1976] 2002) *The World in a Frame: What We See in Films* (Chicago, IL: University of Chicago Press).

Britton, Andrew. (1992) "Betrayed by Rita Hayworth: Misogyny in *The Lady from Shanghai*," in Ian Cameron, ed., *The Movie Book of Film Noir* (London: Studio Vista).

Buckland, Warren, ed. (1995) *The Film Spectator: From Sign to Mind* (Amsterdam: Amsterdam University Press).

Buscombe, Edward. (2000) *The Searchers* (London: British Film Institute).

Butte, George. (2017) *Suture and Narrative: Deep Intersubjectivity in Fiction and Film* (Columbus, OH: Ohio State University Press).

Carroll, Noël. (2006) "Introduction to Part IV (Film Narrative/Narration)," in Noël Carroll and Jinhee Choi, eds., *Philosophy of Film and Motion Pictures: An Anthology* (Oxford: Blackwell), pp. 175–84.

Carroll, Noël. (2007) "*Vertigo* and the Pathologies of Romantic Love," in David Baggett and William A. Drumin, eds., *Hitchcock and Philosophy: Dial M for Metaphysics* (Chicago, IL: Open Court), pp. 101–14.

Carroll, Noël, Laura T. Di Summa, Shawn Loht, eds. (2019) *The Palgrave Handbook of the Philosophy of Film and Motion Pictures* (Cham, Germany: Palgrave Macmillan).

Cavell, Stanley. (1979a) *The Claim of Reason: Wittgenstein, Skepticism, Morality, and Tragedy* (Oxford: Oxford University Press).

Cavell, Stanley. (1979b) *The World Viewed: Reflections on the Ontology of Film (Expanded Edition)* (Cambridge, MA: Harvard University Press).

Cavell, Stanley. (1981) *Pursuits of Happiness: The Hollywood Comedy of Remarriage* (Cambridge, MA: Harvard University Press).

Cavell, Stanley. (2005) *Cavell on Film*, ed. William Rothman (Albany, NY: State University of New York Press).

Ceplair, Larry, and Steven Englund. (1983) *The Inquisition in Hollywood: Politics in the Film Community, 1930–1960* (Berkeley, CA: University of California Press).

Chion, Michel. (2004) *The Thin Red Line* (London: British Film Institute).

Clark, T. J. (2014) "Face to Face with Rembrandt," *London Review of Books*, 36:23, December 4, https://www.lrb.co.uk/v36/n23/tj-clark/world-of-faces (last accessed October 12, 2020).

Cohen, Hubert I. (2010) "*Red River* and *The Searchers*: Deception in the Modern Western," *Film Criticism*, 35:1 (Fall), pp. 82–102.

Cronan, Todd. (2013) *Against Affective Formalism: Matisse, Bergson, Modernism* (Minneapolis, MN: University of Minnesota Press).

Currie, Gregory. (2006) "Why Irony Is Pretence," in Shaun Nicols, ed., *The Architecture of the Imagination: New Essays on Pretence, Possibility, and Fiction* (Oxford: Oxford University Press), pp. 111–33.

Currie, Gregory. (2010) *Narratives and Narrators: A Philosophy of Stories* (Oxford: Oxford University Press).

Clayton, Alex. (2016) "V. F. Perkins: Aesthetic Suspense," in Murray Pomerance et al., eds., *Thinking in the Dark: Cinema, Theory, Practice* (New Brunswick, NJ: Rutgers University Press) pp. 208–16.

Danto, Arthur C. (2006) "Moving Pictures," in *Philosophy of Film and Motion Pictures: An Anthology*, ed. Noël Carroll and Jinhee Choi (Oxford: Blackwell), pp. 100–12.

Dardenne, Luc. (2019) *On the Back of Our Images*, trans. Jeffrey Zuckerman (Chicago, IL: Featherproof).

Davis, Mike. (1990) *City of Quartz: Excavating the Future in Los Angeles* (London: Vintage).

de Beauvoir, Simone. (1953) *The Second Sex*, trans. and ed. H. M. Parshley (London: Jonathan Cape).

Deleuze, Gilles. (2005a) *Cinema 1: The Movement-Image* (London: Continuum).

Deleuze, Gilles. (2005b) *Cinema 2: The Time-Image* (London: Continuum).

Dews, Peter. (2010) "Nature and Subjectivity: Fichte's Role in the Pippin/McDowell Debate in the Light of His Neo-Kantian Reception," in Jürgen Stolzenberg, and Oliver-Pierre Rudolph, eds., *Wissen, Freiheit, Geschichte. Die Philosophie Fichtes im 19. und 20. Jahrhundert. Band I.* (Leiden: Brill/Rodopi), pp. 235–50.

Dimendberg, Edward. (2004) *Film Noir and the Spaces of Modernity* (Cambridge, MA: Harvard University Press).

Doniger, Wendy. (2005) *The Woman Who Pretended to Be Who She Was: Myths of Self-Imitation* (Oxford: Oxford University Press).

Dreyfus, Hubert. (2003) "Existential Phenomenology and the Brave New World of *The Matrix*," *Harvard Review of Philosophy*, 11:1 (Spring), pp. 18–31.

Frampton, Daniel. (2006) *Filmosophy* (London: Wallflower).

Fukuyama, Francis. (1989) "The End of History?," *National Interest*, no. 16 (Summer), pp. 3–18.

Gibbs, John, and Douglas Pye, eds. (2005) *Style and Meaning: Studies in the Detailed Analysis of Film* (Manchester: Manchester University Press).

Grant, Barry Keith. (2003) "Introduction: Spokes in the Wheels," in Barry Keith Grant, ed., *John's Ford's* Stagecoach (Cambridge: Cambridge University Press, 2003).

Gunning, Tom. (2000) *The Films of Fritz Lang: Allegories of Vision and Modernism* (London: British Film Institute).

Hansen, Miriam Bratu. (2012) *Cinema and Experience: Siegfried Kracauer, Walter Benjamin, and Theodor W. Adorno* (Berkeley, CA: University of California Press).

Hegel, G. W. F. (1988) *Phänomenologie des Geistes* (Hamburg, Germany: Felix Meiner Verlag).

Hegel, G. W. F. (2010) *The Science of Logic*, trans. and ed. George Di Giovanni (Cambridge: Cambridge University Press).

Hegel, G. W. F. (2018) *The Phenomenology of Spirit*, trans. and ed. Terry Pinkard (Cambridge: Cambridge University Press).

James, Henry. (1977) *The Princess Casamassima* (Harmondsworth, UK: Penguin).

James, Henry. (1986) *The Wings of the Dove* (London: Penguin).

Jones, James. (1998) *The Thin Red Line* (London: Hodder and Stoughton).

Kant, Immanuel. (2007) *Critique of Pure Reason*, trans. and ed. Marcus Weigelt (London: Penguin).

Kitses, Jim. (1969) *Horizons West* (London: Thames and Hudson).

Klevan, Andrew. (2018) *Aesthetic Evaluation and Film* (Manchester: Manchester University Press).

Klevan, Andrew. (2020) "Ordinary Language Film Studies," July 27, https://www.academia.edu/43723219/ORDINARY_LANGUAGE_FILM_STUDIES_ANDREW_KLEVAN_ACADEMIA_EDU_VERSION_JULY_2020 (last accessed August 25, 2020).

Klinger, Barbara. (1994) *Melodrama and Meaning: History, Culture, and the Films of Douglas Sirk* (Bloomington, IN: Indiana University Press).

Korsgaard, Christine M. (1996) *The Sources of Normativity* (Cambridge: Cambridge University Press).

Korsgaard, Christine M. (1997) "The Normativity of Instrumental Reason," in G. Cullity and B. Gaut, eds., *Ethics and Practical Reason* (Oxford: Clarendon Press), pp. 215–54.

LaRocca, David, ed. (2020) *The Thought of Stanley Cavell and Cinema: Turning Anew to the Ontology of Film a Half-Century after The World Viewed* (New York, NY: Bloomsbury Academic).

Lash, Dominic. (2020) *The Cinema of Disorientation: Inviting Confusions* (Edinburgh: Edinburgh University Press).

Lash, Nicholas. (2008) "Recovering Contingency," in *Theology for Pilgrims* (London: Darton, Longman and Todd), pp. 52–67.

Latour, Bruno. (1993) *We Have Never Been Modern*, trans. Catherine Porter (Cambridge, MA: Harvard University Press).

Lear, Jonathan. (1988) *Aristotle: The Desire to Understand* (Cambridge: Cambridge University Press).

Lear, Jonathan. (1990) *Love and its Place in Nature: A Philosophical Interpretation of Freudian Psychoanalysis* (London: Faber and Faber).

Levinson, Jerrold. (2013) "Review of *Fatalism in American Film Noir: Some Cinematic Philosophy*," *Notre Dame Philosophical Reviews*, June 17, https://ndpr.nd.edu/news/fatalism-in-american-film-noir-some-cinematic-philosophy/ (last accessed August 31, 2020).

Lévi-Strauss, Claude. (1963) *Structural Anthropology*, trans. Claire Jacobson and Brooke Grundfest Schoepf (New York, NY: Basic Books).

Lévi-Strauss, Claude. (1981) *The Naked Man (Introduction to a Science of Mythology: 4)*, trans. John and Doreen Weightman (New York, NY: Harper & Row).

Liandrat-Guigues, Suzanne. (2000) *Red River* (London: British Film Institute).

Lodge, David. (2002) *Consciousness and the Novel: Connected Essays* (Cambridge, MA: Harvard University Press).

Lumsden, Simon. (2011) "Hegel, Analytic Philosophy and the Return of Metaphysics," *Parrhesia*, 11, pp. 89–93.

Macarthur, David. (2019) "Naturalism from the Mid-Twentieth Century to the Present," in Kelly Becker and Iain D. Thomson, eds., *The Cambridge History of Philosophy, 1945–2015* (Cambridge: Cambridge University Press), pp. 171–88.

MacDowell, James. (2014) *Happy Endings in Hollywood Cinema: Cliché, Convention and the Final Couple* (Edinburgh, Scotland: Edinburgh University Press).

MacDowell, James. (2016) *Irony in Film* (London: Palgrave Macmillan).

Marx, Karl, trans. Ben Fowkes (1976) *Capital: A Critique of Political Economy, Volume One* (Harmondsworth, UK: Penguin Books in association with New Left Review).

McGinn, Colin. (2005) *The Power of Movies: How Screen and Mind Interact* (New York, NY: Random House).

Miller, D. A. (2016) *Hidden Hitchcock* (Chicago, IL: Chicago University Press).

Moran, Richard. (2017) *The Philosophical Imagination: Selected Essays* (Oxford: Oxford University Press).

Mulhall, Stephen. (2020) "What a Genre of Film Might Be: Medium, Myth, and Morality," in *LaRocca*, pp. 88–104.

Mullarkey, John. (2009) *Refractions of Reality: Philosophy and the Moving Image* (Basingstoke, UK: Palgrave Macmillan).

Mulvey, Laura. (1989) *Visual and Other Pleasures* (Basingstoke, UK: Palgrave).

Nannicelli, Ted, and Paul Taberham, eds. (2014) *Cognitive Media Theory* (New York, NY: Routledge).

Nietzsche, Friedrich. (1990) *Beyond Good and Evil*, trans. R. J. Hollingdale (London: Penguin).

Nietzsche, Friedrich. (1997) *On the Genealogy of Morality*, trans. Carol Diethe (Cambridge: Cambridge University Press).

Nussbaum, Martha. (1995) *Poetic Justice: The Literary Imagination and Public Life* (Boston, MA: Beacon Press).

Orpen, Valerie. (2003) *Film Editing: The Art of the Expressive* (London: Wallflower).

Osborne, Peter. (2013) "More than Everything: Žižek's Badouian Hegel," *Radical Philosophy* 177 (Jan/Feb), pp. 19–25.

Perez, Gilberto. (1998) *The Material Ghost: Films and their Medium*. (Baltimore, MD: Johns Hopkins University Press).

Perez, Gilberto. (2019) *The Eloquent Screen: A Rhetoric of Film*. (Minneapolis, MN: University of Minnesota Press).

Perkins, V. F. (1972) *Film as Film* (London: Penguin).

Perkins, V. F. (2020) *V.F. Perkins on Movies: Collected Shorter Film Criticism*, ed. Douglas Pye (Detroit, MI: Wayne State University Press).

Pinkard, Terry. (2017a) *Does History Make Sense? Hegel on the Historical Shapes of Justice* (Cambridge, MA: Harvard University Press).

Pinkard, Terry (2017b) "The Form of Self-Consciousness," in *Zuckert and Kreines*, pp. 106–20.

Pomerance, Murray. (2011) "Some Hitchcockian Shots," in Thomas Leich and Leland Poague, eds., *A Companion to Alfred Hitchcock* (Chichester, England: Wiley-Blackwell), pp. 237–52.

Potts, Neill. (2005) "Character Interiority: Space, Point of View and Performance in Hitchcock's *Vertigo* (1958)," in *Gibbs and Pye*, pp. 85–97.

Price, Brian. (2019) "The Philosophical Hitchcock: *Vertigo* and the Anxieties of Unknowingness," *New Review of Film and Television Studies*, 17:4, pp. 500–7.

Pye, Douglas. (1996) "Genre and History: *Fort Apache* and *The Man Who Shot Liberty Valance*," in Ian Cameron and Douglas Pye, eds., *The Movie Book of the Western* (London: Studio Vista), pp. 111–22.

Pye, Douglas. (2007) "Movies and Tone," in John Gibbs and Douglas Pye, eds., *Close-Up 02* (London: Wallflower), pp. 1–80.

Pye, Douglas. (2013) "Seeing Fictions in Film," *Projections*, 7:1 (Summer), pp. 131–8.

Redding, Paul. (2018) "Robert Pippin's Hegel as an *Analytically Approachable* Philosopher," *Australasian Philosophical Review*, 2:4, pp. 355–64.
Rödl, Sebastian. (2007) *Self-Consciousness* (Cambridge, MA: Harvard University Press).
Rorty, Richard. (2002) "Comments on Pippin on James," *Inquiry*, 45:3, pp. 351–8.
Rosenbaum, Jonathan. (2009) "Buried Clues, True Grit," in Bert Cardullo, ed., *Committed Cinema: The Films of Jean-Pierre and Luc Dardenne; Essays and Interviews* (Newcastle-upon-Tyne, UK: Cambridge Scholars), pp. 2–9.
Rothman, William. (2004) *The "I" of the Camera: Essays in Film Criticism, History, and Aesthetics* (2nd ed.) (Cambridge: Cambridge University Press).
Rothman, William. (2020) "*Film as Film* and the Personal," in LaRocca, pp. 121–6.
Rushton, Richard. (2013) *The Politics of Hollywood Cinema: Popular Film and Contemporary Political Theory* (Basingstoke, UK: Palgrave Macmillan).
Rushton, Richard. (2014) "Empathic Projection in the Films of the Dardenne Brothers," *Screen*, 55:3 (Autumn), pp. 303–16.
Russell, Francey. (2018) "I Want to Know More about You: On Knowing and Acknowledging in *Chinatown*," in Garry L. Hagberg, ed., *Stanley Cavell on Aesthetic Understanding* (Cham, Germany: Palgrave Macmillan), pp. 3–35.
Ryle, Gilbert. (1949) *The Concept of Mind* (Harmondsworth, UK: Penguin).
Scarry, Elaine. (1999) *On Beauty and Being Just* (Princeton, NJ: Princeton University Press).
Seeley, William, and Noël Carroll. (2014) "Cognitive Theory and the Individual Film: The Case of *Rear Window*," in Nannicelli and Taberham, pp. 235–52.
Shetley, Vernon. (1999) "Incest and Capital in *Chinatown*," *MLN*, Dec., 114:5, pp. 1092–109.
Shuster, Martin. (2017) *New Television: The Aesthetics and Politics of a Genre* (Chicago, IL: University of Chicago Press).

Sinnerbrink, Robert. (2011) *New Philosophies of Film: Thinking Images* (London: Continuum).

Slugan, Mario. (2019) *Noël Carroll and Film: A Philosophy of Art and Popular Culture* (London: Bloomsbury Academic).

Smith, Murray. (2011) "On the Twofoldness of Character," *New Literary History*, 42:2 (Spring), pp. 277–94.

Smith, Murray. (2014) "'The Pit of Naturalism': Neuroscience and the Naturalized Aesthetics of Film," in Ted Nannicelli and Taberham, pp. 27–45.

Srinivasan, Amia. (2015) "Normativity without Cartesian Privilege," *Philosophical Issues*, 25, pp. 273–99.

Stoutland, Frederick. (2011) "Introduction: Anscombe's *Intention* in Context," in Anton Ford, Jennifer Hornsby, and Frederick Stoutland, eds., *Essays on Anscombe's* Intention (Cambridge, MA: Harvard University Press).

Suther, Jensen. (2020) "The Logic of Critical Theory," *Radical Philosophy* 208 (Autumn), pp. 97–9.

Teague, David W. (1997) *The Southwest in American Literature and Art: The Rise of a Desert Aesthetic* (Tucson: University of Arizona Press).

Thomas, Deborah. (2005) "Knowing One's Place: Frame-Breaking, Embarrassment and Irony in *La Cérémonie* (Claude Chabrol, 1995)," in *Gibbs and Pye*, pp. 167–78.

Thompson, Michael. (2008) *Life and Action: Elementary Structures of Practice and Practical Thought* (Cambridge, MA: Harvard University Press).

Trahair, Lisa. (2016) "Belief in this World: The Dardenne Brothers' *The Son* and Søren Kierkegaard's *Fear and Trembling*," *SubStance*, 45:3, pp. 98–119.

Travis, Charles. (2006) *Thought's Footing* (Oxford: Oxford University Press).

Vogler, Candace. (2017) "The Moral of the Story" *Critical Inquiry*, 34:1 (Autumn), pp. 5–35.

Welsch, Tricia. (2000) "Sound Strategies: Lang's Rearticulation of Renoir," *Cinema Journal*, 39:3 (Spring), pp. 51–65.

Whalen, Tom. (1999) "'Maybe All Men Got One Big Soul': The Hoax within the Metaphysics of Terrence Malick's *The Thin Red Line*," *Literature/Film Quarterly*, 27:3, pp. 162–6.

Williams, Bernard. (1973) *Problems of the Self: Philosophical Papers 1956–1972* (Cambridge: Cambridge University Press).

Williams, Bernard. (1993) *Shame and Necessity* (Berkeley, CA: University of California Press).

Wilson, George. (2011) *Seeing Fictions in Film: The Epistemology of Movies* (Oxford: Oxford University Press).

Wittgenstein, Ludwig. (2001) *Tractatus Logico-Philosophicus*, trans. D. F. Pears and B. F. McGuinness (London: Routledge).

Wittgenstein, Ludwig. (2009) *Philosophical Investigations*, trans. G. E. M. Anscombe, P. M. S. Hacker, and Joachim Schulte, ed. P. M. S. Hacker and Joachim Schulte (Chichester, UK: Wiley-Blackwell).

Wollheim, Richard. (2015) *Art and Its Objects* (2nd ed.) (Cambridge: Cambridge University Press).

Wood, Michael. (2005) *Literature and the Taste of Knowledge* (Cambridge: Cambridge University Press).

Yacavone, Daniel. (2015) *Film Worlds: A Philosophical Aesthetics of Cinema* (New York, NY: Columbia University Press).

Zborowski, James. (2016) *Classical Hollywood Cinema: Point of View and Communication*. (Manchester: Manchester University Press).

Žižek, Slavoj. (2012) *Less Than Nothing: Hegel and the Shadow of Dialectical Materialism* (London: Verso).

Žižek, Slavoj. (2014) *Absolute Recoil: Towards a New Foundation of Dialectical Materialism* (London: Verso).

Zuckert, Rachel, and James Kreines, eds. (2017) *Hegel on Philosophy in History* (Cambridge: Cambridge University Press).

Zuckert, Rachel, and James Kreines. (2017) "Introduction," in *Zuckert and Kreines*, pp. 1–12.

Filmography

All That Heaven Allows (1955) Dir. Douglas Sirk, USA: Universal.
Barry Lyndon (1975) Dir. Stanley Kubrick, USA: Warner Bros.
Batman (1966) Dir. Leslie H. Martinson, USA: William Dozier.
Batman (1989) Dir. Tim Burton, USA: Warner Bros.
Caught (1949) Dir. Max Ophüls, USA: MGM.
Chinatown (1974) Dir. Roman Polanski, USA: Paramount.
Citizen Kane (1941) Dir. Orson Welles, USA: RKO.
Double Indemnity (1944) Dir. Billy Wilder, USA: Paramount.
Groundhog Day (1993) Dir. Harold Ramis, USA: Columbia.
Hiroshima mon amour (1959) Dir. Alain Resnais, France: Argos.
Inception (2010) Dir. Christopher Nolan, USA: Warner Bros.
In the Heat of the Night (1967) Dir. Norman Jewison, USA: United Artists.
Johnny Guitar (1954) Dir. Nicholas Ray, USA: Republic.
La Cérémonie (1995) Dir. Claude Chabrol, France: MK2.
M (1931) Dir. Fritz Lang, Germany: Nero-Film.
Man of the West (1958) Dir. Anthony Mann, USA: United Artists.
North by Northwest (1959) Dir. Alfred Hitchcock, USA: MGM.
On the Waterfront (1954) Dir. Elia Kazan, USA: Columbia.
Out of the Past (1947) Dir. Jacques Tourneur, USA: RKO.
Rear Window (1954) Dir. Alfred Hitchcock, USA: Paramount.
Red River (1948) Dir. Howard Hawks, USA: United Artists.
Ride the High Country (1962) Dir. Sam Peckinpah, USA: MGM.
Scarlet Street (1945) Dir. Fritz Lang, USA: Universal.
Shadow of a Doubt (1943) Dir. Alfred Hitchcock, USA: Universal.
Shane (1953) Dir. George Stevens, USA: Paramount.
Sherlock Jr. (1924) Dir. Buster Keaton, USA: MGM.
Stagecoach (1939) Dir. John Ford, USA: United Artists.
Star Wars (1977) Dir. George Lucas, USA: 20th Century Fox.
Talk to Her (Hable con ella) (2002) Dir. Pedro Almodóvar, Spain: El Deseo.
The Big Sleep (1946) Dir. Howard Hawks, USA: Warner Bros.
The Child (L'enfant) (2005) Dir. Jean-Pierre and Luc Dardenne, Belgium: Sony Pictures Classics.

The Dark Knight (2008) Dir. Christopher Nolan, USA: Warner Bros.
The General (1926) Dir. Buster Keaton, USA: United Artists.
The Golden Bowl (2000) Dir. James Ivory, USA: Merchant Ivory.
The Gunfighter (1950) Dir. Henry King, USA: 20th Century Fox.
The Hunger Games (2012) Dir. Gary Ross, USA: Lionsgate.
The Lady from Shanghai (1947) Dir. Orson Welles, USA: Columbia.
The Lusty Men (1952) Dir. Nicholas Ray, USA: RKO.
The Maltese Falcon (1941) Dir. John Huston, USA: Warner Bros.
The Man Who Shot Liberty Valance (1962) Dir. John Ford, USA: Paramount.
The Matrix (1999) Dir. Lana and Lily Wachowski, USA: Warner Bros.
The Promise (*La promesse*) (1996) Dir. Jean-Pierre and Luc Dardenne, Belgium: Les Films du Fleuve.
The Room (2003) Dir. Tommy Wiseau, USA: Wiseau-Films.
The Scarlet Empress (1934) Dir. Josef von Sternberg, USA: Paramount.
The Searchers (1956) Dir. John Ford, USA: Warner Bros.
The Shootist (1976) Dir. Don Siegel, USA: Paramount.
The Son (*Le fils*) (2002) Dir. Jean-Pierre and Luc Dardenne, Belgium: Les Films du Fleuve.
The Thin Red Line (1998) Dir. Terrence Malick, USA: 20th Century Fox.
The Turin Horse (2011) Dir. Béla Tarr and Ágnes Hranitzky, Hungary: T. T. Filmműhely.
The Virginian (1929) Dir. Victor Fleming, USA: Paramount.
The Wild Bunch (1969) Dir. Sam Peckinpah, USA: Warner Bros.
Vertigo (1958) Dir. Alfred Hitchcock, USA: Paramount.
Winchester '73 (1950) Dir. Anthony Mann, USA: Universal.
Written on the Wind (1956) Dir. Douglas Sirk, USA: Universal.
Young Ahmed (*Le jeune Ahmed*) (2019) Dir. Jean-Pierre and Luc Dardenne, Belgium: Les Films du Fleuve.

Index

Abrams, Nathan 9
Adorno, Theodor W. 28–9, 94–5, 99, 200, 202, 227 n.5, 233 n.28
agency 6, 7–9, 19, 30–2, 36, 50–1, 84, 89, 99, 109–45, 147, 160, 183, 214–15, 224 n.16, 230 n.10
All That Heaven Allows (Sirk) 179, 190, 191, 193, 195–9, 217 n.1, 227 n.4
allegory 18, 72, 75, 78, 140, 236–7 n.16
Allen, Woody 181
Almodóvar, Pedro 6, 147–9, 151–7, 226 n.2
Althusser, Louis 215
"analytic" vs "continental" philosophy 2–3, 6, 7, 199–209, 217 nn.3–4, 241 n.22
Anders, Glenn 129
Anscombe, Elizabeth 29–30, 32, 111, 202, 217 n.3, 228 n.3, 232 n.20, 235 n.6
apperception 5, 6, 27, 42–7, 112, 222 n.9, 222–3 n.11
Arendt, Hannah 61, 184
Arlen, Richard 75
Austin, J. L. 2, 51, 180, 223 n.14
Austin, Mary 66
autonomy 5, 29, 35–6, 41, 42, 54, 218 n.5

Bancroft, George 68
Barker, Jess 133
Barry Lyndon (Kubrick) 190
Barthes, Roland 138
Batman 93
Bataille, Georges 202
Bazin, André 67–8, 115
Beckett, Samuel 113, 183
Bel Geddes, Barbara 167

Bennett, Joan 133
Bernstein, Charles 204
Bernstein, J. M. 207–8, 242 n.25
Bessette, Eliot 117, 135–7, 186–8
Beyond Good and Evil (Nietzsche) 160, 166–7, 176–7
Big Sleep, The (Hawks) 100, 117, 131
Bilimoria, Purushottama 184–5
Boetticher, Bud 64
Bogart, Humphrey 100, 131, 172
Bordwell, David 10, 182, 218 n.6, 219 n.11, 238–9 n.3
Bouchey, Willis 71
Brando, Marlon 112
Brandom, Robert 3, 33, 200, 202, 217 n.3, 219 n.10, 230 n.10
Brandon, Henry 83
Braudy, Leo 232 n.19
Bresson, Robert 113
Brian, Mary 76
Britton, Andrew 127–8, 231 n.14
Brodie, Steve 123
Burr, Raymond 17
Burton, Tim 93
Buscombe, Edward 226 n.8
Butte, George 61, 243 n.2

Cámara, Javier 151
Carroll, Noël 46, 48, 55, 205–6, 223 n.12
Caught (Ophüls) 208
Cavell, Stanley 2, 7, 10, 51, 101, 104, 107, 139, 158, 165–6, 173, 175, 180, 183, 203, 204, 208, 218 n.7, 229 n.8, 236 n.11, 237 n.18, 240 n.11, 242 n.24, 244 n.4
Caviezel, Jim 103
Cérémonie, La (Chabrol) 91, 226 n.2

Cézanne, Paul 37
Chabrol, Claude 91
Chandler, Raymond 117
Chaplin, Ben 105
character (in films) 49, 50, 60–4,
 67–9, 71, 75, 85–6, 93–6, 102–8,
 111–20, 127–8, 131, 134–6,
 138, 140–5, 149, 157–8, 168,
 170, 172, 175, 186, 188–90, 193,
 196–7, 215, 225 n.3, 226 n.2,
 229 n.7, 233 n.6, 234–5 n.3., 236
 n.15, 241 n.16, 243 n.3
Chienne, La (Renoir) 134
Chinatown (Polanski) 89, 92–102,
 149, 227 n.4, 227 nn.7–8
Chion, Michel 103, 107
Citizen Kane (Welles) 13, 49
Clark, T. J. 169
Clayton, Alex 194
Clift, Montgomery 67
cognitivism 199–200, 202, 205,
 223 n.14, 241 n.21
Cohen, Hubert I. 83–4, 232 n.24
Cook Jr., Elisha 131
Cooper, Gary 75–6
Cotton, Joseph 156
Coy, Walter 84
Crawford, Joan 194
Cronan, Todd 244 n.6
Currie, Gregory 191–2, 194,
 204
Curtis, Ken 85

Danto, Arthur 221 n.5, 222–3 n.11
Darcy, Georgine 17
Dardenne brothers 6, 109, 137–45,
 155, 162, 187, 207–8, 233
 nn.26–28, 238–9 n.3
Darwin, Charles 31–2, 118–19, 142
Davis, Mike 95
de Beauvoir, Simone 229 n.5
de Corsia, Ted 130
Deleuze, Gilles 4, 12, 57, 141–2, 202,
 204, 232 n.22, 233 n.1, 242 n.25
Derrida, Jacques 202

Descartes, René 8, 28, 33, 41, 60,
 142, 189, 202, 218 n.5, 220 n.1,
 232 n.22
Devine, Andy 61
Dews, Peter 231 n.12
Dimendberg, Edward 115
Döblin, Alfred 183
Doniger, Wendy 168, 184
Double Indemnity (Wilder) 131
Douchet, Jean 18
Douglas, Kirk 121
Dreiser, Theodore 183
Dreyfus, Hubert 11
Dunaway, Fay 99
Duryea, Dan 133

Elsaesser, Thomas 186–7, 189
Emerson, Ralph Waldo 7
Emma (Austen) 183
Evelyn, Judith 17

Ferguson, Frances 184
*Film as Film: Understanding and
 Judging Movies* (Perkins) 13, 38
film noir 6, 109, 115–37, 186,
 202, 206
Flamant, Georges 134
Flaubert, Gustave 113
Fleming, Rhonda 123
Fleming, Victor 75
Fontane, Theodor 183
Ford, John 1, 59, 62, 67, 74, 78, 83,
 86, 87, 94, 113, 181, 225 nn.3–4,
 238–9 n.3
Foucault, Michel 202
Frampton, Daniel 12–13
Frank, Nino 115–16
Freud, Sigmund 18, 31–2, 118–19,
 142, 163, 173, 185
Fukuyama, Francis 90, 226 n.1

gender 34–5, 133, 184, 232 n.18
Genealogy of Morality, On the
 (Nietzsche) 160
General, The (Keaton) 46, 223 n.12

genre 51, 63, 67, 102, 123, 132, 170, 172, 229 n.8, 243 n.3
Géricault, Théodore 39–41
Geuss, Raymond 2
Godard, Jean-Luc 113
Golden Bowl, The (Ivory) 212, 243 n.2
Golden Bowl, The (James) 212
Gourmet, Olivier 140
Grahame, Gloria 172
Grandinetti, Dario 151
Grant, Barry Keith 69
Grant, Cary 45
Greenberg, Clement 38
Greer, Jane 120
Groundhog Day (Ramis) 181
Gunfighter, The (King) 64
Gunning, Tom 134, 183

Hansen, Miriam Bratu 227 n.5
Hardy, Thomas 183
Hawks, Howard 1, 59, 80, 83, 100, 117, 211, 238–9 n.3
Hayward, Susan 89
Hayworth, Rita 120, 231 n.14
Hegel, G. W. F. 2–3, 5, 7–9, 11, 27, 28, 30, 33–9, 42–4, 51, 90–2, 109–13, 119, 147, 160–1, 166, 182, 184–5, 200–3, 206, 214–15, 217 n.4, 218 n.5, 220–1 n.3, 221 n.5, 222 n.9, 222–3 n.11, 226 n.1, 227 n.5, 229 n.4, 231 n.12, 233 n1, 235 n.5, 237 n.18, 238 n.1, 239 n.9, 241 n.22
Heidegger, Martin 7, 28–9, 36, 44, 202
Helmore, Tom 162
Hickock, Wild Bill 68–9, 225 n.3
history 2, 4, 7–9, 16, 28, 31, 33–8, 41, 50–1, 54, 56, 65, 80, 82, 90–1, 94–6, 98, 114–15, 119, 182, 184, 189, 218 n.5, 219 n.10, 220 n.1, 235 n.5, 236 n.13, 237 n.18, 241 n.19, 243–4 n.4
Hitchcock, Alfred 1, 3, 6, 10–26, 147–8, 155, 162–77, 184, 185,
198, 205–6, 207–8, 224 n.18, 236 n.13, 236 n.15, 238–9 n.3
Hobbes, Thomas 220 n.1
Hollywood 4, 7, 59, 61, 102, 114, 132, 181–3, 229 n.9, 231 n.14, 236–7 n.16, 238–9 n.3
Houlgate, Stephen 200
Hudson, Rock 195
Hume, David 28
Hunter, Jeffrey 83, 226 n.8
Huston, John 95, 131
Huston, Virginia 123
Huston, Walter 76

Ibsen, Henrik 183
imagination 26, 45–9, 140, 192
imaginative seeing 47–9, 140
In a Lonely Place (Ray) 147, 155–6, 172–5
In the Heat of the Night (Jewison) 53
interpretation 5, 10–11, 15–22, 25, 32, 36, 53, 55, 60, 67, 71, 75, 77–8, 98, 103–4, 106, 113–14, 117, 125, 127–8, 135–7, 159, 161, 167, 169, 176, 180–2, 199, 203, 206, 208, 214, 218 n.6, 218 n.9, 219 n.11, 219 n.13, 222 n.10, 227 n.6, 235 n.4, 238 n.2, 244 n.6
irony 20, 25–6, 68–9, 82, 95, 103, 106–7, 119, 127, 129, 135, 168, 179, 186–99, 206, 239 nn.9–10, 240 nn.12–13, 241 n.17
irrationality 35, 60, 81, 100, 110, 124, 166

James, Henry 56, 113, 132, 150, 169, 211–13, 243 n.2
Johnny Guitar (Ray) 179, 190, 193–4, 240 n.14
Jones, James 101
Jordan, Dorothy 84

Kafka, Franz 113, 183
Kant, Immanuel 2, 6–8, 10–11, 28, 33, 35, 41–4, 47, 49, 112, 135,

151, 222 nn.8–9, 222–3 n.11,
   223 n.13, 230 n.10
Keaton, Buster 46, 223 n.12,
   234–5 n.3
Kellogg, John 123
Kelly, Grace 16
Kennedy, Arthur 89
Kierkegaard, Søren 143, 202
King Lear (Shakespeare) 183
Kitses, Jim 66
Klevan, Andrew 3–4, 182, 195–8,
   217 n.2
Klinger, Barbara 195, 238–9 n.3
Korsgaard, Christine 110–11, 119,
   184, 228 n.1
Koteas, Elias 102
Kreines, James 8
Krutch, Joseph Wood 66
Kubrick, Stanley 190
Kürnberger, Ferdinand 94

Lacan, Jacques 215
Lady from Shanghai, The (Welles)
   116, 120, 128–32, 136
Lang, Fritz 48, 109, 117, 131, 134–5,
   232 n.19
Lash, Dominic 234–5 n.3
Lash, Nicholas 218 n.5
Latour, Bruno 28–9
Lear, Jonathan 150, 173, 220 n.2,
   222 n.9, 231 n.11, 238 n.1
Levinas, Emmanuel 7, 202,
   233 n.28
Levine, Susan S. 184
Levinson, Jerrold 136
Lévi-Strauss, Claude 66, 97, 224 n.1
Liandrat-Guiges, Suzanne 67
Libet, Benjamin 31
Locke, John 28, 42
Lodge, David 211–13
Longuenesse, Béatrice 200
Lorre, Peter 48
Lusty Men, The (Ray) 59, 64, 89–
   90, 132
Lyotard, Jean-François 202

M (Lang) 48
Macarthur, David 31
Macbeth (Shakespeare) 9
MacDowell, James 191–9, 213, 240
   n.13, 241 n.15
MacMurray, Fred 131
Making Meaning (Bordwell) 10
Makkai, Katalin 184
Malick, Terrence 89, 94, 102–3,
   238–9 n.3
Maltese Falcon, The (Huston) 131
Man of the West (Mann) 64
Man Who Shot Liberty Valance, The
   (Ford) 59, 61–2, 64, 68, 71–5,
   77–81, 97, 105, 126, 225 nn.3–6,
   242–3 n.27
Manet, Édouard 37–8
Mann, Anthony 133
Mantell, Joe 100
Marèse, Janie 134
Marinne, Morgan 140
Martinson, Leslie H. 93
Marvin, Lee 68
Marx, Karl 31–2, 61, 82, 118–19, 142,
   185, 202
Matrix, The (Lana and Lily
   Wachowski) 11
McDowell, John 139, 200, 202, 217 n.3
McGinn, Colin 3
Merchant of Venice, The
   (Shakespeare) 50
Merleau-Ponty, Maurice 44
Michie, Elsie B. 184
Miles, Vera 24, 61, 71, 85
Miller, D. A. 21–2, 24
Minima Moralia (Adorno) 94
Mitchell, Thomas 68
Mitchum, Robert 89, 120–2, 125
modernism and modernity 5, 6, 8,
   27–41, 68, 91–2, 115, 118, 137,
   207–8, 214, 218 n.5, 220 n.1,
   221 n.5, 227 n.8, 229–30 n.9,
   236 n.13
Modleski, Tania 184
Moran, Richard 40, 47, 235 n.6

moral psychology 6, 60, 65, 147–77, 214, 242 n.25
Morissette, Alanis 193
Mulvey, Laura 18
Musil, Robert 113, 183

Nagl, Ludwig 138
narration 12–15, 27, 41, 49–52, 92, 99, 105, 114, 120, 126, 128, 186–7, 198, 213, 223–4 n.15, 224 n.16, 228 n.9
Newton, Isaac 28
Nicholson, Jack 98
Nietzsche, Friedrich 6, 7, 10–11, 16, 31–2, 35, 61, 118–19, 142, 147, 149, 158–62, 166–7, 176–7, 185, 214, 233–4 n.1, 235 nn.4–5, 235 n.7, 236 n.11
Niles, Ken 123
Nolan, Christopher 93
Nolte, Nick 102
normativity 5, 29–41, 44, 54, 95, 99, 113, 118, 182, 204, 214, 220 n.2, 222 n.7, 229 n.8, 229–30 n.9, 230 n.10, 235 n.5, 242 n.25
Novak, Kim 162, 170, 236 n.15
Nussbaum, Martha 159

O'Keeffe, Georgia 66
Ó Maoilearca, John 203–4, 207, 242 n.24
On the Waterfront (Kazan) 112
Ophüls, Max 198, 208
Orpen, Valerie 17
Osborne, Peter 2
Othello (Shakespeare) 9, 53
Otto, Miranda 105–7
Ouédraogo, Rasmané 139–40
Out of the Past (Tourneur) 116, 120–6, 128, 135–6

Palmer, Belinda 100
Pasolini, Pier Paolo 141
Perez, Gilberto 71–2, 75, 79, 82–3, 86, 105, 183, 213

Perkins, V. F. 10, 13, 21, 38, 92, 181, 183, 193, 208, 214, 219n, 236–7 n.16, 239 n.5
phenomenology 8, 44, 49, 200, 223 n.14
Phenomenology of Spirit, The (Hegel) 3, 237–8 n.18
Philosophical Investigations (Wittgenstein) 192, 221–2 n.6
Philosophy of Right (Hegel) 237–8 n.18
Pinkard, Terry 8, 25, 33, 43, 65
Pinker, Steven 8
Pippin, Robert B.
  After the Beautiful 36–9, 182, 207, 221 n.5, 222–3 n.11
  Douglas Sirk: Filmmaker and Philosopher 1, 241 n.19, 243–4 n.4
  Fatalism in American Film Noir: Some Cinematic Philosophy 1, 61, 109, 113, 115–37, 186, 202, 218–19 n.9, 229 n.7, 229–30 n.9, 231 nn.13–15, 231–2 n.16, 232 nn.17–18
  Filmed Thought: Cinema as Reflective Form 1, 5, 7, 13–26, 51–2, 55–6, 92–108, 138–45, 148–58, 161–2, 173–5, 184, 187, 189–90, 193–9, 206, 227 nn.7–8, 228 n.10, 232 n.25, 233 n.28, 236–7 n.16, 239 n.9, 240 n.12, 240 n.14
  Hegel's Idealism: The Satisfactions of Self-Consciousness 2, 7–8, 43
  Hegel's Practical Philosophy: Rational Agency as Ethical Life 11–12, 59, 109–12, 139, 184, 214, 218 n.5, 220 n.2, 229 n.4
  Henry James and Modern Moral Life 56, 211
  Hollywood Westerns and American Myth: The Importance of Howard Hawks

and John Ford for Political
Philosophy 1, 4, 7, 59–87, 89,
105, 225 nn.4–6, 226 nn.7–8
*Modernism as a Philosophical
Problem: On the
Dissatisfactions of European
High Culture* 35–6, 42, 147,
220 n.1, 233–4 n.1
*The Philosophical Hitchcock:
Vertigo and the Anxieties of
Unknowingness* 1, 52, 54–6,
162–73, 175, 177, 183, 185,
207, 235 n.8, 235–6 n.9, 236
nn.13–15, 237–8 n.18
Polanski, Roman 89, 93–6, 149,
227 n.7, 238–9 n.3
political psychology 6, 59–87, 93,
101–2, 104, 160, 207, 225 n.6
Pomerance, Murray 21, 24, 183
Portrait of a Lady, A (James) 169
Potts, Neill 236 n.15
Price, Brian 49
Promise, The (Dardenne brothers)
138, 139–40
Psycho (Hitchcock) 24
psychoanalysis 18, 67, 95, 117,
173
psychology 6, 59–87, 93, 101–2, 104,
138, 142–3, 147–77, 207, 213–
14, 225 n.6, 235 n.6, 242 n.25
Pursuits of Happiness (Cavell) 10,
229 n.8
Pye, Douglas 14, 78, 224 n.16,
225 n.5, 226 n.3

rationality 8, 28, 31, 33, 35, 41, 60,
81–2, 99, 109–15, 145, 147,
184–5, 201, 231 n.12
Ray, Nicholas 59, 89–90, 132, 147,
155, 172, 175, 179, 190, 193–4,
198, 238–9 n.3
Rear Window (Hitchcock) 205–6
Red River (Hawks) 59, 62, 67, 80–3,
211, 226 n.7
Redding, Paul 217 n.4

reflective form 13, 52, 104, 127, 142,
151, 172, 182, 188, 205, 211,
218–19 n.9, 220 n.1, 232 n.22
Renier, Jérémie 139, 233 n.26
Renoir, Jean 132, 134, 232 n.19
Ricoeur, Paul 31
Ride the High Country
(Peckinpah) 64
Ritter, Thelma 16
Roberts, Roy 97
Robinson, Edward G. 131
Rödl, Sebastian 139, 232 n.21,
236 n.10
Rorty, Richard 2–3
Rothman, William 172, 183, 239 n.5
Roux, Tony 125
Rushton, Richard 144–5, 185
Russell, Bertrand 7
Russell, Francey 101
Ryle, Gilbert 202, 232 n.23

Savage, Jon 106
Scarlet Empress, The (von
Sternberg) 190
Scarlet Street (Lang) 116–17, 131–6
Scarry, Elaine 159
Schelling, Friedrich 202
Searchers, The (Ford) 59, 62, 63,
83–7, 99, 137, 226 n.8
Seeley, William 205–6
self-consciousness 6, 13–15, 18–19,
35, 41–9, 66, 68, 112, 115, 147,
194, 205, 211–12, 215, 221 n.5,
222 n.9, 232 n.22, 242 n.26
Sen, Amartya 184–5
Shadow of a Doubt (Hitchcock) 6,
147–9, 155–8, 161, 168
Shakespeare, William 9, 50
Shane (Stevens) 64
Shayne, Konstantin 207
Shetley, Vernon 96–7, 100–1, 227 n.8
Shootist, The (Siegel) 64
Simon, Michel 134
Simpsons, The (Groening) 181
Sinnerbrink, Robert 201, 238n

Sirk, Douglas 1, 179, 187–90, 193, 195–9, 238–9 n.3, 241 nn.16–19, 243–4 n.4
skepticism 135, 165–6, 173, 175–6, 180, 224 n.18, 237–8 n.18
slavery 34
Sloane, Everett 129
Smith, John Dee 103
Smith, Murray 205, 222n, 242 n.26
Son, The (Dardenne brothers) 140–4, 233 n.26
Soupart, Isabella 141
Srinivasan, Amia 229–30 n.9
Stagecoach (Ford) 59, 68–71, 224–5 n.2
Steele, Bob 131
Stewart, James 12, 15, 68, 162
Stieglitz, Alfred 66
Stoutland, Frederick 228–9 n.3
subjectivity 8–9, 16, 19–20, 35–6, 39, 56, 60, 65, 75, 77, 114, 119, 141–3, 149, 169, 182, 185, 202, 207–8, 218 n.5
Suther, Jensen 27, 200

Talk to Her (Almodóvar) 6, 147–9, 151–7, 226 n.2
Talton, Alix 174
Tarantino, Quentin 234 n.2
Teague, David W. 66
television 16
Thin Red Line, The (Jones) 101
Thin Red Line, The (Malick) 89, 94, 101–8, 228 n.10
Thomas, Deborah 226 n.2
Thompson, Michael 139, 161, 201
Thus Spoke Zarathustra (Nietzsche) 10–11, 16
Tolstoy, Leo 183
Toulmin, Stephen 220n
Tourneur, Jacques 109, 113, 116, 121, 136
Towne, Robert 95
Tractatus Logico-Philosophicus (Wittgenstein) 93

tragedy 17, 64, 100, 101, 167, 175, 229–30 n.9, 237–8 n.18
Trahair, Lisa 141–4, 232 n.22
Travis, Charles 57
Trevor, Claire 68
Trumpener, Katie 184
Turin Horse, The (Tarr and Hranitsky) 41
Tyler, Tom 68

Vertigo (Hitchcock) 3, 5–6, 11, 18, 25–6, 55–6, 147, 162–77, 185, 207–8, 236 n.13, 236 n.15, 237–8 n.18
Virginian, The (Fleming) 75–7
Vogler, Candace 158, 234–5 n.3
von Sternberg, Josef 190
voyeurism 15–19, 21, 24, 25

Ware, Helen 76
Watling, Leonor 151
Wayne, John 63, 67, 68, 71, 83
Welles, Orson 109, 113, 116, 120, 126–8
Western (film genre) 59–87
Whalen, Tom 228 n.11
Wild Bunch, The (Peckinpah) 64
Wilder, Billy 131
Williams, Bernard 47–8, 60–1, 217 n.3, 223 n.13, 229–30 n.9
Wilson, George 45–8, 92, 183, 200, 223 n.12
Wilson, Mark 7
Winchester '73 (Mann) 133
Wings of the Dove, The (James) 213, 224 n.18, 234–5 n.3
Wiseau, Tommy 193
Wittgenstein, Ludwig 2, 7, 93, 139, 192, 221–2 n.6, 222 n.10, 229 n.8, 235 n.6, 239–40 n.10, 240 n.11
Wollheim, Richard 221 n.4, 222 n.7, 222 n.10, 222–3 n.11
Wood, Michael 199, 224 n.18, 235 n.4
Wood, Natalie 83

Wood, Robin 183
world (of a film) 6, 14, 40–1, 46–9, 69, 78, 89–108, 118–19, 132, 134, 141–2, 150, 184, 188–9, 232 n.19, 234–5 n.3, 236 n.13, 243 n.3
world-in vs *world-of* 92–4, 96, 105, 108, 150
Wright, Teresa 156
Written on the Wind (Sirk) 241 n.17
Wyman, Jane 195

Yacavone, Daniel 92–4, 150, 221 n.5
Young Ahmed (Dardenne brothers) 138
Young, Carleton 71

Zacharasiewicz, Waldemar 138
Zborowski, James 217 n.2, 239 n.8
Žižek, Slavoj 206–7, 242–3 n.27
Zuckert, Rachel 8
Zwerling, Darrell 96

www.ingramcontent.com/pod-product-compliance
Lightning Source LLC
Chambersburg PA
CBHW052218300426
44115CB00011B/1743